THE MONETARY
GEOGRAPHY
OF AFRICA

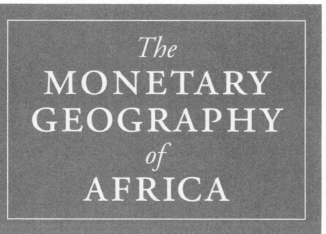

The
MONETARY
GEOGRAPHY
of
AFRICA

PAUL R. MASSON

CATHERINE PATTILLO

BROOKINGS INSTITUTION PRESS
Washington, D.C.

Library of Congress Cataloging-in-Publication data

Masson, Paul R.
The monetary geography of Africa / Paul R. Masson and Catherine Pattillo.
   p.   cm.
Includes bibliographical references and index.
ISBN 0-8157-5500-7 (cloth : alk. paper)
1. Monetary policy—Africa. I. Pattillo, Catherine A. (Catherine Anne) II. Title.
HG1325.M377 2004
332.4'96—dc22   2004020089

Typeset in Adobe Garamond

Composition by Circle Graphics
Columbia, Maryland

Printed by R. R. Donnelley
Harrisonburg, Virginia

To Betsy

and

To Dave, Camille, and David Michael

Contents

Foreword   ix

Preface   xiii

Acknowledgments   xv

Abbreviations and Acronyms   xvii

1   Monetary Union in Africa: Past, Present, and Future   1

2   African Currency Regimes since World War II   12

3   Criteria for Currency Unions or the Adoption
of Another Currency   33

4   African Monetary Integration in Practice:
CFA Franc Zone and South African CMA   45

5   Experiences of Countries in Managing
Independent Currencies   77

6   Proposed Single Currency for West Africa   95

7   Regional Integration in SADC   113

8 EAC and COMESA 129

9 A Single Currency for Africa? 147

10 Africa's Monetary Geography in the Coming Decades 162

Appendixes

A Calibration of the Model 171

B Country Vignettes 182

References 197

Index 207

Maps

Figure 1-1. Political Divisions of Africa xx

Figure 1-2. GDP per Capita at PPP Exchange Rates, 2002 2

Figure 2-1. Currency Areas, 1964 18

Figure 2-2. Exchange Rate Volatility against the U.S. Dollar, 2000–01 28

Figure 2-3. Exchange Rate Volatility against the Euro, 2000–01 29

Figure 9-1. Membership in Regional Arrangements 149

Foreword

W hat has taken the place of the cold war as the defining division in world politics? One answer is the chasm between, on the one hand, those who feel that they are benefiting from globalization and, on the other, those who feel left behind. Today the split is, very roughly, 50-50; but the gap between the two is widening, and because of unsustainable population growth in poorer regions of the world the ratio of globalization's self-perceived winners and losers is shifting in the wrong direction.

Africa is a continent especially afflicted by this trend. Hence the importance of this book by Paul Masson, who was in 2002–03 a visiting fellow in the Economic and Governance Studies programs at Brookings, and Catherine Pattillo, who is a senior economist at the International Monetary Fund and has written widely on African issues.

Africa has had a bad half century. In the 1950s, per capita income levels were about the same in many African countries as in Asian countries at that time. Ghana's per capita GDP, for instance, equaled that of South Korea. But over the intervening decades, many Asian countries have experienced explosive economic growth and dramatic improvements in education, health, and well-being. Africa, by contrast, has been left behind. Indeed, in a number of African countries per capita incomes have actually fallen over the past several decades.

The causes of the differential performance have been much discussed. Among the most important are surely inadequate government policies in a number of areas. In too many African countries, kleptocratic leaders of authoritarian regimes held on to power by rewarding their supporters and attracting grants from both sides in the cold war. Instead of investment in productive activities, aid has led to enrichment of politicians and their coteries. Countries have followed inward-looking policies that have protected domestic cartels rather than benefiting from trade liberalization.

While monetary policy is by no means the only factor in economic development, it has its role to play. Most African countries abandoned colonial currencies at independence and created new currencies and their own central banks. These new moneys soon lost their value—except, notably, in the former French colonies—even if nominally pegged to some international currency. They became inconvertible and access to foreign exchange was rationed, opening the door to corruption and inefficiencies in allocation. In a number of countries, inflation was used as a way to close the gap between excessive government spending and meager tax revenues.

African populations and policymakers have become aware of the inadequacies of past policies and governance structures. As early as the 1980s and 1990s there were moves in some countries to liberalize domestic economies and open them to foreign competition: to stress export development rather than import replacement, to make currencies convertible in the context of exchange rate flexibility. The end of the cold war has removed some of the sources of aid available to African dictators, as well as the unquestioning support of the donors. More attention is now being given to whether aid will serve the purpose of development. On the African side, the newly created African Union is attempting to mobilize peer pressure to improve governance and government policies through the New Partnership for African Development, or NEPAD.

One way countries can apply peer pressure is through regional organizations. Regional integration may also yield other economic benefits through improved transportation and communication links and expanded trade. In this regard, several groups of African countries have come up with plans for regional integration that would also include currency unions—that is, the replacement of existing national currencies with a new, supranational currency. The hope is that a regional currency will stimulate other aspects of regional integration, especially expanded trade, and produce lower inflation, since the new central bank will be (at least nominally) independent from national treasuries. Doubtless, too, the example of Europe is at the forefront of the minds of proponents of currency unions, who hope to see the creation of an African currency to rival the euro.

Since resources—financial, technical, and personnel—are in short supply in Africa, it is important to look hard at whether the recent enthusiasm for monetary integration is justified. If the expected benefits are not likely to be forthcoming, then governments are better advised to devote resources to other essential activities that aim to improve health, stimulate investment, and boost economic development.

Paul and Catherine take a hard look at the economic benefits and costs— and also the apparent political motivations—of proposed monetary unions in western, eastern, and southern Africa, as well as the proposal for a single African currency. Moreover, they for the first time present a history of the use of currencies and monetary policies on the African continent since World War II. And they go on to speculate as to what Africa's "monetary geography" will look like two decades from now.

The authors highlight some of the limitations of assuming that the European example can be translated directly to the African context. First, ensuring the independence of the regional (or continental) African central banks will not be easy, since there is no evidence that monetary unions will in themselves discipline fiscal policies. Therefore, government deficits will tend to put upward pressure on inflation. Second, levels of intraregional trade are much lower in Africa than in Europe and are likely to remain so, limiting the gains from a single currency. Finally, a continentwide currency will not have a major global impact while Africa's economic size (in terms of GDP) remains modest.

We at Brookings are proud that this book bears our imprint, since it is an example of a project that cuts across subject areas in addressing some of the most important issues facing the world today: poverty reduction and economic development.

STROBE TALBOTT
President, Brookings Institution

Washington, D.C.
October 2004

Preface

This book describes the present use of currencies in Africa as well as their use in the recent past and attempts to draw conclusions concerning the evolution of exchange rate regimes in the future. Before getting into the substance, two questions need to be answered: what is the meaning of monetary geography, and why is it an interesting topic for Africa? We have adapted the term *monetary geography* from the title of a book published by Benjamin Cohen in 1998, *The Geography of Money*. In that book, Cohen argues forcefully that money has become "deterritorialized," that is, the circulation of a particular money is no longer coterminous with the country of issue. A prime case in point is the creation of the euro, which is not associated with a single country but rather with a supranational central bank. In addition, foreign currencies circulate widely in many developing countries because of uncertainty about the ability of the domestic currency to maintain its value. Thus in this book we are concerned with the use of money, whether within the issuing country's borders or outside of them. We are especially interested in the potential spread of regional currency areas. In keeping with the geographical notion, we will rely on maps to convey some of the key data not only on the use of moneys but also on the economic variables that influence their use and determine their value.

This brings us to the second question: why is that an interesting topic in Africa today? In fact, Africa is arguably a more useful laboratory than is

Europe for studying the use of money. It contains two monetary unions characterized by joint decisionmaking among sovereign states that have existed for some forty years—the two CFA franc zones—and a monetary area between South Africa and smaller neighboring countries, in which South Africa sets monetary policy, that dates back to the early years of the twentieth century. This justifies a more thorough look at the African experience than has been attempted thus far, in notable contrast to the European case, which has received enormous attention. Moreover, the African continent has several projects for further monetary unions that are intended to culminate in a single African currency. So there is a great need for analysis of the advisability of the monetary union projects and for research into how best to proceed. We hope that this book goes some way toward meeting those needs. The views expressed here, however, are those of the authors and do not represent those of the Brookings Institution, the International Monetary Fund, or other institutions discussed.

The book is intended for policymakers (and general readers) as well as economists with technical training. Some of our conclusions are based on a quantitative assessment of the economic costs and benefits of monetary unions and hence on calculations that necessarily rely on some sort of economic model. In order to make the policy implications clear, however, we try to put the technical details on the model in appendixes. The nontechnical reader can skip over them.

Acknowledgments

W e would like to thank a great number of our colleagues at the IMF
and World Bank, UN Economic Commission for Africa, WAMI,
other official institutions, and in academe. Our collaboration began when
Christian François, then in the IMF's African Department, suggested that we
analyze the proposed monetary union for ECOWAS. Each of us had earlier
worked on currency issues for Africa, and we are grateful for the encouragement of Paul Collier, Ernesto Hernández-Catá, and Charles Humphreys in
that regard. Our work on ECOWAS was greatly assisted by the hospitality and
information provided by WAMI in Accra, Ghana, and especially by Ernest
Addison, Rebiliy Asante, Siradiou Bah, and Michael Ojo. This book grew out
of our earlier collaboration as well as involvement with the CFA franc zone by
Masson, who would like to thank his collaborators in that work at the IMF,
especially Ousmane Doré, Christian Durand, Papa Ousmane Sakho, Pierre
van den Boogaerde, and Johannes Wiegand; the BCEAO and the BEAC for
hospitality provided in Dakar, Senegal, and Yaoundé, Cameroon, respectively;
and Philippe Bonzom, Christian DeBoissieu, Patrick Guillaumont, Sylviane
Guillaumont-Jeanneney, Célestin Monga, and Marc-Olivier Strauss-Kahn for
interesting discussions on the book's topics. We would like to thank Ratna
Sahay and Miguel Savastano, who supported Pattillo's work on the book.
    The book itself has benefited from comments from several of those listed
above as well as Christopher Adam, Luis de Azcarate, Hugh Bredenkamp,

Donal Donovan, Pierre Ewenczyk, A. Laure Gnassou, John Green, Charles Harvey, Eric Helleiner, Jacqueline Irving, Christiane Kraus, Luca Ricci, Klaus-Walter Riechel, Jon Shields, Meshack Tjirongo, Romain Veyrune, and many others in the IMF African Department. Benjamin Cohen encouraged us to undertake the project, which is inspired by his own work, and gave us detailed comments on the outline. Gerald Helleiner generously read through a late draft, making detailed comments as well as highlighting contentious issues. Ashoka Mody provided some data for chapter 5.

The building blocks for our book were presented at various conferences, including the American Economic Association annual meeting (New Orleans, January 2000); *Caisse des Dépots et Consignations/Centre d'Etudes Prospectives et d'Informations Internationales* conference on monetary unions (Santiago, Chile, March 2002); regional currency areas conference sponsored by the UN Economic Commission for Africa (Accra, Ghana, October 2002); and seminars at the Bank of Canada and University of Aix-Marseille. We would like to thank Frank Bohn, Agnès Bénassy-Quéré, Patrick Osakwe, Malcolm Knight, and Gilles Nancy for offering us the opportunity to present our ideas in conferences and seminars. A conference at the Bank for International Settlements on regional currency areas (September 2002) provided insights and useful contacts, for which we are grateful to Philip Turner and John Hawkins.

Indispensable inputs to our analysis of Southern Africa, Botswana, and SADC were obtained thanks to Masson's visits to Pretoria, South Africa, and Gaborone, Botswana. The visits were arranged with the kind assistance of Lambertus van Zyl and Donald Stephenson. Masson would especially like to thank, among the many whom he met there, Werner Brümmerhoff, Derek Hudson, Keith Jefferis, Brian Kahn, Christopher Loewald, Elias Masilela, Oduetse Motshidisi, Andrew Motsomi, Jay Salkin, and Moeketsi Senaoana.

We would especially like to acknowledge our debt to our close collaborators. Xavier Debrun has coauthored with us several papers on monetary unions in Africa, and this book builds on that work. Heather Milkiewicz put together much of the data used in this book, has mastered the technology of creating maps, and has done much of the statistical analysis. Manzoor Gill and Nese Erbil also provided some excellent research assistance.

Finally, Masson would like to thank the Brookings Institution, and, in particular, Carol Graham and Robert Litan, for providing excellent facilities and support without which the book would not have been possible. Thanks also are extended to Randi Bender and Janet Walker for their conscientious editing and Eric Haven for his careful research verification as well as Vicki Chamlee for proofreading and Julia Petrakis for indexing.

Abbreviations and Acronyms

AEC African Economic Community. Created by the 1991 Abuja Treaty.

AMU Arab Maghreb Union. A regional group that includes Algeria, Libya, Mauritania, Morocco, and Tunisia.

APRM African Peer Review Mechanism. An instrument of NEPAD that will review countries' performance in the area of governance and exert peer pressure to improve it.

AU African Union. A pan-African organization whose Constitutive Act entered into force in 2001. The AU aims to bring about economic and political integration.

BCEAO *Banque Centrale des Etats de l'Afrique de l'Ouest.* Central bank of WAEMU.

BEAC *Banque des Etats de l'Afrique Centrale.* Central bank of CAEMC.

CAEMC Central African Economic and Monetary Community (or, in French, CEMAC, which stands for *Communauté Economique et Monétaire de l'Afrique Centrale*). Comprises Cameroon, Central African Republic, Chad, Equatorial Guinea, Gabon, and Republic of the Congo. Uses the CFA franc issued by the region's central bank, the BEAC.

CFA franc zone A common currency area that uses the CFA franc, which is pegged to the euro with the assistance of the French Treasury. Its African members comprise two groups of countries (plus Comoros), WAEMU and CAEMC, each with its own central bank and currency. In the group of countries represented in WAEMU, franc CFA in French stands for *franc de la Communauté Financière Africaine,* while for those countries in CAEMC, franc CFA means *franc de la Coopération Financière en Afrique centrale.*

CFAF   CFA franc.

CMA   Common Monetary Area. Comprises South Africa, Lesotho, Namibia, and Swaziland.

COMESA   Common Market for Eastern and Southern Africa. Extending from Egypt in the north to Namibia in the south.

EAC   East African Community. Composed of Kenya, Tanzania, and Uganda.

ECB   European Central Bank.

ECCAS   Economic Community of Central African States. An embryonic grouping of CAEMC countries and their neighbors in central Africa.

ECOMOG   ECOWAS Military Observer Group.

ECOWAS   Economic Community of West African States. Founded in 1975, comprises those countries in WAEMU and WAMZ, plus Cape Verde and Liberia.

EMS   European Monetary System. A transitional regime leading to the EMU.

EMU   European Economic and Monetary Union. The common currency area based on the euro.

ERM   Exchange rate mechanism of the European Monetary System.

EU   European Union. A grouping of (at present) twenty-five countries, twelve of which belong to the EMU.

IMF   International Monetary Fund.

MMA   Multilateral Monetary Agreement. The 1992 agreement that governs the CMA.

NEPAD   New Partnership for African Development. A 1999 initiative of Presidents Mbeki (South Africa), Wade (Senegal), Bouteflika (Algeria), and Obasanjo (Nigeria) to encourage African countries to work together in order to improve governance and further development.

NOFP   Net Open Forward Position.

OAU   Organization of African Unity. The predecessor (with the AEC) to the AU.

OCA   Optimum currency area.

OECD   Organization for Economic Cooperation and Development. Grouping of the developed countries.

OHADA   *Organisation pour l'Harmonisation du Droit des Affaires en Afrique* (Organization for the Harmonization of Business Law in Africa). Agreement on common business law involving mainly Francophone African countries.

PPP Purchasing power parity. The PPP exchange rates are exchange rates that keep constant relative purchasing power.

REC Regional Economic Community. Considered building blocks of the African Union. The principal RECs are AMU, COMESA, ECCAS, ECOWAS, and SADC.

REER Real Effective Exchange Rate. A measure of the average exchange rate against all other currencies, adjusting for differences in price levels.

RMS Root mean square.

SACU South African Customs Union. Includes Botswana, Lesotho, Namibia, South Africa, and Swaziland.

SADC Southern African Development Community. Goals are to foster successful economic and social development among members states: Angola, Botswana, Democratic Republic of the Congo, Lesotho, Malawi, Mauritius, Mozambique, Namibia, Seychelles, South Africa, Swaziland, Tanzania, Zambia, Zimbabwe.

SARB South African Reserve Bank. The central bank of South Africa, which issues the rand.

UDEAC *L'Union Douanière des Etats de l'Afrique Centrale* (Central African Customs Union).

UDEAO *L'Union Douanière des Etats de l'Afrique de l'Ouest* (West African Customs Union).

WAEMU West African Economic and Monetary Union (in French, UEMOA, which stands for *Union Economique et Monétaire Ouest-Africaine*). Members (Benin, Burkina Faso, Côte d'Ivoire, Guinea-Bissau, Mali, Niger, Senegal, and Togo) use the CFA franc issued by their central bank, the BCEAO.

WAMI West African Monetary Institute. Located in Accra, Ghana, is the precursor to the central bank for WAMZ.

WAMZ West African Monetary Zone, which is to be established by July 2005 with a common central bank and a single currency. Its prospective members include the Gambia, Ghana, Guinea, Nigeria, and Sierra Leone.

Figure 1-1. *Political Divisions of Africa*

1

Monetary Union in Africa: Past, Present, and Future

Africa finds itself at an important juncture in its history as the twenty-first century gets under way. There is widespread consensus that Africans must take responsibility for their destiny. Nearly fifty years have passed since the beginning of decolonization and early hopes of rapid development have faded. In recent decades, the continent has suffered from abysmal economic performance. Africa has failed to benefit from the increase in prosperity experienced by the rest of the world, prosperity resulting from expansion of trade and other aspects of globalization. Instead, African countries have become increasingly marginalized, with their share of world exports falling from already low levels of 4 percent in 1980 to 1.6 percent in 2000. Per capita incomes almost everywhere on the continent have declined relative to world averages and have fallen in absolute terms in a number of countries. Figure 1-1 provides a conventional country map of the continent, and figure 1-2 classifies the countries into ranges of per capita GDP. Incomes are very low when compared to the typical developing country, except for southern and northern Africa, even when calculated using PPP exchange rates, as is the case in figure 1-2.[1]

---

1. PPP exchange rates correct for differences in the cost of living when calculating real incomes across countries. Using market exchange rates would give much lower U.S. dollar income levels, because prices (in particular of nontraded goods and services) are very low in these countries.

Figure 1-2. *GDP per Capita at PPP Exchange Rates, 2002*

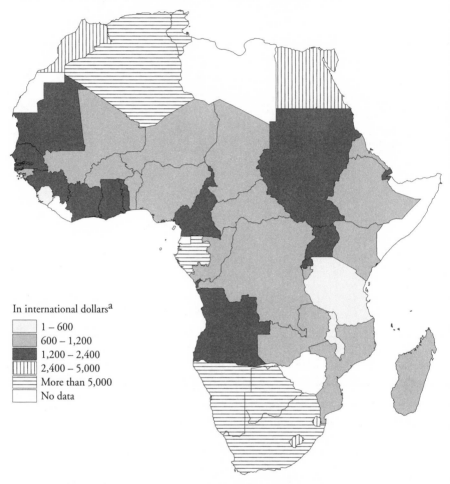

In international dollars[a]

	1 – 600
	600 – 1,200
	1,200 – 2,400
	2,400 – 5,000
	More than 5,000
	No data

Source: World Bank, World Development Indicators database (2004).
a. An international dollar would buy in the cited country a comparable amount of goods and services a U.S. dollar would buy in the United States.

The causes of this poor performance are many and diverse, and include inappropriate development strategies that are dependent on inward-looking policies meant to capture rents rather than foster growth; obstacles to trade, especially in agricultural products, imposed by OECD countries; undemocratic politics that have produced kleptocratic leaders; and the persistence of tribal and ethnic conflicts leading to civil strife and wars with neighboring countries.

Africa since independence has seen a series of regional integration initiatives aimed at defusing conflicts and promoting economies of scale in production and distribution. Starting in the mid-1980s, some countries liberalized payments and trade regimes in an attempt to stimulate growth. Despite a few success stories, however, there has not been a generalized takeoff toward rapid growth or expansion of trade. With the passage of time, there has been increasing recognition in Africa by the general population and their leaders of the need to carry out further structural changes and take responsibility for the success or failure of economic policies. This has led to a stronger consensus in favor of formulating outward-looking and efficiency-enhancing policies, making leaders accountable for their shortcomings, and favoring regional cooperation. The formation of the AU and its implementation plan, NEPAD,[2] are manifestations of this determination. The summit of African leaders in Lusaka, Zambia, in July 2001 heralded the replacement of the OAU and the creation of NEPAD, and the inaugural summit for the AU took place in Durban, South Africa, in July 2002.

Another manifestation has been the renewed impetus given to subregional integration initiatives, in particular, projects to create monetary unions. Monetary unions, groupings of countries sharing a common currency and central bank, are a particular type of monetary integration linking countries. The popularity of these unions has been dramatically increased by the creation of the euro zone in January 1999 and the January 2002 introduction of euro notes and coins to replace the German deutsche mark, French franc, Italian lira, and other currencies of the (at present) twelve member countries. Box 1-1 explains some of the forms that monetary integration can take.

There are a number of regional monetary integration initiatives presently being considered in Africa. In West Africa, ECOWAS since its formation has had the objective of constructing a free trade area and single currency union. The absence of any progress on the latter led a subset of ECOWAS countries to propose a second monetary zone—this in addition to the existing CFA franc zone in West Africa, known in English as WAEMU—as a fast track to the creation of the unified West African monetary zone. The timetable, which was set back by a few years, now calls for the creation of this second monetary zone, or WAMZ, by July 2005. This zone will include some or all of the following countries: the Gambia, Ghana, Guinea, Nigeria, and Sierra Leone. Such a monetary union would overlap closely with an earlier colonial grouping, the West African Currency Board. WAMZ would be subsequently merged with WAEMU to achieve the goal of a single West African currency.

2. See this book's Abbreviations and Acronyms section.

Box 1-1. *Types of Monetary Integration*

The European Commission's study to prepare for economic and monetary union and a subsequent article distinguish between three types of monetary integration.[1] Each type would involve current and capital account convertibility, but they are distinguished by whether there are separate currencies (and central banks) and, if so, whether their parities are perfectly fixed.

—An informal exchange rate union consists of separate currencies whose parities are fixed but only within margins (and central parities can be adjusted). The EMS's exchange rate mechanism after August 1993 is an example.

—A formal exchange rate union has separate currencies, but rates fluctuating within narrow or zero margins, and a strong degree of coordination among the central banks. In Africa, the CMA is an example, since the currencies of Lesotho, Namibia, and Swaziland are linked one for one with the South African rand.

—A full monetary union involves a single currency and central bank. The euro zone and both of the CFA franc zones would be examples of full monetary union.

We would add two other types of monetary integration, namely[2]:

—Adoption of another country's currency (often called dollarization or, by extension, euroization). In this case, there is only a single currency but not monetary union, since the country issuing the currency does not take into account the goals of the dollarizing country. Examples of dollarized countries are Ecuador, El Salvador, and Panama. There are several examples in Africa of countries using other countries' currencies temporarily before issuing their own (for instance, Botswana upon independence used the rand but in 1976 issued its own currency, the pula, and Eritrea used the Ethiopian birr for a period after independence).

In East Africa, Kenya, Tanzania, and Uganda have agreed to revitalize the EAC, which was effectively dissolved in the 1960s. The project envisions a single currency (at an unspecified future date), in effect reestablishing the currency union constituted around the East African shilling that was in place at the time of independence.

Southern Africa has been exploring regional integration in the context of SADC to build on the long-standing but more restricted SACU and the CMA. Though the focus of SADC is on trade and structural policies, some

—A currency board, in which a country pegs to another currency with zero margins, and the link between the two currencies is institutionalized through a mechanism that limits the money supply in the currency board country to the quantity of reserves held in the other currency. Countries operating currency boards include Bulgaria, Djibouti, and Estonia.

Within these five types of arrangements, it is interesting to distinguish those in which decisions on monetary policy (or coordination of exchange rate policies) are symmetric (that is, reflect the interests of all countries) from those that are asymmetric. By their very nature, dollarization and currency boards are asymmetric—countries adopt or peg to another currency unilaterally; there is no shared responsibility for monetary policy. But the first three arrangements can differ in their degree of asymmetry. The ERM was designed to be symmetric (with a parity grid defined around a basket currency, the European Currency Unit, or ECU), but in practice, given the superior credibility of the Bundesbank and strength of the German economy, it operated to an extent asymmetrically. Full monetary union is likely to be symmetric, since the creation of a single supranational central bank is likely to involve institutions that represent all countries, but this is not necessarily the case, nor is it true of formal exchange rate unions. In particular, in the CMA, South Africa, given the size of its economy, effectively sets monetary policy for the zone; the other countries peg their currencies to the rand. In discussing projects for monetary integration within SADC (chapter 7), we give some attention to the issue of whether an exchange rate or monetary union would be symmetric or asymmetric.

1. Emerson and others (1991), and Cobham and Robson (1994).
2. See Hawkins and Masson (2003).

consideration is also being given to expanding the CMA centered on the rand, which now includes Lesotho, Namibia, South Africa, and Swaziland, to include other SADC countries. An expanded monetary zone could involve shared monetary policy responsibility by South Africa's Reserve Bank with neighboring central banks.

A feature of regional cooperation in Africa is the existence of overlapping regional integration initiatives. For instance, COMESA includes most of the countries of SADC but also Egypt, Sudan, and East African countries and has a different timetable for trade liberalization. The CFA franc zones overlap partially with ECOWAS, as only one of the two CFA zones, WAEMU, is part of West Africa. Both WAEMU and ECOWAS have criteria for regional surveillance, but not identical ones, and dismantling of trade restrictions has proceeded differently in the two organizations. Overlapping initiatives with sometimes conflicting provisions may prove to be an obstacle to achieving the objectives of each; at the very least, they squander resources of expertise and money, which are in short supply in Africa.

In this book we focus on the effects of monetary arrangements, so we will not dwell on other aspects of regional integration, except to the extent that they are relevant to potential gains from introducing a common currency or other forms of monetary cooperation. This is not to deny that these other aspects may not be important. Indeed one of our themes is that it may well be a mistake to hope that monetary integration will be a substitute for directly addressing problems in other areas, such as regional conflicts, poor transportation links, or inadequate governance.

How did exchange rate regimes evolve into their current constellation? Roughly speaking, African countries can be divided into three groups: countries colonized by France, countries colonized by other European powers, and countries of southern Africa (also at one time colonized by European powers but with a quite separate history). A review of the history of African monetary arrangements shows that in the early postcolonial period the non-French-speaking colonies largely abandoned their colonial monetary arrangements (which were typically currency boards linked to the British pound sterling, Belgian franc, Spanish peseta, or Portuguese escudo) in favor of the creation of a national central bank and looser exchange rate arrangement, such as an adjustable peg or managed floating. In contrast, the Francophone countries largely retained their institutional structures, which linked them to their neighbors in a multilateral framework as well as to France. There are essentially three reasons for the difference in postcolonial experience. First, the British, Belgian, Spanish, and Portuguese monetary arrangements were bilateral links with the home country and did not have sufficient institutional structure to survive independence. Second, the French made efforts to adapt the CFA franc zone in order to preserve it, while the other colonial powers did not as strongly resist the dissolution of the colonial currency boards. Third, Francophone African countries had stronger political and cultural ties with the metropolitan country before independence, which made the elites in these countries generally more willing to preserve colonial institutions.

The third set of countries mentioned above is found in southern Africa. Lesotho, Swaziland, and Namibia upon independence continued to be part of a zone centered on the rand, the currency of the continent's largest economy, South Africa. Another country in the region, Botswana, abandoned the monetary union and pegs the pula to a basket of currencies (in which the rand is given a large weight, however).

We consider the advantages and disadvantages of monetary integration from the perspective of the traditional criteria for a monetary union as well as from the point of view of providing discipline over fiscal policies and helping to achieve political objectives. The advantages of a common currency (for a region or for the continent as a whole) depend importantly on the savings of transaction costs, and these savings depend on the extent of trade among countries. Unfortunately, data for most African regions do not hold out much promise that savings of transaction costs will be large. In fact, trade within regional groupings (or even with all of Africa) typically is quite low. A new currency will be more attractive if it exhibits more stability (that is, maintains its purchasing power better) than the currencies it replaces. This might be the case if monetary union provides an institutional framework for achieving more discipline over fiscal policies and a sustainable regime that insulates the (regional) central bank from pressures to provide monetary financing. On the other side of the ledger, as stressed by the OCA literature pioneered by recent Nobel Prize winner Robert Mundell, having a common monetary policy is likely to be more constraining the more dissimilar the countries are, as their economies face shocks of a quite different nature (because they export different commodities, for example). Greater labor mobility or compensating flows of capital, achieved in a federation through a system of taxes and transfers, can mitigate the effects of asymmetric shocks. Labor mobility between some countries has been quite high, for instance, to South Africa from neighboring countries. In other countries there are periods of high mobility, but when the economic or political situation changes migrants are expelled, which has occurred in several countries in both West and East Africa. As for fiscal flows between countries, the shortage of financial resources means that they are likely to be severely limited.

We argue that an important source of asymmetry among countries relates to the degree of fiscal discipline. This is likely to be especially important in the African context, since in practice a central bank's independence cannot be guaranteed, even if it is a supranational institution associated with a regional monetary union. As a result, more disciplined countries will not want to form a monetary union with countries (especially if they are large) whose excessive spending puts upward pressure on the central bank's monetary expansion. We sketch out a simple model embodying this feature, as well as the traditional OCA criteria, and calibrate it to African data. It will serve in later chapters to evaluate the economic costs and benefits of various monetary union proposals.

The experience of the currency union countries in Africa (those that are members of the CFA and CMA zones) has been different from that of countries managing independent currencies. The CFA franc zone countries experienced significantly lower inflation than the rest of sub-Saharan Africa, though no better growth performance. And they suffered a period of exchange rate overvaluation and economic crisis in the late 1980s and early 1990s that culminated in a large devaluation in 1994 (cutting in half the value of the currency relative to the French franc). The crisis was due in part to the weakness of commodity prices, the strength of the French franc, overexpansionary fiscal policies in the zone, and excessive direct and indirect monetary financing of government deficits. In recognition of the deficit problem, member countries have attempted to put in place a process of regional surveillance over national fiscal policies in order to enforce greater discipline. Each of the two CFA franc zones has also made progress in creating an effective customs union with a common external tariff. It must be recognized, however, that even these two sets of countries differ considerably: regional surveillance, trade, and cooperation are more advanced in WAEMU than in CAEMC. The CMA countries have also generally benefited from low inflation, thanks to the monetary anchor provided by South Africa's Reserve Bank, and trade linkages are very strong between South Africa and the smaller CMA countries. However, this zone, unlike the CFA, has not been accompanied by regional surveillance over fiscal policies, probably due to the great asymmetry in size that has not favored the establishment of multilateral institutions.

In most of sub-Saharan Africa (with the exception of southern Africa), independent currency regimes have been associated with higher inflation and periodic devaluations—though devaluations have also served in some cases to cushion external shocks, for instance, to the terms of trade. Initially, the official pegs were maintained with exchange controls accompanied typically by inefficiencies and corruption, and parallel exchange markets developed. Under pressure from the Bretton Woods institutions, these countries moved toward liberalizing their payments regimes starting in the mid-1980s to enable current account convertibility and the elimination of parallel markets. In many of these countries, the current exchange rate regime is some form of managed floating.

We apply lessons from both experience and theory to the proposals for regional monetary unions. We consider ECOWAS, which as noted above has a project to create a second monetary zone of mainly Anglophone countries in West Africa (those countries that are not members of WAEMU) by mid-2005. This region, however, faces a major problem because Nigeria has both asymmetric terms of trade shocks (it is a large oil exporter while its potential partners are oil importers) and large fiscal imbalances that would not bode well for the effective independence or monetary discipline of a regional central bank. Any sustainable monetary union among these countries would have to be accompanied by reinforced fiscal discipline through effective regional surveillance and controls. We also consider another possible way toward greater monetary integration in West Africa, namely, through the expansion of the CFA franc zone. We find that indeed a few candidates would both gain and also produce gains for existing WAEMU members but that WAEMU would lose from admitting some of the other ECOWAS countries.

The concept of a full monetary union among the SADC countries of southern Africa seems infeasible at this stage, since a number of countries suffer from the effects of civil conflicts and drought and are far from having converged with the macroeconomic stability of South Africa and its CMA partners. More likely, any progress in achieving monetary integration would involve a limited expansion of the existing exchange rate union constituted by the CMA, and it would likely involve a monetary policy set by South Africa, as in the existing CMA, rather than involve the delegation by that country of monetary policy to a new and untried supranational institution.

Kenya, Tanzania, and Uganda's plan to revive the monetary union that formed part of the EAC, though unlikely to produce enormous economic gains, does seem to be generally compatible with other initiatives that could contribute to greater regional solidarity. However, economic gains would likely favor Kenya, which, unlike the other two countries, has substantial exports to its neighbors. The main issues would be whether the political will now exists to push regional integration ahead and whether it would continue to exist in the future. A wider project (which includes Kenya and Uganda but not Tanzania) is a monetary union among COMESA countries. This regional grouping also partly overlaps with SADC, exhibiting the overlapping regional commitments that prevail in Africa and often lead to inaction and contention. As is the case for SADC, differences in macroeconomic stability, fiscal discipline, and financial development among COMESA countries are great, making it unlikely that such a project is achievable as currently envisioned. Moreover, South Africa is not a member, so that COMESA would not benefit from the track record of monetary stability of South Africa's Reserve Bank.

Does that mean that the goal of a single African currency is beyond reach?[3] Probably, and in any case the idea that currencies should span a continent

3. Robert Mundell has argued that though a common currency would be a good thing, a more realistic goal in the medium term would be a common peg to the euro (Mundell, 2002).

does not make a lot of sense. At present, the euro is the only regional currency with a global role. Creating a single African currency would not likely give it prominence on a world scale, and the single African monetary policy (whatever it was) would impose considerable costs on very dissimilar economies. If exchange rate stability is the primary objective, then stability could be achieved at a much lower cost through a unilateral peg to the dollar, the euro, or a combination of the two, depending on a country's pattern of trade and financial relations. If the objective of a single currency is primarily to demonstrate continental solidarity, we think that since the economic costs would be substantial, a better way should be found to demonstrate that solidarity, for instance, through agreement to dismantle barriers to the movement of goods, people, and capital throughout the region. Of course, regional integration would be abetted by succeeding with the NEPAD initiative. By reducing conflicts, improving governance, eliminating corruption and fiscal excesses, and promoting the rule of law, African countries would become much more attractive partners in regional cooperation.

How will exchange rate regimes in Africa evolve in the short run to medium run in light of developments in the rest of the world? We believe that economic realities suggest that grand new projects for monetary unions are unlikely to be successful, though it is possible that expansion of existing monetary unions may take place, building on the considerable experience and credibility of the CFA franc zone and the CMA. However, enlargement of the CFA franc zone poses institutional problems. Turning to southern Africa, the CMA countries differ considerably in financial development and macroeconomic stability from their neighbors, so any expansion of the CMA is likely to be limited and delayed.

Recently, a great deal of attention has been paid to the hypothesis that countries need to choose between very hard pegs (in the limit, a monetary union) or flexible exchange rates. The intermediate regimes are not sustainable. The main argument relates to the trend toward capital account liberalization, which makes difficult the maintenance of anything but perfectly credible pegs. We consider that this factor is unlikely to dictate the choice of regime for most African countries, which continue not to be completely integrated with international capital markets, as there are capital controls, economic and political risks, and high transactions costs that inhibit capital movements. The absence of perfect capital mobility leaves open the full range of possible regimes, including adjustable pegs.

A major issue concerns the choice between a domestic nominal anchor and some form of exchange rate target. Exchange rate targets are fairly transparent (especially single currency pegs, less so for a basket peg) and do not require

sophisticated financial systems, since the central bank essentially makes the foreign exchange market, buying and selling as necessary. If an exchange rate peg
is preferred, the choice of the anchoring currency is also important. The euro,
launched in January 2002, is already the world's second most important currency, and the euro area is set to expand further. Given the extent of Africa's
trade with Europe, a peg to the euro may be an attractive option.

In this context, the question arises as to whether the EU could play some
role in guaranteeing a peg to its currency, as is done by France for the CFA
franc, now that the euro has replaced the French franc as the anchoring currency. An expansion and transformation of the CFA franc zone would allow
countries joining it to achieve stability with the euro, while at the same time
benefiting from the considerable credibility associated with the CFA franc. It
would be natural to envision the EU assuming France's role of guaranteeing
the currency peg. However, France's EU partners have shown no enthusiasm
for doing so, especially since an enlarged CFA might have more serious budgetary and monetary consequences for Europe than is the case at present.
The question for African countries would then arise of whether to continue
to anchor the CFA to the euro and, if so, how. The three main alternatives
would be a joint float, a currency board with a peg to the euro, or euroization
(the outright adoption by African countries of the euro as their currency). If
the former, the currency would then rely solely on the discipline and independence of the central bank operating a credible domestic monetary anchor.
If the latter, countries would abandon any possibility of monetary independence vis-à-vis Europe, and doing so would likely revive perceptions of colonial dependence as well as produce a loss of the seigniorage that accrues to
countries issuing their own currencies. The currency board option would
allow little or no independence, except symbolic, but would at least raise
some seigniorage for the central bank.

With increasing financial development, a domestic financial target becomes
both more desirable and achievable. This is likely to be the route followed by
the more advanced and larger economies or by regional monetary unions. It is
already practiced in South Africa, which targets domestic inflation and lets the
rand float freely in foreign exchange markets. At present, this is an option that
is open to few of the countries or regions in Africa, but greater institutional and
financial development could make it an attractive option for more—but by no
means all—African countries. In the future, therefore, we see the monetary
geography of Africa as including diverse arrangements—some regional currencies, some countries with independent currencies, and these currencies either
pegged to international currencies or floating—as is currently the case.

2

African Currency Regimes since World War II

Providing historical context for the current constellation of currency areas throws light on the potential success of initiatives toward greater monetary integration. Indeed the proposals to create monetary unions encompassing the countries of ECOWAS in West Africa and of EAC and of COMESA in East and southern Africa, to reinforce or enlarge the CFA franc zone, or to extend the rand area to SADC, to say nothing of the plan to create a single currency for Africa, need to be evaluated in light of past experiences with monetary integration. However, this is not the place for an exhaustive survey of the use of money since the dawn of recorded time. Instead, the experience in the postwar period, both before and after decolonization, seems most relevant to the extent that economies had already acquired some of the structural features that characterize them today. A look at the immediate preindependence experience shows that much of the continent had currencies that were tightly linked to the currency issued by the European colonizer. Moreover, neighboring colonies often shared the same African currency.

This could be used in support of the argument that reestablishing those monetary unions is both feasible and, more speculatively, desirable. However, subsequent history suggests reasons to doubt that assessment, since in most cases those monetary or exchange rate unions were dissolved shortly after independence and each African country now typically has its own currency and independent monetary policy. The two major exceptions are the CFA franc zones in West and Central Africa, which consist mainly of former French countries, and the CMA centered around South Africa and the rand (though the smaller CMA countries do have their own currencies). These cases provide interesting insights into why monetary and exchange rate unions get dissolved and the institutional development needed for their success. Thus the prospects for the continued existence of these zones and the creation of new monetary unions are illuminated by the historical experience.

Precolonial Period

At various times in the world's monetary history, Africa has held an important role, in particular, supplying precious metals that served as money. During the medieval period, the continent was a major source of gold, most of which reached Europe via trans-Saharan trade routes from West Africa to North Africa. From the ninth to the sixteenth century, Africa was a prime supplier of gold to the world economy until it was eclipsed by the gold discoveries in the new world. During the earlier period, "West African gold was absolutely vital for the monetization of the medieval Mediterranean economy and the maintenance of its balance of payments with South Asia."[1]

With the exception of the Asante kingdom in West Africa, gold played a small role for Africa's own monetary use. Instead, a variety of goods served as units of account, including palm oil, cotton cloths, cowrie shells, copper ingots, brass or iron bars, and brass horseshoe-shaped *manillas*.[2] The case of cowries in West Africa has received considerable attention. The shells were imported from the Indian Ocean, so that transport costs limited the expansion of the money supply. However, improved shipping technology in the late nineteenth century led to rampant inflation.[3] The limitations on their usefulness as a form of money, including their weight when carried over long distances, were a reason for the introduction of colonial coinage by the British.[4] However, cowries continued to maintain their role to some extent under British rule, and they still had some exchange value in markets of northwestern Ghana as late as the 1960s.[5]

Despite being overshadowed by other sources of bullion, Africa continued to be a notable supplier of precious metals. The British guinea coin was named after the area in West Africa where the silver was mined, which had unusually

1. Austen (1987, p. 36).
2. Austen (1987, p. 92).
3. Austen (1987, p. 134).
4. Helleiner (2003, p. 170).
5. Johnson (1970).

rich deposits. In the late nineteenth and early twentieth century, South Africa became an important enough source of gold that an interruption of its supply to the London market, when the world economy was on the gold standard or the Bretton Woods gold-exchange standard, would have had implications for the international monetary system.

Colonial Monetary Arrangements

As Africa increased its contacts with European powers, coastal areas tended to adopt European silver coins of various kinds (for example, Austrian Maria Theresa thalers and French five-franc pieces) alongside African commodity currencies.[6]

However, the advent of colonization soon led to the replacement of both African commodity currencies and silver coins by government-issued coins and notes linked to the metropolitan currency.[7] Since the metropolitan governments were on the gold standard, this essentially linked African currencies to gold.

Incorporating Africa into the international monetary system via linkage with the metropolitan currency had both advantages and disadvantages. It facilitated international trade but could discourage internal trade in areas with little access to the official currency. Also, it was a manifestation of dependency on the financial system of the métropole, and it may have inhibited the development of domestic financial institutions.

The Great Depression and Second World War ushered in regimes that, at least in the early postwar years, involved extensive restrictions on the convertibility of the European currencies to which the African colonies were linked. Since European economies had been weakened by the war and their import needs greatly exceeded their export capacities, they all imposed various import restrictions and exchange controls that prevented the free international use of their currencies. So instead of being a link to a single international monetary standard, the colonial monetary arrangements served to tie each African economy much more closely to its colonial power. Payment restrictions were accompanied by import preferences vis-à-vis the metropolitan country that had much the same effect.

This period also saw the creation of monetary institutions that gave further structure to the African monetary arrangements, while maintaining the close

---

6. Ethiopia and Liberia, which did not fall under colonial rule, are discussed in chapter 5.
7. Austen (1987, p. 134).

link with the metropolitan currency. Initially the French franc circulated in France's African colonies, but over time France introduced colonial currencies. After the Second World War, France's tropical African colonies shared the Colonies Françaises d'Afrique (CFA) franc. In 1948 the CFA franc was pegged to the French franc at a rate of one CFA franc to two French francs.[8] The CFA franc served as currency for two separate groupings of sub-Saharan countries, French West Africa and French Equatorial Africa.[9] The French Treasury guaranteed the exchange rate and ensured transferability to and from France and the other territories through potentially unlimited financing provided by an operations account. Until 1955 the right of bank note issue in the CFA franc zones was vested in certain private banks. In 1955 two new public institutions were given responsibility for note issue in West and Central Africa: the Institut d'Emission de l'Afrique Occidentale Française et du Togo (Dahomey, Guinea, Côte d'Ivoire, Mali, Mauritania, Niger, Senegal, Upper Volta, and Togo), and Institut d'Emission de l'Afrique Equatoriale Française et du Cameroun (Cameroun, Central African Republic, Chad, Congo-Brazzaville, and Gabon).[10] Each of these monetary institutes, based in Paris and controlled by the French government, issued a distinct bank note that was the respective monetary area's version of the CFA franc.

The operations account system (which is still in place in the existing CFA franc zones, albeit in modified form) needs to be distinguished from a traditional system based on foreign exchange reserves (such as a currency board or unilateral peg), since the former provides unlimited access to a particular foreign currency, the French franc. In the colonial system, the African countries in the franc zone were obliged to deposit all their earnings in francs and the countervalue of their earnings in foreign currency in their Operations Account with the French Treasury, but had unlimited access to French francs in exchange for their own currency.[11] Access to French francs was not the same as access to foreign exchange (in particular, U.S. dollars), however, since at the time the French franc was not freely convertible into other major currencies. Access to French franc balances was unlimited, since operations account balances could become negative, providing financing for potentially large

8. With the move to the new French franc in 1960, the parity became one CFA franc to 0.02 French francs. This parity remained in effect until the devaluation of the CFA franc on January 11, 1994, making one CFA franc to 0.01 French francs.

9. Also, League of Nations–mandated territories Cameroun and Togo and French-controlled islands in the Indian Ocean, including Madagascar and Comoros.

10. Abdel-Salam (1970, p. 341).

11. Abdel-Salam (1970, p. 340).

balance of payments deficits, but only vis-à-vis the franc zone, because international use of the French franc was restricted.

Most of the British colonies were grouped into three currency boards—the West African Currency Board, Southern Rhodesia Currency Board, and East African Currency Board—in each of which the quantity of money was linked to the amount of sterling assets held by the currency board.[12] The membership of the West African Currency Board included the Gambia, Gold Coast, Nigeria, Sierra Leone, and later the British Cameroons. The Southern Rhodesia Currency Board (or Central African Board after 1954) included Southern Rhodesia, Northern Rhodesia, and Nyasaland. The East African Currency Board grouped Kenya, Tanganyika, Uganda, and later Zanzibar, Aden, Somalia, and Ethiopia. Each of the currency boards was characterized by a fixed parity with the pound sterling, an automatic system of issue, and (in principle) 100 percent sterling cover for the local currency.[13] Thus the British had a quite different mechanism from the French for ensuring the convertibility of their currencies into the metropolitan currency. The currency board's automaticity ensured that the parity vis-à-vis the pound sterling could be maintained and would not be strained by excessive monetary expansion without the British monetary authorities having to provide overdraft facilities.

Spain, Belgium, and Portugal had various arrangements with their colonies that in each case provided for a link with the metropolitan currency. Belgian colonies of the Congo and Rwanda-Urundi formed a monetary union whose currency, the Congolese franc, was pegged to the Belgian franc.[14] Portuguese and Spanish colonies typically used the escudo or peseta, respectively. The British protectorates in southern Africa were linked to the Union of South Africa, the major economy in the region, which was formed in 1910. It had its own currency, the South African pound, which, upon creation of South Africa's central bank (the Reserve Bank of South Africa) in 1921, became the sole circulating medium and legal tender for the small British protectorates of Bechuanaland (Botswana), Basutoland (Lesotho), and Swaziland and also for the League of Nations' trusteeship territory of South West Africa (Namibia). In 1961 the South African pound was replaced by a new currency, the rand, and the monetary union became known informally as the Rand Monetary Area.

12. British protectorates in southern Africa depended on the Reserve Bank of South Africa.
13. Abdel-Salam (1970, p. 346).
14. However, the Belgian authorities had earlier resisted the introduction of a colonial currency in the Congo state before 1908, fearing that it would have allowed Africans to break the link between selling produce to Belgian merchants and buying imports from them (Helleiner, 2003, p. 174).

After Independence

As the movement leading to general decolonization gained strength, Britain and France differed in the arrangements that they proposed for their African colonies. France attempted to preserve and strengthen the currency unions based on the CFA franc by allowing for greater African representation on governing boards and offering a currency guarantee on French franc reserves. The link with the French franc was maintained, as was France's strong influence on monetary policy, while the French Treasury continued to provide a guarantee of convertibility.

In contrast, Britain, which had earlier resisted the creation of colonial central banks, was not as determined (or successful) in influencing the postcolonial monetary policy regimes. In the face of opposition to the colonial currency boards, by the mid-1950s the Bank of England had accepted the idea of replacement of the currency boards by African central banks. For instance, in 1957 (before independence) a high-ranking official of the Bank of England, J. B. Loynes, provided the Nigerian federal government with advice on the establishment of a central bank.[15] Similarly, the Bank of England encouraged the East African Currency Board to take on central banking functions.[16] One by one each of the newly independent countries created its own central bank and currency. Even when these new currencies were to be linked together, as in the EAC (composed of Kenya, Tanzania, and Uganda), the forces of disintegration were irresistible in the absence of external inducements to cooperate. Thus while the former French colonies are still grouped into two currency unions, WAEMU and CAEMC, the former British colonies (with the exception of the British protectorates in southern Africa) all have independent monetary policies and separate currencies. The former Spanish and Portuguese colonies also generally have their own currencies, though several of them in fact have joined one of the CFA zones (Equatorial Guinea joined CAEMC in 1985, and Guinea-Bissau joined WAEMU in 1997) or linked their currencies to the euro (Cape Verde has done so, with the financial assistance of Portugal), also producing exchange rate stability vis-à-vis the CFA franc.

15. Crick (1965, p. 363). However, Helleiner (2003, p. 199) points to earlier hostility to the creation of central banks. Apparently, the Bank of England's opposition was only abandoned after it appeared that most colonies upon independence were determined to leave the currency board.

16. See Crick (1965, p. 391). The recommendation to move to a regional central bank was also made by Dr. Erwin Blumenthal of the Deutsche Bundesbank in a report commissioned in 1962 by the newly independent Tanganyika government (Crick, 1965, p. 404).

Figure 2-1. *Currency Areas, 1964*

Franc zone
Other franc
Pound sterling area
Pound sterling territories

Source: Mládek (1964a, 1964b).

It is true that the former colonies of Britain did tend to remain in the sterling area, in the sense that payments regulations gave preference to transfers vis-à-vis other countries using the pound sterling or linked to it. Figure 2-1 shows what can loosely be called the French franc and pound sterling area countries in Africa in 1964, less than a decade after independence. However, while the franc zone was an institutionally supported monetary union, the sterling area in 1964 was only a loose arrangement mainly based on preferential payments regulations.

The franc area in 1964 included Algeria, Morocco, and Tunisia, which maintained some monetary arrangements with France, though increasingly loose ones; the monetary unions constituted by the two CFA franc zones in West and Central Africa; and the Malagasy Republic and Comoros. The sterling area at this time was characterized not by monetary unions (with the exception of the East African currency union, which disappeared soon after) or operations accounts in sterling, but rather by the following characteristics, which generally applied to member countries: rates of exchange quoted in sterling; official reserves held in sterling; payments and private assets normally routed through or held in London; and freedom of payments made within the sterling area, but restrictions on payments outside.[17] Sterling area countries and territories in 1964 included all former and present British colonies in Africa (including South Africa) except British Cameroons, which merged with French Cameroun, and British Somaliland, which was absorbed in the Republic of Somalia. By this time other colonial powers' currency areas had disappeared or only survived in countries not yet independent, such as Angola and Mozambique, which were part of the Portuguese escudo zone, though these countries had their own bank notes.[18] Mozambique adopted a new currency, the metical, in 1980, five years after independence, and initially its official fixed parity was defined in terms of a basket of six currencies.[19] Upon independence in 1960 (and the independence of the Belgian Congo), Rwanda and Burundi ceased using the Congolese franc and responsibility for issuing the new franc of Rwanda and Burundi was given to a joint monetary institution.[20] However, the economic union did not survive the tribal conflicts that occurred in 1963–64, and each country subsequently adopted its own currency.

The sterling area ceased to have any operational significance with the abandonment of exchange controls by Britain in the late 1970s. Moreover, the breakdown of the Bretton Woods system of fixed but adjustable parities and the advent of generalized floating of the currencies of the major powers had led many African countries to loosen their exchange rate links with the former colonial power and to devalue or abandon their exchange rate parities with the metropolitan currency. However, the CFA franc zone retains, with

---

17. Mládek (1964b).

18. The escudo zone broke down before independence because of payments imbalances, and the colonial escudos were made inconvertible in the metropolitan currency. See Valério (2002).

19. See *Indian Ocean Newsletter* (1986).

20. See Institut Royal des Relations Internationales (1963).

the financial support of France, the fixed peg to the French franc, despite a devaluation that occurred in 1994.

Dissolution of British Currency Boards

Seeds of the dismemberment of currency boards in western and eastern Africa were already planted before independence. The boards' rigidity and automaticity evoked the criticism by British academics that they could not be managed flexibly enough to attain such policy objectives as stimulating economic activity, and forcing colonies to hold reserves in London detracted from their use of their savings to foster development.[21] Sterling balances yielded at the time very low rates of interest, stimulating demands that the colonies be allowed to hold a more diversified portfolio of assets. In any case, despite resistance from the Bank of England, which feared that African central banks would be subjected to political pressures and would be ineffective if capital markets were not in place, the British authorities succumbed to the criticisms (including those of economists from the U.S. Federal Reserve and World Bank) and agreed to dismantle the currency boards and set up central banks in each of the colonies.[22]

The Central African Currency Board was abolished in April 1956. It was replaced by the Central Bank of Rhodesia and Nyasaland, which operated until 1964, when the newly independent countries of Malawi, Rhodesia, and Zambia started issuing their own banknotes. In large part because of political frictions and diverging economic interests among the member countries,[23] the monetary area was definitively dissolved in June 1965 and each of the countries created its own central bank.[24] In West Africa, member countries progressively withdrew from the West African Currency Board: Ghana doing so in 1957, Nigeria in 1959, British Cameroons in 1962 (to join the Central African CFA franc zone as part of Cameroun), Sierra Leone in 1963, and the Gambia in 1964. The new currencies in Ghana (the Ghanaian pound, later the cedi) and Nigeria (the Nigerian pound, later the naira) were initially linked at par with sterling but subsequently depreciated.

In East Africa, the former colonies aimed to retain cohesion among the member countries and replace the currency board with some type of monetary union in the context of a new East African Community linking Kenya, Tanzania, and Uganda. However, after protracted negotiations that broke down in 1966, each of the three countries decided to issue its own currency and create its own central bank.[25] The currencies were to be freely convertible at par,

21. Hazlewood (1952).
22. Uche (1997, pp. 152–53); Helleiner (2001).
23. See Birmingham and Martin (1983).
24. Abdel-Salam (1970, p. 347).
25. Abdel-Salam (1970, p. 349).

but subsequent events and political disagreements led to restrictions on convertibility and exchange rate fluctuations, effectively ending the monetary union.[26] Capitalist Kenya and socialist Tanzania were following quite different economic policies, while the Uganda of Idi Amin was practically at war with its neighbors. In these circumstances, the cooperation required to make monetary union work was clearly not present.

Consolidation of the CFA Franc Zone

In contrast to Britain, France moved to shore up the institutions that linked its former African colonies to the French franc by increasing African participation in decisions while maintaining the financing facility embodied in the operations accounts. In 1959 the Instituts d'Emission were transformed into central banks, called the BCEAO and the BCEAEC (subsequently renamed BEAC). Their headquarters were initially in Paris, but provisions were made for them to move to Africa. In addition to the currency issue, the two central banks were authorized to extend credit to commercial banks and the treasuries of the member countries. Starting in 1966, each central bank could grant short-term loans to a national treasury equal to 10 percent of the country's fiscal receipts. In 1970 this limit was raised to 15 percent in exceptional circumstances, and in 1972–73 the limit was boosted to 20 percent, accompanied by abandonment of restrictions on the exceptional nature of full access and the short maturity of the loans.[27] The agreements establishing the central banks provided for each of them to pool the foreign exchange reserves of their member countries and to maintain a separate operations account at the French Treasury. The boards of the two banks now included both French and African representatives.[28]

The former French colonies upon independence chose to remain in the CFA franc zone and participate in the regional central bank, with the exception of Guinea and Mali,[29] which chose an anticapitalist path of national self-reliance rather than integration with the world economy.[30] Both countries created their own central banks and currencies. It is hard to say whether the decision of the other, nonsocialist, countries to remain in the franc zone was due to a calculation of the benefits of monetary stability and the financing guarantee of the operations account or due to the advantages of maintaining other links with France. Cultural links with the former metropolitan power

26. Cohen (1998, p. 73).
27. Vinay (1988, p. 24).
28. Abdel-Salam (1970).
29. Mali subsequently reached agreement with France in 1967 on the conditions for Mali to rejoin the CFA franc zone, and, after a period of pegging to the French franc with French support, Mali did so in 1984.
30. Yansané (1984).

remained strong, as France had long welcomed the participation of African elites in French life, for instance, honoring the contributions of poet (and later statesman) Léopold Senghor by naming him to the *Académie Française* and making Félix Houphoët-Boigny (later Côte d'Ivoire's first president) a French cabinet minister. In any case, the French government was keen on maintaining the monetary relationship with African countries and exerted pressures to induce them to continue to participate.[31] French desire to preserve the franc zone and the African leaders' concurrence seem to have more to do with shared interests of a small transnational group of key policymakers than with any clear economic interest, however, as Stasavage argues convincingly.[32] He documents the close personal ties of African leaders with France and the fact that they resisted calls for a more active exchange rate policy from their populations. Conversely, French policy was decided by African hands, often in the face of the French public's indifference or opposition.

The economic performance of the CFA franc zone clearly demonstrates that price and monetary stability were important features of the continuing link with a currency of a major economic power. Indeed Boughton argues that considered alone, monetary union among the African members of the CFA franc zone would not seem to yield obvious benefits.[33] Instead, France needs to be considered an integral part of the system and a source of benefits that include discipline, credibility, and stability in international competitiveness. This, however, may be too negative a view of a purely African monetary union since it ignores the advantages of having a supranational central bank that is at least partially insulated from pressures from national treasuries, an issue discussed later in this book. It is also noteworthy that even in 1970 an observer could say that "one of the fundamental ills of the CFA franc system is that it had given its member countries an essentially overvalued currency,

---

31. Monga and Tchatchouang argue that the continued existence of the CFA franc zone was primarily the result of French pressure rather than the wishes of the African colonies, which were given independence on the condition that they would sign cooperation accords with France (Monga and Tchatchouang, 1996, p. 23). E. Helleiner notes that the harsh treatment that France accorded to Guinea and Mali served as a caution to the others. He also suggests that aside from these two countries, the leaders of Francophone African countries were more conservative in their economic philosophy than their Anglophone counterparts and hence did not want to create their own central banks for the purpose of engaging in activist monetary policies (Helleiner, 2003, p. 212). Mundell suggests that the different choices of policy regime made by leaders of Francophone and Anglophone African countries were related in part to their different economic training. Keynesian heterodoxy in monetary matters was much more in vogue in London than in Paris in the postwar period (Mundell, 1972).

32. Stasavage (2003).

33. Boughton (1991).

which has seriously impaired the competitiveness of their export products, and has tied their economies to French markets."[34] This ill became evident in the course of the 1980s and led to an economic crisis that culminated in the devaluation in 1994 of the CFA franc.

The CFA franc zone was further modified in 1972–73 by new treaties between France and the African members. In Central Africa, the central bank was renamed the BEAC, its headquarters moved to Yaoundé, Cameroun, as of 1977, and an African named as governor. In West Africa, similarly, the BCEAO headquarters was moved to Dakar, Senegal, in 1978 and henceforth was headed by an African, the first governor being Abdoulaye Fadiga. France, responding to African critiques that its monetary policy was too rigid and did not promote development, made token changes intended to placate politicians.[35] The requirements for holding reserves in the operations account were loosened somewhat. These provisions are still in effect: holdings of the operations account need only constitute 65 percent of total reserves, but emergency measures are to be taken if the ratio of reserves to the central bank's sight liabilities decline below 20 percent or if the operations account balance becomes negative. The limit on lending to national treasuries was raised to 20 percent of their fiscal receipts in the previous year. France provided an exchange rate guarantee for reserves in the operations account, compensating for any decline in the value of the French franc against the Special Drawing Right (SDR).[36] This guarantee and generous remuneration of French franc balances (linked to the French money market rate) made the requirement to hold 65 percent of reserves in the operations account not constraining. Indeed it was in the interest of African central banks to hold reserves in excess of the minimum, because in effect they were being paid an interest rate whose high level reflected an exchange rate risk to which they were not exposed.[37] As a counterpart for the overdraft facilities of the operations account, France retained some representation on the bodies in each central bank that made monetary policy decisions. However, that representation was a minority one.[38]

Despite these changes, Madagascar and Mauritania chose to quit the CFA franc zone rather than sign the new treaties with France. Madagascar's decision was the result of a choice in favor of a planned economy, while Mauritania's

34. Abdel-Salam (1970, p. 345).

35. Stasavage (2003, ch. 3).

36. Vinay (1988, annex 6).

37. Vizy (1989, p. 47).

38. There are currently two French representatives (out of a total of eighteen) on the board of the BCEAO and three (out of thirteen) on the board of the BEAC. See A. Laure Gnassou, "La BCE doit tisser des liens avec les banques centrales africaines de la zone franc," *Le Monde*, June 18, 2001.

decision reflected its lack of solidarity with its West African neighbors, with whom it had had ethnic conflicts.[39]

The 1994 devaluation was a major event that risked destroying the CFA franc zones. The decision to devalue came after years of wrangling; devaluation was advocated early on by the IMF and World Bank but resisted by both the French and African authorities. France signaled a change in its position at a meeting of the Franc zone in Abidjan, Côte d'Ivoire, in September 1993, when it made clear that it would only provide aid to countries having agreed to pro-grams with the Bretton Woods institutions (the IMF and World Bank).[40] The depth of the economic and financial crisis eventually forced African heads of state to accept the fact that there was no alternative to devaluation, and on Jan-uary 11, 1994, the decision was announced to cut the value of the CFA franc in half, from fifty to the French franc to 100.[41] Instead of destroying the mone-tary union or cutting the link with the French franc, the commitment to a fixed parity was reiterated and the two African zones agreed on measures that would reinforce their cooperation on fiscal policy, banking supervision, and regional free trade.[42] The framework for enhanced cooperation was embodied in treaties setting up the WAEMU and CAEMC, respectively.

Creation of Southern Africa's CMA

As mentioned above, the British protectorates in southern Africa adopted the South African currency. After they became independent in the late 1960s, Botswana, Lesotho, and Swaziland continued to use the rand as the sole cur-rency in circulation, without any formal agreement with the South African government. However, informally these three nations and the Republic of South Africa constituted the rand area. There were no internal restrictions on payments within the zone, and the smaller members imposed similar pay-ments restrictions outside the zone to those of South Africa.

In 1969 after a customs union agreement was renegotiated with South Africa, attention turned to formalizing and adapting monetary relations between the smaller countries and South Africa. This led eventually, in Decem-

---

39. Parmentier and Tenconi (1996, p. 39).

40. See Parmentier and Tenconi (1996, p. 155). Stasavage maintains that the decision by Edouard Balladur (the French prime minister at the time) to restrict support granted to African governments reflected both the much smaller proportion of French officials with CFA franc zone backgrounds in his government and the rivalry between Balladur and Jacques Chirac for the 1995 presidential nomination (Stasavage, 2003, chapter 5).

41. The Comoros franc was devalued by half this amount, from fifty to the French franc to seventy-five.

42. See, for instance, Clément and others (1996). For the lead up to the devaluation, see, for instance, Boughton (1993).

ber 1974, to a formal agreement recognizing the Rand Monetary Area linking Lesotho and Swaziland with South Africa; Botswana had decided to withdraw from the monetary union. The agreement provided that the rand would be legal tender and exchangeable at par within Lesotho and Swaziland, but the latter would have the right to issue their own currencies, whose note issue would be backed 100 percent by rand deposits with the SARB.[43] There would be no restrictions on transfers of funds within the union or on access of the smaller countries to South Africa's capital markets. The smaller countries would apply substantially the same foreign exchange controls as South Africa for transfers outside the area, though they could apply their own regulations on foreign direct investment. Among exchange rate unions with a dominant member, South Africa was unique in that it agreed to share seigniorage on the basis of an estimate of the rand currency circulating in the other two member countries. Swaziland established its own monetary authority and began to issue its own currency, while Lesotho did not. Botswana continued to use the rand on an informal basis until the introduction of the pula in August 1976, which was pegged to the U.S. dollar until 1980, at which time it was it was pegged to a basket of currencies. Botswana's decision to have its own currency and, on occasion, to vary its exchange rate peg and the basket or currency to which it is pegged has allowed the authorities to insulate the economy to some extent from fluctuations in the demand for its exports, in particular, diamonds.[44]

The Rand Monetary Area was replaced in July 1986 by the CMA as a result of agreement among the three countries to accommodate certain concerns of Swaziland. The MMA made Namibia an independent member of the CMA in February 1992, though the latter had long been a de facto member of the rand zone. As was the case for the Rand Monetary Area, the CMA is a formal exchange rate union in which monetary policy is effectively set by South Africa but where the smaller members have the right to issue their own currencies. There are no restrictions on transfers of funds within the CMA, and the smaller countries' currencies are convertible into rand at a one-to-one rate. They are not legal tender in South Africa, however. Namibia and Lesotho issue their own currencies (as does Swaziland), but they have to be fully backed by prescribed rand assets (the latter is not true for Swaziland).[45]

South Africa introduced a dual currency system in 1979, which applied to payments outside the CMA. The commercial rand rate was determined in the market subject to reserve bank intervention, while the financial rand, which applied to most nonresident portfolio and direct investment, floated cleanly

43. d'A. Collings and others (1978, p. 102).
44. Masalila and Motshidisi (2003).
45. Van Zyl (2003).

(except for some intervention in the early 1990s), with market thinness making the rate volatile. One of the objectives was to break the link between domestic and foreign interest rates and to insulate the capital account from certain categories of capital flows.[46] The financial rand was abolished in 1983 and some capital controls on residents liberalized, but following large depreciations of the single rate associated with gold price weakness and the debt crisis in 1985, the financial rand was reintroduced and controls tightened again. The dual currency system remained in effect until exchange rate unification in 1995. The objective of the reserve bank's intervention in the commercial rand market during the period 1979–99 has been characterized as aiming to maintain the profitability and stability in the gold industry by smoothing the real rand price of gold with, as a consequence, a highly variable real exchange rate. After 1988, however, the real rand gold price was allowed to fall and the reserve bank was more active in limiting movements of the real exchange rate.[47]

The continued existence of an exchange rate union based around South Africa's currency is evidence of the mutual advantage of a exchange rate stability and the circulation of rand throughout the area (much of the revenues of the smaller countries comes from remittances from workers in South Africa). The willingness of South Africa to listen to the concerns of its neighbors, as evidenced by the various adaptations of the monetary union over time, has also contributed to its success. The relative size of the countries is a factor in the durability of the relationship, as there is no doubt where the responsibility for monetary policies lies.[48]

Today's Exchange Rate Regimes

The international environment in which African currencies function is very different today compared to what prevailed in the early postcolonial period. In that earlier period, the British pound sterling and French franc zones (see figure 2-1) were essentially comprised of countries with currencies fixed to the two European currencies. Since both the franc and pound sterling were pegged to gold via the U.S. dollar, albeit with possible changes in parities,[49] African currencies exhibited exchange rate stability against all other major reserve currencies. Three major events have occurred in the meantime, two external and one internal, with significant effects on the monetary geography of Africa.

---

46. Aron, Elbadawi, and Kahn (2000).
47. Aron, Elbadawi, and Kahn (2000).
48. Cohen (1998) argues that the existence of a hegemonic power is a strong factor favoring the survival of common currency areas.
49. There was a devaluation of the pound in 1967 and the franc in 1969.

The first major event started in 1973, when the central banks of countries issuing the major currencies no longer attempted to maintain parities, either against the dollar or against gold. Thus an African country's choice of which currency to use as an anchor could have major repercussions on its effective exchange rate (that is, a weighted average of its exchange rate against other currencies), since the major currencies now fluctuated among themselves. In particular, countries that pegged to a European currency could experience a large, real appreciation if the dollar was weak, and vice versa. Movements of European currencies among themselves could have similar effects. While the formation of the EMS and the progressive hardening of exchange rates between pairs of EMS currencies during the 1980s limited the latter problem, the exchange rate crises in 1992–93 exacerbated intra-European exchange rate volatility once again, especially after Britain and Italy were forced to leave the exchange rate mechanism in September 1992. Movements among the exchange rates of the major currencies thus made exchange rate pegs more difficult for the African countries, as is also true for other developing countries.

The second major event involved the recognition by policymakers in developing countries that payments restrictions needed to prop up pegged exchange rates produced widespread inefficiencies, in environments where fiscal discipline did not exist and inflation resulted in a continual decline in competitiveness. In particular, exchange controls and rationing of foreign exchange opened up widespread opportunities for corruption and distortions across sectors. As a result of this realization and pressures from official lenders, African countries moved to liberalize their international payments and to give greater weight to market forces in the determination of their exchange rates. Many countries therefore moved to greater exchange rate flexibility (though not to free floating), either abandoning exchange rate parities or allowing greater fluctuations around them. As a result, in 2001 most countries exhibited substantial exchange rate volatility against the two most important reserve currencies, the dollar and the euro (figures 2-2 and 2-3, respectively).

The principal exception was constituted by the countries of the two CFA franc zones, WAEMU and CAEMC. As indicated in figure 2-3, the two CFA francs are perfectly stable against the euro (at a rate of 655.967 CFAF to one euro) and have been since the introduction of the latter on January 1, 1999, at which time the euro replaced the French franc as the anchor for the CFA francs.[50]

50. As a result of an agreement reached in March 1998, Cape Verde is also linked to the euro at a fixed parity, with the convertibility of the Cape Verde escudo guaranteed by Portugal (Alibert, 1999).

Figure 2-2. *Exchange Rate Volatility against the U.S. Dollar, 2000–01ᵃ*

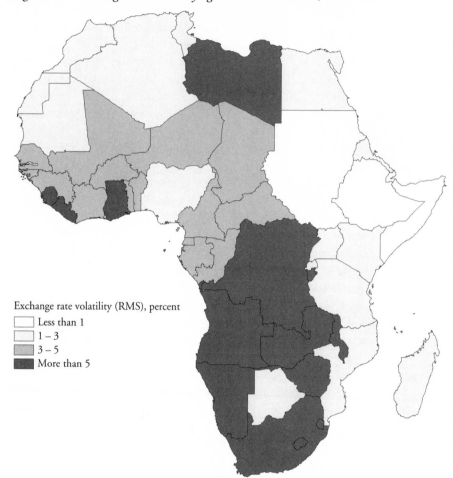

Exchange rate volatility (RMS), percent
- Less than 1
- 1 – 3
- 3 – 5
- More than 5

Source: IMF, International Financial Statistics database (2002).
a. Monthly data.

The official exchange rate classification published by the IMF to some extent reflects this reality, as a majority of African countries in 2001 practiced either managed floating or independent floating—twenty-six out of fifty-two countries (see table 2-1). Aside from the countries of the CFA and CMA zones (excluding South Africa, which as the anchor of the CMA was classified as independently floating against the rest of the world), few African countries had hard pegs or currency board arrangements (the list includes

Figure 2-3. *Exchange Rate Volatility against the Euro, 2000–01*[a]

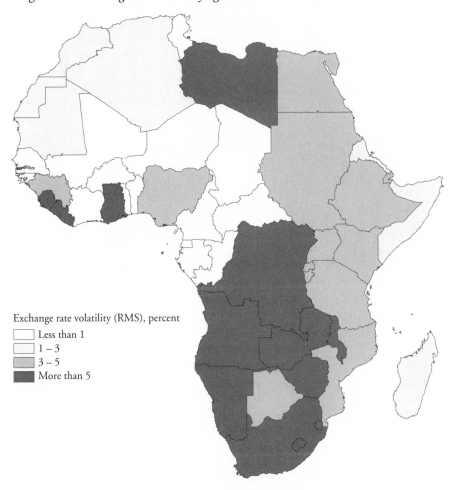

Exchange rate volatility (RMS), percent

☐ Less than 1
☐ 1 – 3
☐ 3 – 5
■ More than 5

Source: IMF, International Financial Statistics database (2002).
a. Monthly data.

only Botswana, which pegs to a basket, Djibouti, Eritrea, Libya, Morocco, Seychelles, and Zimbabwe). Only one country, Egypt, was classified as having a "pegged exchange rate with horizontal bands."

An alternative classification created by Levy-Yeyati and Sturzenegger on the basis of the actual behavior of exchange rates and reserves broadly supported the existence of intermediate and floating rate regimes, albeit with some differences with respect to some of the countries officially declared as

Table 2-1. *African Currencies and Exchange Arrangements*

Country	Currency	Article VIII acceptance date[a]	IMF[b]	Exchange arrangement Levy-Yeyati & Sturzenegger[c]	Reinhart & Rogoff[d]
Algeria	Algerian dinar	Sep-97	MF	FL	2
Angola	New kwanza		MF	IN	—
Benin	CFA franc	Jun-96	NL	FX	1
Botswana	Pula	Nov-95	P	FX (1976)	2
Burkina Faso	CFA franc	Jun-96	NL	FL	1
Burundi	Burundi franc		MF	FL (1991)	3
Cameroon	CFA franc	Jun-96	NL	FX	1
Central African Republic	CFA franc	Jun-96	NL	FX	—
Chad	CFA franc	Jun-96	NL	FX	1
Comoros	Comoro franc	Jun-96	P	FX	—
Congo, Republic of the	CFA franc	Jun-96	NL	FX	5 (1997)
Congo, Dem. Rep. of the	New zaire		IF	IN (1995)	—
Côte d'Ivoire	CFA franc	Jun-96	NL	FX	1
Djibouti	Djibouti franc	Sep-80	CB	FX	—
Egypt	Egyptian pound		BH	FL	1
Equatorial Guinea	CFA franc	Jun-96	NL	FX	1
Eritrea	Birr		P	—	—
Ethiopia	Birr		MF	FL (1999)	—
Gabon	CFA franc	Jun-96	NL	FX	1
Gambia, the	Dalasi	Jan-93	IF	FL	2
Ghana	Cedi	Feb-94	MF	IN	3
Guinea	Guinea franc	Nov-95	MF	IN (1998)	3
Guinea-Bissau	CFA franc	Jan-97	NL	FX	1
Kenya	Kenyan shilling	Jun-94	MF	FL	3
Lesotho	Loti (plural maloti)	Mar-97	P	FX	1
Liberia	Liberian dollar		IF	FX (1997)	2
Libya	Libyan dinar		P	FL	—
Madagascar	Malagasy franc	Sep-96	IF	FL	4
Malawi	Kwacha	Dec-95	IF	IN	3
Mali	CFA franc	Jun-96	NL	FX	1
Mauritania	Ouguiya	Jul-99	MF	FL (1997)	2
Mauritius	Mauritian rupee	Sep-93	MF	IN	2
Morocco	Dirham	Jan-93	P	FL (1990)	2
Mozambique	Metical		IF	FX	—
Namibia	Namibian dollar	Sep-96	P	FX	—
Niger	CFA franc	Jun-96	NL	FX	1
Nigeria	Naira		MF	FL	3

Table 2-1. *African Currencies and Exchange Arrangements (Continued)*

Country	Currency	Article VIII acceptance date[a]	IMF[b]	Exchange arrangement	
				Levy-Yeyati & Sturzenegger[c]	Reinhart & Rogoff[d]
Rwanda	Rwanda franc	Dec-98	MF	FL	—
São Tomé and Principe	Dobra		IF	FL	—
Senegal	CFA franc	Jun-96	NL	FX	1
Seychelles	Seychelles rupee	Jan-78	P	IN (1995)	—
Sierra Leone	Leone	Dec-95	IF	IN	—
Somalia	Somali shilling		IF	FX (1981)	—
South Africa	Rand	Sep-73	IF	FL	4
Sudan	Sudanese pound		MF	FL (1998)	—
Swaziland	Lilangeni	Dec-89	P	FX	1
Tanzania	Tanzanian shilling	Jul-96	IF	FL (1999)	3
Togo	CFA franc	Jun-96	NL	FX	1
Tunisia	Tunisian dinar	Jan-93	MF	2	2
Uganda	Ugandan shilling	Apr-94	IF	FX	3
Zambia	Kwacha		MF	FX	5
Zimbabwe	Zimbabwe dollar	Feb-95	P	IN	2

a. Acceptance of Article VIII of the IMF's Articles of Agreement commits a country to currency convertibility for international payments for goods and services.

b. IMF classification, as of 2001.

    NL   Exchange arrangements with no separate legal tender.

    CB   Currency board arrangement.

    P   Conventional pegged arrangement.

    BH   Pegged exchange rate within horizontal bands.

    PC   Crawling peg.

    BC   Crawling band.

    MF   Managed floating with no preannounced path for the exchange rate.

    IF   Independently floating.

c. Levy-Yeyati and Sturzenegger, 2002 (last year available in parentheses).

    Three-way classification

    FL   Float.

    IN   Intermediate (dirty; dirty/crawling peg).

    FX   Fix.

d. Reinhart-Rogoff, 2000 (last year available in parentheses).

    1   Fixed.

    2   Crawling peg or band.

    3   Managed floating/widely crawling band/moving band.

    4   Freely floating.

    5   Freely falling.

peggers (see table 2-1).[51] A different classification scheme also based on observed behavior is provided by Reinhart and Rogoff, who classify most countries as pegging to the euro (principally the CFA franc zone countries) or to the rand; having a de facto peg, crawling or not, with respect to the euro or the dollar; or having managed floating.[52] Only two countries at the end of 2001 were free floaters, namely Madagascar and South Africa, while a novel category, freely falling, applies to some flexible-rate countries in earlier periods, for instance, Republic of the Congo during 1975–97 (last year that data was available), Nigeria during 1991–96, and Zambia from 1985 to August 2001.

The third major event is the creation of the euro, which is likely to have further significant repercussions for Africa and influence on the evolution of exchange regimes in the future. The peg to the euro provides both a potentially more stable anchor for African currencies than a peg to the French franc (because the euro is based on a larger, and more economically diversified, geographic area), and it insulates a greater fraction of African trade from exchange rate fluctuations. In addition, the successful launch of the euro has stimulated interest elsewhere in monetary unions, including in Africa. We will discuss in later chapters whether that renewed interest is warranted and also review in chapter 4 the experience of the two existing monetary and exchange rate unions in Africa, the CFA and CMA zones.

The experience with African monetary unions in the postcolonial period underscores the importance of political forces in leading to their dissolution or, in the case of the French involvement with the CFA franc zone, in encouraging their continued existence. Either a strong shared commitment to regional integration in its various dimensions or a hegemonic power willing to support other members seems to be essential for the durable success of a monetary union.[53] Whatever the economic costs and benefits, therefore, and in the absence of an external guarantor or hegemonic power, political solidarity among member countries will be crucial to make a success of current monetary union projects. The continued episodes of regional conflict suggest that the bases for such solidarity do not seem to exist among many of the candidates for regional monetary integration in Africa—but the same could have been said of Europe in the immediate postwar period.

51. Levy-Yeyati and Sturzenegger (2002).
52. Reinhart and Rogoff (2002).
53. Also necessary is a shared commitment to macroeconomic stability.

3

Criteria for Currency Unions or the Adoption of Another Currency

Currency regimes, in particular the adoption of a common currency in the context of regional integration, have been in the spotlight for more than four decades. In recent years, a more intense interest in developing-country monetary unions, especially in Africa, can be attributed to the EU's successful launch of the euro zone. Despite extensive economic analysis and some agreement on the factors that would produce costs and benefits, economists often cannot reach a consensus on whether the benefits of a currency regime in a particular region outweigh the costs, much less a general presumption that monetary unions are necessarily a good thing.[1] Nevertheless, there is considerable political support for the idea, often in the context of a desire to further regional solidarity, which suggests that the economic literature has not paid sufficient attention to the political dimension. We argue that some of the existing literature is less applicable to Africa than to Europe because Africa faces fundamental problems, such as a lack of central bank independence and severe fiscal distortions leading to overspending and pressures to monetize deficits, that are not prevalent in Europe.

1. This is in contrast to the sweeping statement by John Stuart Mill that separate currencies are a form of "barbarism" and that the common interest would require moving to a single world currency. While there are some supporters of this view (for example, Cooper, 1984), it is certainly not generally held at present.

The economics literature on optimum currency areas (OCAs) is derived in large part from the seminal article by Robert Mundell.[2] In a nutshell, a common currency can save on various types of transactions costs, but a country abandoning its own currency gives up the ability to use monetary policy to respond to asymmetric shocks, which are shocks that impact it differently from the other countries in the union. Those costs, in turn, can be minimized by greater flexibility of the economy, in particular, through labor mobility, wage and price flexibility, and fiscal transfers. The likelihood of asymmetric shocks depends inversely on how diversified a country's economy is and how similar its production and export structures are relative to its partners in the monetary union.

The analysis, when applied to Europe, usually has assumed that institutional design issues by and large have been resolved. In particular, the central bank can be insulated by statute from having to finance government spending (in Europe, this is ensured by a no-bailout provision preventing the central bank from lending to governments, buttressed by a history of central bank independence, particularly in Germany). The main danger is that fiscal policy may indirectly put pressures on monetary policy. For instance, if a country got into trouble servicing its debt, the central bank might be led to ease monetary policy to lower the treasury's interest costs and prevent a financial crisis. The Stability and Growth Pact to which euro zone countries have to commit themselves was aimed at minimizing that danger in Europe. Though there is considerable controversy at present about the effectiveness of the pact, and several governments have breached the deficit ceiling (3 percent of GDP), there is no immediate concern that the ECB's independence is being put in peril.

In Africa, however, the institutional challenges are at least an order of magnitude greater. Existing national central banks generally are not independent, and countries with their own currencies have often suffered periods of high inflation because those central banks have been forced to finance public deficits. Hence the interest in the African context is in whether the creation of a regional central bank can be a vehicle for solving precommitment and credibility problems that bedevil existing central banks. If so, they may be able to provide an "agency of restraint,"[3] producing a central bank that is more independent and exerts greater discipline over fiscal policies than do national central banks.

A further important motivation for monetary union in Africa is to provide impetus for greater regional integration. Monetary union is often seen as an important symbol of regional solidarity, one that is likely to reinforce popular (and hence political) support for regional initiatives. In Europe that aspect

2. Mundell (1961).
3. Collier (1991).

was important, but the implementation of a monetary union (envisioned some forty years ago) followed, rather than preceded, deep structural integration, the creation of other regional institutions, and the experience of close intergovernmental cooperation. A common currency that is not supported adequately by institutions and regional solidarity may fail, and this would harm, not help, other regional integration initiatives. There are examples of this, including the ruble zone at the dissolution of the Soviet Union and monetary union in the EAC shortly after independence. Thus it is unrealistic to assume that creating a common currency will necessarily enhance integration. On the contrary, a strong political commitment to common regional goals and the presence of other economic institutions that make sticking with the monetary union in every country's interest are necessary to ensure its success and continued existence.

A model based on our previous work (which serves throughout this book as the basis for evaluating monetary projects) integrates the idea of asymmetry of shocks with the absence of institutions effectively able to insulate the central bank from pressures to finance deficits and to produce overexpansionary monetary policies. Though monetary unions reduce somewhat the bias toward monetary expansion (because by fixing the exchange rate between countries in the monetary union, the union reduces the scope for beggar-thy-neighbor monetary policies or competitive devaluations), the composition of the monetary union is crucial. Not only would a country not want to join in a monetary union with another country that faced very different external shocks (for example, to its terms of trade)—at least if that country was large enough to matter—it would also not want to link to a country that had much less disciplined fiscal policies. The latter country would cause the central bank to produce higher inflation, and this would have adverse consequences on the first country's welfare. Measuring fiscal discipline is difficult, but we attempt to do so using measures of institutional development and absence of corruption. In particular, we find that African countries with their own monetary policies tend to suffer from higher inflation the lower they score on measures that proxy for diversion of spending and taxes to purposes that do not reflect social needs. Instead, these diverted funds may just serve the private objectives of the government in power, which may tolerate corruption as a way of rewarding its supporters, for instance. Though our research focuses on fiscal distortions and shock asymmetries, we do not neglect political factors, which we also highlight as important influences on the potential success or failure of monetary union projects.[4] Appendix A provides some more

4. A point forcefully made by Cohen (2000).

details concerning the model and its calibration, forming the basis for its application in subsequent chapters.

OCAs

If there were no nominal frictions, so that wages and prices were perfectly flexible, then it would surely be optimal from an economic perspective to have but a single world currency (at least if that currency were well managed).[5] For various reasons, however, there is stickiness of wages and prices that opens the door for monetary policy to have a significant effect on economic activity. This stabilization role for monetary policy in the face of shocks to the domestic economy is all the more valuable the greater the magnitude of those shocks and the less important are other available shock absorbers.

Mundell emphasized labor mobility as the key shock absorber that could compensate for the lack of flexibility of prices and a fixed exchange rate. When the region where they lived was hit by a negative shock, workers could migrate to regions that had better employment prospects. Thus an OCA would exhibit high labor mobility within the area and relatively low labor mobility outside it. Others suggested that financial transfers could also provide a shock-absorbing role; income losses could be partially offset by payments from areas that were relatively favorably affected.[6] There is a considerable literature examining the role of federal taxes and spending in compensating for asymmetric shocks in existing federations.[7] Since multinational monetary unions typically would not provide for such financial transfers, or at least not to the extent of fiscal federations, they would need other forms of flexibility if faced with large asymmetric shocks.

The OCA approach to the cost-benefit analysis of monetary unions emphasizes three key factors that need to be quantified:

—Potential losses from membership in a monetary union depend on the extent that a country faces large shocks that are asymmetric, that is, differ from those of potential partners in the monetary union. If all countries faced the same shocks (and were affected in the same way by them), then a common monetary policy would be optimal.

—Potential gains depend on the saving of transactions costs that are incurred by changing currencies, and the higher these transactions costs the

5. There are many good surveys of the OCA literature. A recent one containing an extensive bibliography is Hawkins and Masson (2003).

6. For example, Kenen (1969).

7. For example, Sala-i-Martin and Sachs (1993); Bayoumi and Masson (1995).

greater is actual (or potential) trade between the countries.[8] Countries that would not benefit from trade would not gain from using the same currency. However, currency union may in itself stimulate an increase in trade.[9]

—The losses are mitigated by the extent that other shock absorbers exist, in particular, factor mobility and financial transfers. Asymmetric shocks would not be a serious problem for a monetary union if economies were sufficiently flexible.

The above three factors have formed the basis for much of the discussion of the costs and benefits of monetary union in Europe and other regions. In Europe, the gains were seen to be significant given the extent that EU countries trade among themselves. Moreover, losses due to asymmetric shocks, at least for most EU countries, were considered relatively small given the similarity of their economies (diversified manufacturing and services sectors and relatively low dependence on commodity exports).[10] Other shock absorbers are widely recognized to be present in only very limited form: labor mobility is low and fiscal transfers through the EU budget are small (and not linked to asymmetric shocks), but countries perform stabilization policy effectively through national fiscal policies.[11]

In Africa, the scope for significant gains and factors attenuating losses are much reduced. Asymmetric shocks, in many cases, are likely to be more important. African countries are often dependent on only a few export commodities, whose prices frequently do not move together; intraregional trade is low, so the scope for saving on transactions costs is limited; and the availability of such shock absorbers as labor mobility and financial transfers is inhibited by ethnic conflicts and a general lack of financial resources. This generally negative assessment of monetary unions leads us to consider other arguments that go beyond the OCA approach.

Agency of Restraint

Losing the ability to use monetary policy is not worrisome if that policy instrument is misused. On the contrary, a new regional central bank might be able to produce a better monetary policy because it was more independent of any particular government. In turn, this independence might force

8. Frankel and Rose (1998).

9. Rose (2000).

10. Nevertheless, even in Europe there was considerable disagreement on whether the Economic and Monetary Union (EMU) would produce net gains, and the issue remains open for the EU countries not yet members. See, for instance, U.K. Treasury (2003).

11. Bayoumi and Masson (1995).

greater discipline on fiscal policies, that is, provide an agency of restraint for them.

Some informed observers have argued that the theoretical advantage of having monetary policy in reserve to offset asymmetric shocks is in practice not worthwhile.[12] They argue that instead of offsetting asymmetric shocks, monetary policy has typically just produced inflation, no doubt because of an absence of effective central bank independence and because of a lack of public support for low inflation. Hence tying the hands of the monetary authorities would be a good thing. One way of doing so would be to constrain monetary policy in the context of a monetary union.

Though there have been a few exceptions, the experience of African countries with independent currencies has not been notably successful in approximating price stability, and it is doubtful whether monetary policy changes that occurred were optimal responses to asymmetric shocks. Instead, in many countries monetary policy has been dictated by the need to finance fiscal policy. In the absence of central bank independence and debt markets where governments could finance themselves, persistent deficits have led to excessive money creation, as governments have used seigniorage to plug the gap between expenditure and taxes.

A monetary union with a regional central bank might avoid this pitfall. Each country in the union would have less influence over the actions of the central bank than they would have in a national setting; this could enhance the central bank's independence and its ability to resist pressures to provide monetary financing. No longer able to obtain seigniorage revenue on demand, governments would bite the bullet and tailor their spending to their revenues (or if they borrowed, they would be subject to the discipline exerted by financial markets).

Experience contradicts this sanguine assessment. The CFA franc zone has two regional central banks, yet the independence of the two central banks was compromised in the 1980s by large countries bypassing limits on monetary financing through borrowing by state-owned banks.[13] This led to a serious economic downturn and a banking crisis, culminating in the 1994 devaluation. Since then, both WAEMU and CAEMC have attempted to put in place additional institutional mechanisms to reinforce fiscal discipline. On its own, monetary union is unlikely to ensure that a regional central bank will be able to resist pressures for monetization.

---

12. For instance, Hausman, Panizza, and Stein (2001) have made this argument for Latin America.

13. Guillaume and Stasavage (2000).

Though the weaknesses of existing national central banks makes it natural to envision creating new institutions, there is no guarantee that a regional central bank would do better. Regional development banks and public investment funds in Africa have sometimes been viewed as just another opportunity for capturing rents or funneling revenues. Hence the design of adequate safeguards is key. We have argued elsewhere, in the context of West Africa, that it is essential to complement a well-designed institutional framework for the central bank with regional surveillance over fiscal policies that includes sanctions on those governments that run excessive deficits.[14] This conclusion, we would argue, has general relevance to the continent. However, making such sanctions effective is a difficult challenge, given past unwillingness of African leaders to criticize their peers in neighboring countries.

In Europe too, despite greater institutional development and a longer historical record of macroeconomic stability, the project of monetary union was attractive in part because it built on the monetary institution with the greatest reputation for monetary rectitude—the German Bundesbank. African countries may not be able to benefit from as credible a model but should in any case attempt to use what credibility exists rather than rely on the presumptive credibility gains that might accrue to an untried institution. The two existing African monetary or currency unions, the CFA franc zone and CMA, because they have track records of stability and institutional development, are likely to be more credible than de novo monetary unions.

Enhancing Regional Integration and Solidarity?

Politicians often favor monetary unions because they are a symbol of regional solidarity. It is believed that the creation of such a symbol may bring about forces that lead to stronger regional linkages in other areas too, creating a virtuous circle of closer integration. For instance, monetary union could increase trade, lead to harmonization of fiscal policies, and integrate financial markets. In turn, these changes would increase the net benefits from having a common currency.

In fact, monetary unions display very different degrees of integration in other areas.[15] The Eastern Caribbean Currency Union has no coordination of fiscal policies, low trade between member countries, and no harmonization of capital controls. Even the CFA franc zone, despite a more than fifty-year

14. Masson and Pattillo (2002).
15. Surveyed in Masson and Pattillo (2001).

history, exhibits little financial integration, as banking systems tend to be segmented and regional financial markets rudimentary.[16] Coordination of fiscal policies emerged in earnest only following the 1994 devaluation, which brought home to leaders the deficiencies of the existing system.

An influential paper by Rose offers empirical evidence in support of the contention that membership in a currency union should increase intraregional trade by a factor of about three.[17] We revisit that evidence in the African context in chapter 4, for the two existing monetary unions (the CFA franc zone and the CMA), and provide some support for Rose's estimates. This enhances the advantages of forming monetary unions in Africa. Even if that estimate is accepted, however, the fact remains that given low per capita income and concentration on primary commodity exports, it is likely that trade within African regional groupings will remain small relative to trade with Europe or Asia.

In Europe, the debate over whether creation of the monetary union should precede other forms of integration or rather come later, in a sense crowning the successes in other fields, was resolved in favor of the latter position. It was felt that the dangers of introducing monetary union when countries were not sufficiently integrated for them to form an OCA outweighed the symbolic value of its early creation. Other regions illustrate the possibility that an inadequately designed monetary union or one with insufficiently committed countries may harm, not help, the cause of regional integration. This was the case for the ruble zone at the breakup of the Soviet Union and the monetary union based on the East African shilling, which broke down as each of the EAC member countries attempted to extract seigniorage at the expense of the others.[18]

Though the goal of African unity receives much lip service, the reality in Africa is much different. Countries that are members of the same regional organization, which has the goal to achieve the closest form of integration, are often engaged in overt or covert warfare through supporting rebel groups. Examples include conflicts in Sierra Leone, Liberia, Côte d'Ivoire, Rwanda, Democratic Republic of the Congo, Angola, and Sudan. As mentioned above, hostilities among member governments helped to sink the EAC. The idea that the existence of a monetary union could effectively curb warlike impulses is dubious, though some organizations, like ECOWAS, have had success in stabilizing and mediating regional conflicts.[19] At most, the stability

16. Regional banking supervision was put in place during the 1990s in both regions and may over time help to achieve greater financial integration.

17. Rose (2000).

18. Masson and Pattillo (2001).

19. ECOWAS, which does not (yet) have a common currency, nevertheless has a regional military force that has intervened in Liberia and Sierra Leone.

afforded by a common currency could dampen the negative economic effects of civil conflicts. But it seems likely that in the end, hostility between members of a monetary union would simply destroy it. We discuss later in this book the prospects for a single African currency, which is the goal of the AU.

This is not to deny that political objectives are important to the formation of monetary unions, but rather to argue that rhetoric and reality need to be aligned. The continued existence of the CFA franc zone and the CMA is due in large part to the perceived political self-interest of the major power (or at least, of its key policymakers)—France in the former case, South Africa in the latter. While economic advantage may be part of the story, other factors were at least as important: security as well as regional and global influence. As Cohen notes, the commitment of a hegemonic power is often a precondition for making a monetary union work.[20]

Augmented OCA Model with Fiscal Distortions

The model we use to analyze monetary union is described in fuller, technical detail in our previous work with Xavier Debrun.[21] The model is based on the OCA literature, which focuses on asymmetries of shocks, but further identifies another important asymmetry, political distortions affecting fiscal policy decisions. The model focuses on the monetary impact of country-specific differences in preferences over the size of the government and differences in distortions (political or structural) affecting fiscal policy (either through tax collection costs, diversion of spending, or corruption). The regional central bank is assumed not to be fully independent but to set monetary policy to reflect the average preferences of the countries in the region (including their tolerance for fiscal deficits). As a result, a pair of countries that were very different with respect to the fiscal distortion would be unattractive partners for a monetary union, because the central bank would produce undesirable outcomes for one or both of them.

In particular, it is assumed that policymakers manipulate fiscal policy to serve their own private objectives. The political distortion is modeled as a wedge between the true socially optimal level of public expenditure (reflecting the population's demand for public goods in the country) and the level targeted by the government. We posit that the government's spending target exceeds the social target by the amount of public resources policymakers wish to devote to the exclusive benefit of themselves and their supporters. For

20. Cohen (1998).
21. Debrun, Masson, and Pattillo (2002).

instance, ministers may systematically hire too many civil servants among their constituents to provide a given service to the general public and may approve spending on wasteful infrastructure projects. This shows up as higher spending than is socially desirable. This political distortion adds a source of divergence among states that is highly relevant in the African context.

Central banks have two incentives to generate inflation. On the one hand, since they are assumed not to be independent of the government, they reflect the government's trade-off between the costs of tax distortions and inflation. On the other hand, following the insight of Barro and Gordon, they have incentives to stimulate output or cushion the effects of negative supply shocks by monetary expansion.[22] We extend their model along the lines of Martin to encompass another effect of monetary expansion—namely, depreciation relative to trading partners, which increases exports or cushions their decline.[23] This is the classic beggar-thy-neighbor critique of flexible exchange rates, namely, that countries may try to engineer a competitive devaluation in order to stimulate output and employment at home, at the expense of other countries. In Martin, this works through direct investment, though another channel operates through the price of intermediate inputs. Expansionary monetary policies in one country cause regional bottlenecks for such inputs as cement and machinery, because these goods, though they may be imported from abroad, also are subject to congestion at ports and higher transport costs within the region.

Whatever the channel, systematically using monetary policy to stimulate output is self-defeating, as individuals and firms anticipate the higher inflation and economic activity does not rise. Hence a flexible exchange rate regime may be suboptimal, even from the standpoint of the distorted objectives of the government. The government's decision to join a monetary union thus will depend on whether the new regime helps to reduce this distortion without at the same time unduly limiting the government's flexibility. Monetary union reduces the central bank's incentive to expand monetary policy because now the central bank internalizes the cost to other countries in the region, as they share the same currency. However, asymmetries (both of shocks and fiscal policy distortions) can still be a serious problem that may produce a welfare loss relative to an independent currency.

In the formal model, we consider two benchmark regimes. Under the first regime (autonomy), each country simultaneously sets monetary and fiscal instruments, considering its neighbors' decisions as given. This regime assumes complete discretion and flexible exchange rates. Under the second regime

---

22. Barro and Gordon (1983). See Jensen (2003) for a modern reinterpretation.
23. Martin (1995).

(monetary union), fiscal policies remain under the responsibility of national authorities while monetary policy is under the control of a central bank that maximizes a weighted sum of member states' objective functions, leading to the same inflation rate for all the member states. Again, there is no reason to believe that a commitment device would be available to the supranational central bank, so that instead it reflects the objectives of the member governments proportionally to their weight in the union. However, the big difference with respect to monetary autonomy is that a single government now has a limited impact on joint decisions. Moreover, conflicting demands by different member states may cancel out to the benefit of all.

What are the incentives to form a regional currency union? First, if all countries in the region were identical and subject to the same shocks, then a currency union including all countries would be desirable for all. In such a configuration, the loss of monetary autonomy does not entail any cost since, in line with the OCA literature, the common monetary policy optimally corresponds to everyone's needs. Moreover, all countries benefit from lower inflation because the common central bank internalizes the beggar-thy-neighbor effect of autonomous policies. In that sense, it is spontaneously more conservative than a national central bank because the regional central bank cannot exploit the competitive devaluation channel that is available to national central banks (or alternatively, it cannot bid up the price of intermediate goods or compete for foreign direct investment through increasing competitiveness). Hence monetary unification provides institutions that are spontaneously able to deliver a more conservative (that is, anti-inflationary) monetary policy. As a corollary, the gains from monetary unification tend to increase with the seriousness of the inflationary bias, and these gains depend positively on the degree of regional trade integration. In other words, all other things being equal, a group of high-inflation countries would expect to gain more from monetary unification than a group of low-inflation countries, and countries that trade little would not see much benefit from a common currency.

Second, structural cross-country differences (that is, differences in size, political distortions, or social spending targets) do not necessarily reduce the net gains from monetary unification for all member states. On the one hand, differences in governments' financing needs are a source of cost because the unionwide inflation rate will only by chance coincide with a country's desired trade-off between seigniorage and tax revenues. On the other hand, differences in financing needs may also be a source of gains depending on the country's position in the distribution of financing needs. More specifically, a government with a relatively high financing need may get additional benefits from participating in a monetary union with more fiscally conservative neighbors (that is, countries with lower financing needs) because the latter will exert restraining pressures on the central bank. From the point of view of big spenders, what could be called imported monetary restraint represents an extra disciplinary benefit that partly addresses the inflationary bias they face under autonomy. By contrast, the small spenders will incur additional losses stemming from the excessive demands of the big spenders for monetary financing, pushing them further away from the low inflation equilibrium. As the model assumes that the pressure exerted by a country on the central bank is proportional to the country's size, the country sizes and financing needs are critical influences on the feasibility of monetary unions: countries with low fiscal distortions will not agree to a monetary union with large undisciplined neighbors.

Third, the model captures the essence of the OCA theory with respect to asymmetric shocks. It assumes that the unionwide inflation target of the common central bank will only accommodate the common component of supply disturbances, that is, the average shock across the countries in the union. In our empirical work, these shocks are identified with terms of trade disturbances, consistent with much evidence of developing countries' vulnerability to these largely exogenous shocks. The fact that the central bank cannot tailor its monetary policy to different shocks facing each country makes abandoning an independent monetary policy in the face of country-specific shocks costly, and underscores the role of the joint distribution of supply disturbances in influencing feasible monetary unions.

Appendix A describes the calibration of the model to African data. Essentially, we use the available 1995–2000 data on African countries' government revenue, spending, and inflation to fit the model and estimate the model's parameter values. The comparison of outcomes for these variables across countries with independent currencies and those in monetary unions helps pin down the disciplining effect of a common currency (through its reduction of the temptation to produce inflation and depreciation). Though limited by data problems, the results of this exercise are broadly supportive of the model. Inflation depends positively and significantly on the size of spending targets and negatively on the extent of trade that is internal to the monetary union. Thus this empirical application of the model to historical data gives us some confidence that it may shed some light on the economic advantages of monetary union projects. We recognize that this leaves open some of the political motives behind these projects, and we discuss them on a case-by-case basis in later chapters.

4

African Monetary Integration in Practice: CFA Franc Zone and South African CMA

The prospects for monetary integration in Africa are best analyzed by first studying the two existing monetary or formal exchange rate unions on the continent. These are the CFA franc zone (or, to be more precise, the two regions composing it, namely, WAEMU and CAEMC)[1] and the CMA based on South Africa's rand. These examples of monetary integration also have the advantage (for our purposes) of having been in place for a long time, albeit having evolved somewhat over the course of their existence. Monetary union in southern Africa dates back to the early years of the twentieth century, becoming subsequently an exchange rate union (as is explained in box 1-1), as the smaller countries issued their own currencies. The CFA franc zone was formed at the time of the Second World War. Given the amount of time since each was created, the effects of monetary integration should have shown themselves by now.

---

1. Each region issues a distinct version of the CFA franc. In West Africa it is known as the franc of the Communauté Financière Africaine, and in Central Africa it is the franc of Coopération Financière en Afrique Centrale. Thus the two currencies are distinguishable and not freely exchangeable, and they may face different devaluation risk (Vizy, 1989, p. 50). In fact, the CFA franc zone also includes Comoros, with its own currency and central bank, and France, which guarantees the parities of the three currencies against the euro. See the annual report of the *Zone Franc* (Bank of France, 2002).

Some have claimed that monetary union itself will greatly stimulate trade and promote fiscal discipline and regional convergence, and data for these existing monetary arrangements can help test these hypotheses. Arguably, the experiences of the existing African monetary unions will be more relevant to other proposed monetary unions in Africa than, for instance, developments in the EU, because there may be special characteristics and common features that prevail on the continent, including a relatively similar level of institutional development. At the very least, a detailed examination of the existing African unions can supplement a more inclusive but broad-brush econometric analysis of country examples drawn from a global sample.

CFA Franc Zone

France created the CFA franc zone during its colonial occupation of Africa, but unlike other regional monetary arrangements imposed by European powers, the zone survived decolonization due in part to France's efforts to maintain it. France continues to provide a guarantee of convertibility of the CFA franc into the euro at a fixed exchange rate parity. The number of CFA francs per French franc, which had remained unchanged for almost fifty years, was increased by a factor of two in 1994, helping to resolve a long crisis that was associated with the overvaluation of the CFA franc.

The fixed peg to the euro (before 1999, to the French franc) considerably constrains the scope for an independent monetary policy in the CFA franc zone. Accordingly, a key indicator guiding monetary policy is the reserve cover ratio, which is the ratio of foreign exchange reserves to the short-term liabilities of the central bank. When that indicator falls below 20 percent for three consecutive months, emergency measures must be taken by the central bank to protect the parity, namely, increases in official interest rates and reductions in refinancing ceilings. An agreement with France provides for at least 65 percent of each central bank's reserves to be held with the French Treasury in an operations account. If that account goes into deficit for thirty days, then specific measures are triggered, which are the reduction by 20 percent of refinancing ceilings for countries in deficit and by 10 percent for countries whose surplus is less than 15 percent of its money supply. This limits the potential liability of the French Treasury and provides an extra rule-based element of credibility to the existing parity.

Reserves for WAEMU and CAEMC are pooled at the respective central banks. However, these reserves are attributed to each of their respective member countries, as is the monetary circulation (with a grid used to estimate the shares of each country in the total currency outstanding). Similarly, monetary programming in each of the two regions is built up from country-by-country estimates of GDP growth (leading to an estimate for money demand) and credit demand from the private and public sectors. The latter produces individual country ceilings for central bank credit to the economy. In fact, however, these ceilings are not rigidly enforced.[2] It is questionable if a country-by-country monetary programming exercise makes sense in an integrated monetary area. If there is a single monetary policy (as is the case for WAEMU and CAEMC separately), the distribution of the money supply across countries should have little importance and be purely endogenous and demand determined.[3] Similarly, in an integrated banking system, it should not matter whether a loan is made from a bank in country A to a firm or individual in country B nor what proportions of total bank assets are held in each of the two countries.

The two regions composing the CFA franc zone have regional institutions that supervise their respective banking systems: for WAEMU it is the Commission Bancaire, located in Abidjan, Côte d'Ivoire; for CAEMC it is the Commission Bancaire d'Afrique Centrale (COBAC), located in Bangui, Central African Republic. Banks in each region in principle can establish branches in any member country. Banks need only obtain a single banking permit, the *agrément unique,* to operate within either WAEMU or CAEMC. However, in practice banks do not operate across borders, nor does either region have an effective regional money market. In addition to the *agrément unique,* banks need to get the permission of the national finance ministry to set up shop, and this seems to be used as a means to protect local banks. Thus there are restrictions on banks' ability to operate in several countries and banks are reluctant to lend across borders in either region.[4] Another feature that interferes with creation of a level playing field is the existence of bank reserve requirements that are differentiated by country.

Continued use of a country-by-country monetary programming exercise in part reflects the reality that neither WAEMU nor CAEMC is, in fact, a perfectly integrated monetary zone. Another factor explaining the monetary programming exercise's existence is that the loans made by the central bank to national treasuries are subject to a ceiling that is equal to the country's fiscal revenues in the previous year. This situation will change with the implementation of decisions made in both WAEMU and CAEMC to eliminate

2. Parmentier and Tenconi (1996, pp. 133–43).

3. Ndiaye (2000) finds that there is not much heterogeneity across national money demands in West Africa, so that a WAEMU money demand function performs well compared to individual country demand functions.

4. IMF (2002b); Hernández-Catá and others (1998).

monetary financing of treasuries. The elimination of monetary financing would ease the move to a system in which there was an overall refinancing target for the zone, and lending by the central bank involved repo or other operations with commercial banks, regardless of their location in the zone. In WAEMU, the Council of Ministers decided in September 2002 that the BCEAO (the central bank of WAEMU) would not provide new government financing as of January 2003 and that outstanding balances would be repaid over a period of ten years. The timetable for a similar phaseout in CAEMC had yet to be finalized at the time of this writing.

Similarly, the constraint on monetary policy that is imposed by the peg to the euro would imply, in the limiting case of perfect capital mobility (and a perfectly credible peg), that the central bank was obliged to follow interest rates set by the ECB. Neither official rates nor money market rates exactly track those in the euro area. In fact, there can occasionally be large discrepancies that persist for months. Though freedom of capital movements between WAEMU and CAEMC, on the one hand, and France (now the euro zone), on the other hand, is enshrined in regulations, in practice there are administrative frictions and de facto restrictions that make capital mobility less than perfect. This, and doubts that the parity will remain fixed forever, help explain the existence of interest differentials. While imperfect capital mobility affords some degree of independence of monetary policy, imperfect credibility puts additional constraints on the central bank, forcing it to maintain higher interest rates than in the euro zone. Moreover, the attempt to exploit systematically any available independence would surely raise questions concerning the commitment of the central bank to the exchange rate parity against the euro and might provoke much larger capital movements than normal.

Other Aspects of Regional Integration

The CFA franc zone regions, over time, have also reinforced other aspects of cooperation among their member countries in three areas: trade, structural policies, and macroeconomic surveillance. Encouraging regional trade through a free trade area has long been an objective, and each zone has had several trade pacts, which met with mixed success as agreed measures were not always implemented and in practice internal trade was not free of barriers.[5] Regional structural policies and macroeconomic coordination were largely absent dur-

---

5. In West Africa, a customs union (the UDEAO), formed in 1966, had a uniform tariff of 50 percent on all intrazone trade, and its successor, created in 1974, had preferential tariff rates that applied only to a limited number of manufactures. In Central Africa, the UDEAC similarly had preferential tariffs, but these were later restricted in scope. See Parmentier and Tenconi (1996).

ing the first forty years of the CFA franc zone. However, the crisis leading to the 1994 devaluation reinforced the recognition that monetary union needed to be accompanied by other aspects of regional cooperation and buttressed by tighter restrictions on borrowing from the central bank by national treasuries. Accordingly, the member countries in each zone agreed to form regional economic and monetary unions, creating the existing WAEMU and CAEMC,[6] whose objectives are to promote regional integration and macroeconomic policy coordination. Economic integration and coordination are promoted by new supranational institutions (in addition to the existing central banks): a commission in WAEMU and an executive secretariat in CAEMC.

In each case, a common external tariff, with three or four rates ranging up to 30 percent, has been put in place, creating customs unions in the two regions, though consistent application of the tariff rates for imports from outside the region remains to be achieved, and the transition to tariff-free intraregional trade is not complete. Structural policy coordination has included establishing a common business law, OHADA,[7] and harmonizing indirect taxes on which, however, more progress has been made in WAEMU than in CAEMC. In particular sectors, governments have agreed to joint projects and harmonization, for example, in the areas of telecommunications, transportation, agriculture, and industrial policy. These various initiatives have as objectives to facilitate cross-border linkages and reduce business costs.

A third important area for cooperation has been regional surveillance over macroeconomic policies. In this regard, member countries have recognized that fiscal policy, if not disciplined, has the potential to interfere with the proper functioning of a monetary union. Indeed the 1994 devaluation was provoked in part by the fiscal excesses of some of the larger countries, in particular Côte d'Ivoire and Cameroon, which also managed to extract seigniorage through borrowing from the central bank by state-controlled banks. In instituting criteria for fiscal policy convergence, the two regions have been guided by the example of the EU, which has used criteria for the public deficit and debt ratios to GDP as conditions for countries to join the EMU[8] and then as ongoing conditions to be satisfied within the EMU, according to the provisions of the Stability and Growth Pact.

---

6. The WAEMU treaty was signed in 1994 and approved by all member countries during that year. The CAEMC treaty, also signed in 1994, went into effect in 1998, when it replaced the UDEAC.

7. The treaty, signed on October 17, 1993, in Port Louis, Mauritius, has been ratified by sixteen countries: all the members of UEMOA and CAEMC, Comoros, and Guinea.

8. The EU also imposes criteria with respect to the rate of inflation, long-term bond rates, and exchange rate stability.

Table 4-1. *WAEMU and CAEMC: Convergence Criteria*

Variable	Reference value
Primary criteria	
Basic fiscal balance (fiscal position excluding grants and excluding public investment financed externally)	At least 0
External public debt/GDP	No more than 70 percent
Rate of inflation	No more than 3 percent
Payment arrears	No accumulation (and reduction of existing stock)
Secondary criteria	
Public sector wage bill/government revenues	No more than 35 percent
Government revenue/GDP	At least 17 percent
Domestically financed public investment	At least 20 percent of tax receipts
Current account deficit, excluding grants/GDP	Less than 3 percent

Source: "La Zone Franc" (www.izf.net [March 2003]).

The current criteria for regional surveillance appear in table 4-1. Though initially the two regions' criteria differed somewhat, they are now essentially the same. In each case, the fiscal deficit measure excludes grants and also spending on public investment that is externally financed. These adjustments are made because including grant revenue may give too rosy a picture of a country's prospects for achieving fiscal policy sustainability. On the expenditure side, projects that are linked to grants also may be associated with temporary, one-off spending, and hence are excluded. Though in practice a distinction should be made between grants and foreign commercial financing, in practice most of the foreign financing for public investment is likely to be on concessional, not commercial, terms. The target for the adjusted deficit is a zero balance.

A ceiling is also specified for total domestic and external debt, which is not to exceed 70 percent of GDP.[9] The origin of the debt, concessional or commercial, is not specified, though the sustainability of a given debt stock would depend significantly on the rate of interest charged. In practice, many of the countries concerned have started from situations of high indebtedness, recently alleviated to some extent by the Highly Indebted Poor Country (HIPC) initiative of the IMF and World Bank to write down the debt they owe and by debt forgiveness by G-7 and other industrial countries.

In addition to criteria on the overall fiscal policies of member countries, the two regions have also targeted specific aspects of their fiscal policies. This has

9. For most countries, domestic debt is small, given the rudimentary state of government bond markets.

included the ratio of fiscal revenues to GDP, considered too low in most member countries; the ratio of public wages and salaries to fiscal revenues, considered too high; and spending on public investment, for which the target is above what most governments spend.

The process of regional surveillance has experienced setbacks in implementation that have hindered achievement of agreed objectives. Difficulties include getting national authorities to produce reliable and comparable data, focusing their attention on the key deficit criterion and away from the multiplicity of secondary criteria, making governments take a serious interest in examining policies in neighboring countries, and creating effective procedures for imposing sanctions in case of noncompliance. In the early years, the central banks in the two regions were the only regional institutions able to marshal data and prepare the necessary documentation for regional surveillance meetings. This responsibility has now passed to WAEMU's commission and CAEMC's executive secretariat. However, data problems persist. The attention given to regional surveillance has increased as experience has been gained. In 1999 WAEMU countries agreed to the Convergence, Stability, Growth, and Solidarity Pact, which mandated a convergence phase over 2000–02 and a stability phase starting in 2003, after which countries would be expected to meet the criteria. However, given the difficulties encountered by countries in meeting the criteria, the heads of state and government of WAEMU decided in January 2003 to postpone the stability phase until January 1, 2006, after which time all member states should meet the primary criteria. CAEMC countries approved new convergence criteria and surveillance procedures in 2001.

Has Monetary Union Increased Trade and Growth and Lowered Inflation?

Adopting a common currency lowers transaction costs for regional trade, since purchasing goods from neighboring countries no longer involves changing currencies. As a result, a monetary union could be expected to increase regional trade, as would forming a free trade area or common market. It may be hard, however, to distinguish the purely monetary union effects from other aspects of regional integration, since the two are often associated, as described above for WAEMU and CAEMC.

Table 4-2 gives the extent of regional trade within these two CFA franc zone regions, between the two of them, and between the zones and France. Trade both between the two regions and with France involves a currency exchange, since neither region's CFA franc is legal tender in the other or in France. However, such an exchange in principle should be free of commission. Intraregional trade is modest, especially within CAEMC, and practically nonexistent between the two regions but is very substantial with France.

Table 4-2. *CFA Franc Zone Trade: Intraregional and with France, 1997–98*[a]

Percent of total trade

Region	WAEMU	CAEMC	CFA[b]
Actual trade			
Intraregional	9.4	2.8	7.8
With France	43.4	32.9	38.7
Predicted trade with currency union dummy			
Intraregional	2.5	2.5	2.2
With France	42.7	38.2	41.2
Predicted trade without currency union dummy			
Intraregional	1.3	1.0	1.2
With France	41.0	36.5	39.5

Sources: Actual data from IMF, Direction of Trade Statistics and International Financial Statistics databases.

a. Actual and predicted by gravity model. Predictions using estimated coefficients from box 4-1.

b. Excluding Comoros.

It is necessary, of course, to have a standard with which to evaluate whether the extent of intraregional trade is out of the ordinary. This is provided by the gravity model, which has been tested extensively and seems to capture well the determinants of bilateral trade between countries. It predicts that larger countries exert a greater gravitational pull on imports and push to exports, that richer countries (in per capita terms) also tend to have higher trade, and that trade diminishes with distance. The model, estimated in log form, generally fits well empirically across a range of countries (but, as discussed later in this chapter, does not do a good job predicting CFA trade). Box 4-1 shows the coefficient estimates when the gravity model is applied to Africa; the estimates suggest that membership in the same currency union has a positive effect on trade between African countries, and this effect is very close to the estimates obtained from the global sample.

It is also of interest to look at the effect of currency union on trade in specific regions. Table 4-2 gives the gravity model's predictions with respect to the CFA regions' internal trade. It can be seen that though intraregional trade in WAEMU is considerably greater than predicted by the gravity model (with or without the currency union dummy), the same is not true of the CAEMC, which actually trades about what the model with the currency union dummy would have predicted. Trade with France is also roughly as predicted by the gravity model. WAEMU results for internal trade are surprising, since the second panel of table 4-2 incorporates the effect of a dummy variable that implies that trade within a currency union is multiplied by about three relative to what it would have been.[10] Thus it seems that WAEMU has been successful in furthering regional integration beyond what would be the case in the usual currency union, while the same is not true of CAEMC.[11]

The evidence is mixed on whether monetary union provides an important stimulus to growth. Evidence from WAEMU and CAEMC initially suggested a positive impact relative to the rest of sub-Saharan Africa.[12] It has also been argued that the existence of France's guarantee of convertibility embodied in the operations account has cushioned the effects of negative shocks by reducing the risk that countries would face a flight from their currency and drying up of sources of access to foreign exchange, which could bring the economy to a halt.[13] However, the CFA franc zone severely underperformed during 1986–93, as the overvaluation of the CFA franc contributed to a persistent economic downturn and adjustment of the exchange rate was difficult given the institutional structure, which requires unanimity among member countries for a parity change. The problem of CFA overvaluation may recur if domestic inflation cannot be kept to levels in the euro zone, especially during periods when the euro is strong against the U.S. dollar.

In contrast, the CFA franc zone has unambiguously delivered better price performance than floating rate or crawling peg regimes in Africa.[14] Inflation is lower in CFA franc zone countries than in the rest of sub-Saharan Africa, no doubt helped by the peg to the French franc, which has anchored the monetary policies of WAEMU and CAEMC. A supranational central bank may also deliver lower inflation in the absence of a peg if it is more independent of national treasuries.

Per Capita Income Convergence

Another objective of regional integration, and one advanced by creating a monetary union, may be to achieve convergence of income levels by stimulating growth in the poorer countries. It is plausible that this would result

10. Rose (2000). See also the comment by Nitsch (2002) and Tenreyro and Barro (2003).

11. The estimated equation also includes a dummy variable for common colonial links with the former metropolitan power. Arguably this effect could be expected to be much stronger for former French colonies than others in Africa, for reasons discussed in chapter 2. But given the common experience of WAEMU and CAEMC, neither a common language nor former colonial links are likely to be the explanation for the high level of WAEMU internal trade. A complicating factor, however, is oil. The CAEMC countries trade little among themselves because they export crude oil, which mainly goes to refineries outside of Africa.

12. Guillaumont and Guillaumont (1984); Devarajan and de Melo (1987).

13. The recent political crisis and civil unrest in Côte d'Ivoire may be an example of this, since the economic impacts, though serious, have not been as dire as in other African countries facing similar situations. Vizy (1989, p. 136).

14. Masson and Pattillo (2001).

Box 4-1. *Gravity Model*

The gravity model is usually specified to include as explanatory variables the product of the two countries' real GDP, both in levels and per capita; the distance between them; and the land areas of the two countries. In addition, a number of dummy variables are included to capture the possible effects of common features of the countries: membership in a free trade area or currency union; a common language, border, or colonizer; and so on. The gravity equation is typically specified in logarithms, so that (time subscripts are omitted),

$$\ln(X_{ij}) = \beta_0 + \beta_1 \ln(Y_i Y_j) + \beta_2 \ln\left(\frac{Y_i}{Pop_i} \frac{Y_j}{Pop_j}\right)$$

$$+ \beta_3 \ln(Area_i Area_j) + \sum_{k=1}^{n} \beta_{3+k} D_k$$

where

    X: the bilateral trade
    Y: real GDP
    Pop: population
    Area: land area
    D: various dummy variables.

The gravity model has been applied to Africa in a number of papers, in particular, to test whether regional trading arrangements have stimulated trade and to explain why Africa generally trades less than other countries. For instance, Hanink and Owusu found that membership in ECOWAS had not promoted trade among its members.[1] Foroutan and Pritchett concluded that the low level of African trade is consistent with the gravity model and is explained by low levels of GDP and distance.[2] However, a more recent study by Subramanian and Tamirisa supports the view that Africa has not taken advantage of trading opportunities and actually is becoming less integrated with the rest of the world.[3]

Of greatest relevance to our study is the effect of membership in a currency union on trade. A widely cited paper, using a global sample, finds that currency unions increase trade by about a factor of three.[4] While it is useful to have the widest sample possible if that sample is homogeneous, it may also be the case that there are particularities in a region that make it not comparable to others. Thus we report here both estimates from the global sample and more limited estimates restricted to Africa.

When we estimate the Glick and Rose model limited to African bilateral trade (including the continent's trade with the rest of the world), the estimated effect of the currency union dummy is almost the same, increasing trade by a factor in excess of three.[5] Not surprisingly, perhaps, the "common language" dummy variable becomes less significant (since the monetary unions in the sample are mainly composed of francophone countries). "Common border" becomes much more important, which is consistent with the poor transportation links between many African countries. Other dummy variables change substantially, including the sign of the "number of islands" and "current colonies" variables.

Log of bilateral trade	Glick and Rose		Africa only with currency union dummy		Africa only without currency union dummy	
	Coefficient	t	Coefficient	t	Coefficient	t
Economic variables, in log form						
Distance	−1.11	−47.28	−1.20	−24.78	−1.25	−25.37
Real GDP	0.93	93.01	1.00	56.89	0.99	56.12
Real GDP per capita	0.46	30.18	0.39	14.90	0.39	14.96
Land area	−0.09	−11.27	−0.17	−12.82	−0.16	−12.02
Dummy variables						
Currency union	1.30	10.15	1.29	7.88	...	...
Common language	0.32	7.68	0.11	1.65	0.16	2.36
Common border	0.43	3.57	1.18	6.68	1.23	6.68
Same regional trade agreement	0.99	7.58	(dropped)		(dropped)	
Number landlocked (0, 1, or 2)	−0.14	−4.21	−0.17	−3.65	−0.17	−3.69
Number islands (0, 1, or 2)	0.05	1.40	−0.17	−2.50	−0.18	−2.53
Common colonizer	0.45	6.45	0.40	4.17	0.53	5.65
Both are current colonies	0.82	3.25	−0.78	−1.89	0.03	0.06
Ever colonized (or by) partner	1.31	10.06	2.05	13.71	2.08	14.03
Part of same nation	−0.23	−0.22	2.20	5.36	1.98	4.20
Constant	−30.58	−81.16	−30.50	−44.09	−23.48	−43.30
Summary statistics						
R^2	0.64		0.51		0.51	
No. observations	219,558		91,791		91,791	

Disentangling the effects of currency union from regional integration initiatives, such as preferential trading areas, is difficult since they often overlap, and the models reported in the table do not include dummy variables for the latter. Though the Glick and Rose study includes dummy variables for regional trading agreements, this dummy is zero for all pairs of African countries because none of these agreements is registered with the World Trade Organization. Another problem is that neither the CMA nor SACU is included in our sample for lack of bilateral trade data among their members.

1. Hanink and Owusu (1998).
2. Foroutan and Pritchett (1993).
3. Subramanian and Tamirisa (2001).
4. Rose (2000). See Glick and Rose (3001) for more details.
5. Since the equation is expressed in logarithms, we need to exponentiate the coefficient to get the effect on the level of trade, and exp(1.3)=3.7.

from increased trade and hence is subject to the above mentioned uncertainties about the effect of a common currency on trade. Related initiatives to liberalize factor movements would also favor growth by allowing capital and labor to move to the locations where they are most productive.[15]

There is an extensive literature testing for convergence, which suggests that it has not operated when all the countries of the world are included. However, there seem to be convergence clubs, such as the OECD, where convergence operates strongly.[16] Jenkins and Thomas assert "there is a growing consensus that convergence clubs exist, where countries with a lower GNP per capita grow more rapidly because they are members of a trade group, or because domestic policy gains credibility by being tied to the domestic policy of a country with a better economic reputation."[17] The precise reasons for the apparent convergence among such groupings are unclear, but since the OECD includes a number of European countries with strong linkages resulting from common membership in regional organizations (the EU, the European Free Trade Association, and so on), it is of interest to explore whether the CFA franc zone also constitutes such a convergence club.

Figure 4-1 shows the evolution of per capita incomes (in real U.S. dollars based on PPP exchange rates) within the two regions of the CFA franc zone over the past few decades. There seems to be no evidence of σ-convergence, that is, a decrease over time in the dispersion of real per capita income levels. The cross-sectional coefficient of variation of per capita GDP confirms this (see figure 4-2). WAEMU countries are more homogeneous than CAEMC countries, with a small downward trend in their cross-sectional variation in the 1990s. For the CAEMC countries, disparities widened in the late 1970s and then again markedly in the 1990s. For comparison, the coefficient of variation across all sub-Saharan African countries is also plotted. That variable indicates a small increase in divergence in the 1990s and a similar pattern in the 1970s to that exhibited by CAEMC. This probably reflects increased inequality between oil-producing and oil-importing countries brought about by the rise in the world oil price.

A second measure of convergence is β-convergence, which is said to occur when, in a cross-section regression of growth rates on initial levels of income per capita, the coefficient (β) is negative. Conditional β-convergence controls for differences in preferences or technology and allows for countries to con-

15. However, equalizing effects on incomes are not unambiguous, since monetary union might lead to agglomeration as businesses migrate to the major metropolitan centers. Results in Tenreyro and Barro (2003) suggest that currency unions lead to greater specialization.

16. Baumol, Nelson, and Wolff (1994).

17. Jenkins and Thomas (1996).

Figure 4-1. *Real PPP per Capita Income*

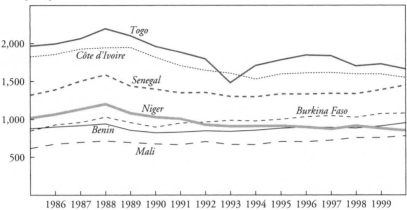

WAEMU Countries
GDP per capita, in 1995 U.S. dollars

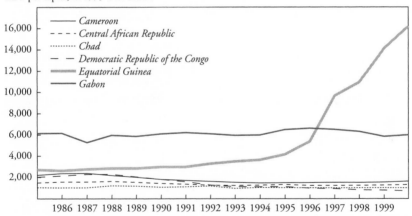

CAEMC Countries
GDP per capita, in 1995 U.S. dollars

Sources: World Bank, World Development Indicators database (2003); and IMF, International Financial Statistics database (2003).

verge to their own steady states. Although widely used, this concept of convergence has been criticized. For example, Quah argues that the evolution of a group of economies should be studied in terms of the dynamics of an entire distribution, rather than average behavior using a cross-section regression.[18] Quah proposes a Markov-chain methodology to estimate the probability that

18. Quah (1996).

Figure 4-2. *CFA Franc Zone Regions: Coefficient of Variation of Real PPP per Capita Income*

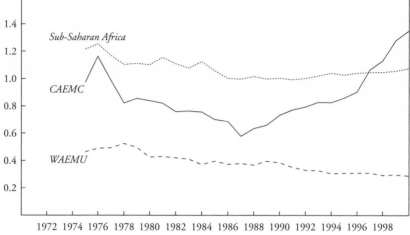

Sources: World Bank, World Development Indicators database (2003); and IMF, International Financial Statistics database (2003).

relatively poorer (richer) countries will raise (lower) their per capita income in the next period.[19]

Our application of the methodology takes countries' per capita GDP in each year relative to the sample average and groups them into five states of relative prosperity. The evolution of the distribution is represented by a 5 × 5 transition matrix whose (j,k)th entry is the probability that a country in income group j transits to income group k in one year.

The results of this analysis for CAEMC and WAEMU are shown in table 4-3. The dominance of the diagonal elements (all over 70 percent) suggests a high degree of persistence. The diagonal entries are higher for CAEMC and tend to increase as one moves up or down the diagonal from the middle. Thus countries that start in the poorest or richest interval have a higher likelihood of remaining there, suggesting a process of divergence. Looking at the off-diagonal elements: countries in group 2 (the second poorest group) are more likely to transit to a poorer group in the following year, while countries in group 4 (the second richest group) have a higher probability of moving into an even richer group the following year. This pattern is again consistent with divergence.

19. Quah (1995).

Table 4-3. *Transition Matrices of Real GDP per Capita, 1975–99*[a]

CAEMC	Initial state no. of observations	Final state Poorest ← 0–0.37	0.37–0.70	0.70–1	1–2.2	→ Richest 2.2+
Poorest	20	0.950	0.050	0	0	0
	61	0.049	0.902	0.049	0	0
	32	0	0.094	0.875	0.031	0
	21	0	0	0	0.947	0.143
Richest	16	0	0	0	0.188	0.813
Total	150					

WAEMU		Final state Poorest ← 0–0.65	0.65–0.80	0.80–1.20	1.20–1.60	→ Richest 1.6+
Poorest	32	0.781	0.219	0	0	0
	48	0.125	0.813	0.063	0	0
	42	0	0.071	0.881	0.048	0
	34	0	0	0.118	0.853	0.029
Richest	19	0	0	0	0.316	0.684
Total	175					

SACU		Final state Poorest ← 0–0.33	0.33–0.67	0.67–1	1–2	→ Richest 2+
Poorest	21	0.905	0.095	0	0	0
	27	0	0.963	0.037	0	0
	19	0	0	0.842	0.158	0
	44			0.045	0.909	0.045
Richest	14	0	0	0	0.214	0.786
Total	125					

Sources: Authors' calculations based on real PPP per capita income in 1995 U.S. dollars from World Bank, World Development Indicators database (2003); and IMF, International Financial Statistics database (2003). Methodology follows Quah (1995).

a. Each country/year real GDP per capita relative to the regional group average is an observation that is grouped into five states of relative prosperity. Intervals are chosen so that the initial number of observations in each state is roughly similar.

The numbers in the left column are the number of country/year observations with starting points in a particular cell. For example, for CAEMC, of the 150 observations (6 countries × 25 years) 61 begin in state 2, and of these, 90.2 percent remained in that state the following year, 4.9 percent moved down into state 1, and 4.9 percent also moved up into state 3.

The evidence for WAEMU is more mixed. On the diagonal, the lowest probabilities register in the upper and lower extremes, indicating that countries in the poorest and richest groups are the least likely to remain in those groups the following year, a pattern consistent with convergence. While the relatively rich countries (group 4) are more likely to become poorer (that is, converge), the relatively poor countries (group 2) are more likely to become poorer (that is, diverge).

Meeting Fiscal Convergence Criteria

As mentioned earlier, an outcome of the 1994 devaluation was greater attention to the need to coordinate macroeconomic policies, in particular fiscal policies.[20] Accordingly, the countries in both WAEMU and CAEMC put in place a regional surveillance procedure that aimed to restrict fiscal deficits and limit public debt. These criteria were buttressed by secondary criteria that aimed to raise government revenues as a fraction of GDP, stimulate investment, and limit the government's wage bill. In addition, since payment arrears are a disguised way of financing deficit spending—one that is especially pernicious—governments agreed also to a criterion that requires reducing or at least not increasing payment arrears. Furthermore, there are criteria that relate to the rate of inflation and to the current account deficit as a ratio to GDP.

Table 4-4 presents recent outcomes for the convergence criteria that relate to fiscal policy for the countries in WAEMU. The key deficit criterion in 2002 is only satisfied by two countries out of eight, Côte d'Ivoire and Senegal. As detailed in Doré and Masson, after an initial period (1995–98) during which considerable progress was made in achieving the convergence criteria, the subsequent period (1999–01) saw either stagnation or backsliding with respect to the criteria.[21] Côte d'Ivoire would seem to constitute an important exception, since it turned a fiscal deficit (defined in terms of the basic balance) of 0.3 percent of GDP into surpluses of 1.7 and 0.3 percent of GDP in 2001 and 2002, respectively. However, as argued in Doré and Masson, this country's fiscal performance can hardly be attributed to increased resolve to achieve fiscal discipline, much less to the regional surveillance criteria of basic budget balance.[22] Instead, during 2000–02 Côte d'Ivoire was gripped by a severe political crisis that led to its external sources of funding drying up. The government accumulated significant domestic and external arrears but also reduced its expenditures, in part because rebels controlled half of the national

20. This section draws on Doré and Masson (2002) and IMF (2002b).
21. Doré and Masson (2002).
22. Doré and Masson (2002).

Table 4-4. *WAEMU: Convergence Criteria Values, 2002*

Country	Basic fiscal balance[a]	Public debt[a]	Inflation rate	Arrears	Wage bill[b]	Public investment[b]	Government revenue[a]	Current account[a]
Benin	−0.2	59.8	2.5	Decrease	32.7	22.0	14.3	−8.2
Burkina Faso	−4.5	66.6	2.4	Decrease	41.1	43.4	12.8	−13.7
Côte d'Ivoire	0.3	107.7	3.0	Increase	44.5	10.6	15.9	−1.0
Guinea-Bissau	−7.3	396.4	3.3	Increase	94.6	5.3	7.5	−21.1
Mali	−1.5	88.3	5.1	. . .	27.0	22.3	14.3	−8.1
Niger	−2.1	91.4	2.8	Decrease	35.9	14.0	10.7	−9.7
Senegal	1.6	69.2	2.4	. . .	29.9	21.7	18.3	−6.2
Togo	−1.0	123.2	3.5	Increase	46.0	9.1	12.6	−14.8
Countries meeting target	2	3	5	5	3	4	1	1

Source: Commission de l'UEMOA, *Rapport semestriel d'éxecution de la surveillance multilatérale* (www.izf. net [December 2002]).
a. As percent of GDP.
b. Percent of government revenues.

territory. Capital expenditure was reduced from 26.7 percent of government revenues in 1998 to 8.8 percent in 2001–02. A similar situation of political crisis prevailed in Togo during 2000–01. Given the large weight of Côte d'Ivoire it is dangerous to rely on averages across WAEMU countries to evaluate the success of regional surveillance.

Factors that a country cannot control also affect the recorded deficit and can complicate an evaluation of the success of regional surveillance. Many of the countries concerned are highly dependent for export revenues and tax receipts on primary commodities whose prices are beyond their control. Thus it is natural to relate the fiscal deficit to changes in a country's terms of trade as well as to a measure of the cyclical position of the economy. An estimated equation regressing the overall budget balance as a ratio to GDP for WAEMU (*OB*) on the output gap (*YGAP*) and the terms of trade (*TOT*) yields the following:[23]

$$OB = -6.3 + 0.293\,YGAP + 0.075\,TOT + \varepsilon,$$
$$(2.24) \qquad\quad (2.68)$$

23. The overall balance was used in preference to the basic balance because data are available for a longer period.

Table 4-5. *CAEMC: Selected Convergence Criteria, Estimates for 2002*

Country	Basic fiscal balance[a]	Inflation rate	Current account[a]
Cameroon	1.3	4.5	−7.2
Central African Republic	−5.6	2.5	−4.8
Chad	−22.3	3.0	−59.6
Dem. Rep. of the Congo	2.2	3.6	0.3
Equatorial Guinea	11.4	6.0	0.1
Gabon	9.0	1.5	−1.8
Countries meeting target	4	3	3

Source: BEAC, *Notes de conjoncture* (www.izf.net [February 2003]).
a. In percent of GDP.

where the *t*-ratios are in brackets. Since these movements are largely exogenous to the countries concerned, it is important to account for the cycle and movements in the terms of trade when evaluating macroeconomic policies in WAEMU. If one sets the variables *YGAP* and *TOT* to their 1994 values and uses the above equation to generate a corrected deficit figure, the budget balance can be shown still to improve over 1995–98, and to deteriorate subsequently, when one excludes Côte d'Ivoire and Togo.[24]

For CAEMC, the contrast between raw data and a corrected deficit figure is even starker, but goes in the other direction. Four of the six member countries (Cameroon, Republic of the Congo, Equatorial Guinea, and Gabon) have substantial production of crude oil and are highly sensitive to changes in the world oil price. Chad also will be in this position in a few years. For these countries, though unadjusted data from the post-1996 period seem to indicate greater budgetary discipline and reinforced regional surveillance (four countries out of six met the deficit criterion in 2002; see table 4-5), that impression is dissipated once account is taken of movements in the terms of trade, for example, by using a constant world oil price based on a decade average to calculate government revenues. On the contrary, recent years have seen a deterioration of the underlying fiscal position, calculated in this fashion, so that such countries as Gabon and Equatorial Guinea are highly vulnerable to a decline in the world price for oil, despite apparently favorable fiscal positions.[25]

In sum the experience with regional surveillance over fiscal positions has been mixed. While an attempt to exert peer pressure over neighboring countries undoubtedly can have positive effects, that pressure to date has been

24. Doré and Masson (2002, figure 5).
25. See discussion in Wiegand (2002).

very light. Future developments may lead to a reinforcement of the process and a willingness to consider sanctions and apply them in cases where overshoots of criteria were the result of policy errors or lack of political will rather than external factors beyond countries' control. Effective surveillance should attempt to distinguish the effects of policy from external forces, especially as concerns the terms of trade. Otherwise governments will easily meet the criteria in times of favorable world market conditions but will have little chance of succeeding when times are bad.

There is little evidence that monetary union itself automatically provides the agency of restraint that would discipline fiscal policies.[26] This conclusion also results from a detailed historical look at the period leading up to the devaluation of 1994. Guillaume and Stasavage document that even the rules on monetary financing were undermined by successful attempts to exert pressure on state-controlled banks to borrow in order to finance government deficits.[27] This was especially true for large countries (Côte d'Ivoire in WAEMU, Cameroon in CAEMC) whose governments could influence the decisions of the central bank.

Monetary Union Costs

Joining a monetary union has costs that are the result of asymmetries across countries. These asymmetries would make a common monetary policy inappropriate for all or some of the potential member countries. In these circumstances (discussed by Mundell in a seminal article and since then by many other economists), separate currencies and flexible exchange rates may be desirable.[28]

It is difficult to assess asymmetries without some standard of comparison. We analyze proposals for a monetary union that would apply to the whole of West Africa—namely, the members of ECOWAS—and show that correlations of shocks to either the terms of trade or to real GDP are considerably higher among the WAEMU countries than with their non-WAEMU neighbors in ECOWAS. Since for any given variable there are a number of bilateral correlations, it is useful to calculate a summary statistic. One alternative would be to average the bilateral correlations, discussed in chapter 6. Another statistic measures the extent that all countries are affected by a common factor, where that factor is constructed to maximize the total variance. This statistic is the percent

26. Masson and Pattillo (2002).
27. Guillaume and Stasavage (2000).
28. Mundell (1961).

Table 4-6. *Proportion of Changes in the Terms of Trade and Real GDP Accounted for by First Principal Component*

	WAEMU 1981–99	CAEMC 1986–99	CFA 1986–99	Sub-Saharan Africa[a] 1986–99
Terms of trade	0.43	0.41	0.34	0.27
Real GDP	0.34	0.34	0.30	0.18

Sources: World Bank, African Development Indicators database (2002); UNCTAD and World Bank. See Cashin, McDermott, and Pattillo (2004).

a. Forty-five countries.

of total variation accounted for by the common factor, the first principal component.[29] Table 4-6 presents the proportion of the regional variance among WAEMU, CAEMC, or all sub-Saharan African countries of the change in the log of the terms of trade or real GDP accounted for by the first principal component. Each of the two regions composing the CFA (WAEMU and CAEMC) exhibits a higher common variation than the rest of sub-Saharan Africa and, therefore, other things equal, would be a better candidate for a monetary union than others in the region.[30] The higher correlations could be caused by the very existence of the monetary union, as countries may have become more similar and their fluctuations more highly correlated.[31] However, this is unlikely to apply to terms of trade correlations, since the choice of which primary commodities to produce would plausibly not have been influenced by the monetary regime, nor are the terms of trade endogenous to a small, open economy. Note that if one combines all the CFA countries, they are much less similar than the two zones are separately, and the correlation for the terms of trade resembles that for the rest of sub-Saharan Africa. This illustrates the fact that CAEMC is an exporter of oil, while WAEMU is an importer.

Another aspect of asymmetry is differences in government spending propensities. This is important for potential monetary unions because monetary policy is likely to be influenced by the need to provide seigniorage to finance government spending—unless central banks are functionally independent

29. Principal components analysis decomposes the total cross-country variance into orthogonal components that are linear combinations of the underlying data. The first principal component is constructed to maximize the explained variance.

30. Of course, any summary statistic hides differences in patterns of bilateral correlations, so a high value for the explained variation may be the result of a few cases of strong comovement. Fielding and Shields (2001) identify groupings of CFA franc zone countries where correlations are highest and suggest that reorganization of the CFA to reflect those groupings might be appropriate.

31. Frankel and Rose (1998).

and prohibited from providing monetary financing to treasuries, which may be difficult to enforce in practice. Thus fiscal asymmetries should make independent currencies more attractive than membership in a common currency area. Again, this is an issue that can only be evaluated by comparison to other sets of countries. We show that differences in spending propensities, and in estimates of spending distortions, are less pronounced among WAEMU countries than in ECOWAS as a whole.

Finally, potential costs from asymmetries can be mitigated by wage and price flexibility, fiscal transfers, and factor mobility between countries of a monetary union. More data is needed to give a definitive answer, but migration between countries of WAEMU seems moderately high, even if there are episodes of backlash against immigration.[32] Fiscal transfers among countries are very limited, while wage and price flexibility is no doubt greater than in most industrial countries, especially in the informal sector.

CMA in Southern Africa

Eclecticism and adaptability characterize the CMA, which groups South Africa, Lesotho, Namibia, and Swaziland. The CMA has evolved from arrangements between the Union of South Africa and the British protectorates in southern Africa plus the League of Nations–mandated territory of South West Africa (now called Namibia). The monetary union continued to encompass these countries upon their independence, though subsequently Botswana left the currency union, and agreements were concluded that allow the smaller members to issue their own currencies. The rand is legal tender in Lesotho and Namibia, but not in Swaziland, and each of these three countries has its own currency. However, none of the currencies is legal tender in South Africa, though each of them circulates to some extent in border areas of that country. Monetary policy is determined by the SARB based on domestic South African objectives. Since 2000 the SARB targets the rate of inflation. Exchange rates within the CMA are not irrevocably fixed, but the currencies have always exchanged one-to-one. South Africa shares seigniorage with Lesotho and Namibia (to compensate for the circulation of the rand in those countries) but not with Swaziland (since the 1986 decision by Swaziland to no longer accept the rand as legal tender).

The currency area is of interest also because Botswana shares many characteristics with the member countries of the CMA but since 1976 is no longer

---

32. Of course, migration may not only be a response to asymmetric shocks but also reflect traditional seasonal patterns or persistent movement from poor rural areas to richer urban (and coastal) areas. World Bank (2000).

part of it. Botswana continues to be a member of the SACU, which links the five countries. Hence Botswana provides interesting evidence on the relative importance of a common currency versus common membership in regional trade pacts in stimulating interregional trade.[33]

The CMA differs from the CFA franc zone by not having put in place regional surveillance over macroeconomic policies (though a larger grouping that includes CMA members, SADC, is beginning to institute such surveillance). Instead, favorable circumstances or the discipline resulting from the inability of the smaller countries to extract seigniorage by running expansionary monetary policies has led to generally sustainable fiscal deficits and low public debt. South Africa itself, though facing significant problems that include high unemployment, has generally followed conservative macroeconomic policies, helping to provide a pole of monetary stability to the region. Despite this, the rand experienced a trend depreciation against both the dollar and the euro until mid-2002, and this allowed CMA countries with higher inflation than South Africa's, in particular Swaziland, to maintain international competitiveness when averaged across all their trading partners, so that deteriorating competitiveness with respect to South Africa was compensated for by increased competitiveness abroad. Since then, the rand has appreciated strongly against the dollar and the euro, and this makes the conditions for achieving growth more difficult for the smaller CMA countries, which may put strains on the monetary union.

Convergence and Integration among CMA Countries

The large disparities in size among the member countries of SACU, and in particular among the CMA countries, are demonstrated in table 4-7. South Africa, with a population of about 43 million and the largest economy in sub-

33. In practice, government revenue from the tariff sharing in SACU has dwarfed any seigniorage received by the smaller CMA countries. The Customs Union Agreement concluded in 1969 provided for a generous share of customs and excise revenues to be paid to Botswana, Lesotho, and Swaziland and as a result constituted upward of 50 percent of government revenues for the latter two countries. Namibia was later included; South Africa received the residual after a complicated calculation that guaranteed certain rates to Botswana, Lesotho, Namibia, and Swaziland (the BLNS countries). A new agreement, signed in October 2002, provides for both more equitable division of revenues and the creation of institutions for joint decision-making and administration of the tariff setting and collection to replace the dominance exerted by South Africa. The new agreement includes a development component favoring the smaller countries (except Botswana); that component is initially 15 percent of the excise pool and is distributed inversely to GDP per capita. Customs revenues are paid disproportionately to the BLNS countries, but excise revenues, minus the development component and the costs of funding SACU institutions, are distributed proportionately to GDP. See McCarthy (2003).

Table 4-7. *SACU: Selected Indicators, 1998–2001*[a]

Indicator	South Africa	Lesotho	Namibia	Swaziland	Botswana
Population (in millions)[b]	42.80	2.15	1.74	1.05	1.60
GDP per capita					
(current U.S. dollars)[b]	2,941	417	2,000	1,297	3,299
GDP growth rate	2.1	3.3	3.2	2.7	6.5
Inflation	5.8	7.7	6.2	7.7	7.4
Broad money growth rate	12.3	7.0	8.4	8.2	22.5
Fiscal position[c]	−1.6	−6.4	−3.5	−1.3	2.1
Government debt[c]	45.5	14.4	...	22.2	9.1
Current account balance[c]	−0.7	−16.5	3.9	−4.1	8.7

Sources: IMF, International Financial Statistics database (2003); and World Bank, African Development Indicators database (2002).
a. Averages.
b. Using data for 2000 only.
c. Percentage of GDP.

Saharan Africa, dominates its smaller neighbors. In per capita income terms, South Africa is much richer than the latter, especially Lesotho and Swaziland. In contrast, Botswana has a higher per capita income level than South Africa.[34]

The extent of intraregional trade and labor mobility is high, resulting in substantial integration, especially for South Africa, Lesotho, and Swaziland. Namibia's economy is larger than Lesotho's or Swaziland's, and it trades more with countries outside the CMA. Changes in Namibia's terms of trade are less well correlated with those of South Africa than is the case for Lesotho and Swaziland. Indeed for this reason Tjirongo concludes that remaining in the CMA is not optimal for Namibia.[35] A contrary view of the net benefits of the CMA for Namibia is given by Alweendo, who stresses the advantages of reduced transactions costs and credibility associated with South Africa's monetary policy.[36]

Data on real per capita income show strong evidence of convergence within the CMA, as the coefficient of variation across countries has declined significantly over the past three decades (see figures 4-3 and 4-4). Thus despite large remaining disparities, it may be argued that this region forms a convergence club.[37] However, convergence is even more evident when Botswana is included,

34. When calculated using current exchange rates. The use of PPP exchange rates gives a different ranking (figure 4-3).
35. Tjirongo (1995).
36. Alweendo (1999).
37. Jenkins and Thomas (1996).

Figure 4-3. *SACU Countries: Real PPP per Capita Income*

GDP per capita, in 1995 U.S. dollars

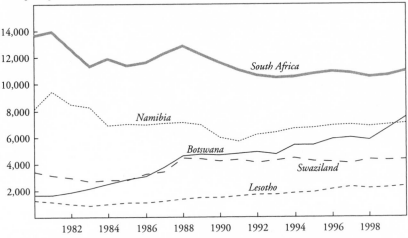

Sources: World Bank, World Development Indicators database (2003); and IMF, International Financial Statistics database (2003).

Figure 4-4. *SACU and the CMA: Coefficient of Variation of Real PPP per Capita Income*

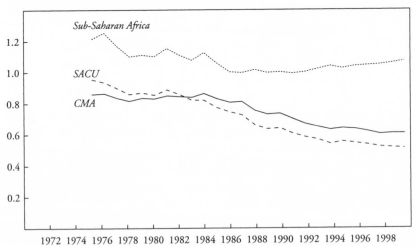

Source: World Bank, World Development Indicators database (2003); and IMF, International Financial Statistics database (2003).

since that country, initially poorer than South Africa, is now somewhat richer in per capita terms. Botswana's real GDP growth averaged 4.8 percent over 1990–2000, compared to 1.7 percent in South Africa, and a more recent period gives a similar ranking (see table 4-7). In any case, convergence in the region does not seem to depend on using the same currency, as Botswana, since 1976, is no longer linked one-to-one to the rand. Botswana's circumstances, however, are fairly unique and hence that country may not provide general lessons concerning currency regimes for other countries.

The transition matrix analysis in table 4-3 is also consistent with convergence for SACU but not as strongly as expected.[38] The pattern of the diagonal probabilities provides mixed evidence for convergence. The off-diagonal entries are more supportive, indicating that relatively poorer countries are more likely to become richer in the following year, and relatively richer countries are more likely to become poorer.

Monetary Policies

South Africa over the past decade has moved from a pegged exchange rate, to a monetary policy with explicit monetary growth targets and a managed float of the rand, and finally to a monetary policy based on a target for the rate of inflation and a free float.[39] Monetary growth targets for M3, a measure of the broad money supply, were preannounced during 1986–98, but structural changes to the financial system made money demand unstable and altered the transmission mechanism. This led, in March 1998, to the replacement of monetary growth targets with M3 guidelines accompanied by an informal inflation target of 1 to 5 percent. In order to reap the credibility benefits from increased transparency, South Africa moved to a formal inflation target in February 2000. The country's minister of finance announced an inflation target of 3 to 6 percent, which was to be achieved by 2002, but in fact was overshot due to strong downward pressures on the rand. The target is formulated for the rate of inflation excluding mortgage interest costs (CPIX), in order to remove the direct effects of the SARB's interest rate policy on consumer prices. The SARB benefits from a long history of independence, which allows it to use the instruments under its control (principally interest rate policy) to achieve its mandated target. However, South Africa is a medium-size, moderately open economy that is strongly influenced by the external environment, and the SARB may miss its target due to external or domestic

38. Using the Quah (1995) methodology, Jenkins and Thomas (1998) find evidence for convergence in SACU and divergence in SADC.

39. See Casteleijn (2001) for a detailed discussion.

shocks. Escape clauses excusing the SARB from reaching the inflation target include developments arising from a sharp rise in the international oil price and international financial contagion. The effort to lower inflation suffered a big setback in the last quarter of 2001, when the rand depreciated sharply. A range of contributory factors has been cited, including declines in world commodity prices, looser monetary conditions, and delays in the privatization program.[40]

Since 1994 South Africa has experienced four periods of unusually severe balance of payments pressure, or currency crises, in 1994, 1996, 1998, and 2001. During the first three episodes, increases in the NOFP played a key role.[41] By the end of 1994, the NOFP had reached the equivalent of 12 percent of GDP. Subsequently, the rand came under frequent attack, and the SARB experienced very large reserve losses and made large forward sales of reserves, which eroded the progress in lowering the NOFP that had been achieved during calmer periods. Each of the crises, except the last, was characterized by sharp increases in the NOFP, increases in interest rates, and sharp depreciations. However, by 2001 a shift of policy had intervened. The NOFP was at a substantially lower level than in earlier crises, and it did not increase during this crisis, as the reserve bank refrained from intervening to support the rand.

The different response of the SARB to the 2001 situation compared to earlier episodes indicated the increased attention given to the inflation rate rather than to the exchange rate per se (though changes in the latter, if permanent, would feed through into domestic prices).[42] In 2001 the SARB did not raise interest rates as sharply nor intervene in the foreign exchange market. Consequently, growth was not significantly impacted and confidence in the management of the economy remained high, as signaled by a rise in the Johannesburg stock exchange. In 2002 the rand recouped most of its 2001 losses, and after appreciating further, its dollar exchange rate at year-end 2003 was less than seven rand to the U.S. dollar, a value last seen in 2000. The appreciation reversed the inflationary pressures triggered by the earlier crisis, and inflation was well within its 3 to 6 percent target band.

Exchange rate flexibility has served South Africa well, arguably preventing some of the worst effects of contagion from the 1997–98 financial crises in Asia.[43] An exchange rate peg to a major international currency (euro or dollar) might have led to a major crisis hitting South Africa, given the extent of its

40. As noted above, however, the rand's depreciation has since been reversed, suggesting that a multiyear average target for inflation might remove the effect of such transitory factors.

41. The NOFP is the central bank's forward liabilities in foreign currency minus its assets.

42. See the discussion in IMF Staff Country Report 02/244, box 2.

43. Mussa and others (2000).

Table 4-8. *Proportion of Changes in the Terms of Trade and Real GDP Accounted for by First Principal Component*

	CMA 1981–99	SACU 1981–99	Sub-Saharan Africa 1986–99[a]
Terms of trade	0.44	0.36	0.27
Real GDP	0.43	0.37	0.18

Sources: World Bank, African Development Indicators database (2002); UNCTAD and World Bank. See Cashin, McDermott, and Pattillo (2004).

a. Forty-five countries.

capital account liberalization and the sophistication of its financial markets. However, the smaller CMA countries (whose currencies are pegged to the rand) do not benefit equally from the flexibility of the rand, since the shocks hitting them are not the same as those impinging on South Africa—the shocks that influence the setting of monetary policy for the CMA by the SARB.

Table 4-8, which reports on the asymmetry of shocks to the terms of trade shocks and to real GDP growth, suggests that these countries behave quite similarly. Some evidence on the extent of trade integration within the CMA is provided in table 4-9. Trade with South Africa is obviously very important to the smaller members of the CMA, but the gravity model gives mixed evidence on whether it may have been favored by the currency union. For Swaziland, the gravity model with currency union dummies exactly predicts the extent of South African trade, while Namibia and Lesotho's trade with South Africa is considerably under predicted. Botswana's trade with South Africa is bracketed by the predictions of the two versions of the model, making

Table 4-9. *CMA and SACU: Trade with South Africa*

		CMA		
	Botswana	Lesotho	Namibia	Swaziland
Actual trade, 2001				
Percent of total trade	40	85	55	70
Percent of GDP	42	104	47	112
Prediction of gravity model, 1997[a]				
Percent of total trade				
without currency union dummy	45	38	18	47
Percent of total trade				
with currency union dummy	39	64	39	70

Source: IMF Staff Country Report 03/21, box 4 (2003).

a. Predictions for 1997, using estimated coefficients from box 4-1.

it hard to conclude anything about the effect of currency union on trade within the CMA.

Given the small size of Swaziland, Lesotho, and (to a lesser extent) Namibia, payments to and from South Africa, including settlements of exports and imports and workers' remittances, are a very large proportion of GDP. Hence the advantages of a common currency (reduction in transactions costs and the absence of exchange rate volatility when converting among CMA countries' currencies) likely dominate the potential costs (loss of monetary policy autonomy). This no doubt provides an explanation for the durability of the relationship among the CMA countries. The willingness of South Africa to accommodate the concerns of its smaller neighbors also is an important part of the story. Cohen describes the use of the rand in Lesotho and Namibia as a case of "dollarization" and argues that these countries are willing to make the rand legal tender because of side payments by South Africa, in the form of offering to stand as the lender of last resort to their domestic banking systems and of providing direct compensation for the seigniorage involved.[44]

Nevertheless, the CMA's durability should not be taken to imply that there are no potential stresses affecting the monetary union. The CMA countries all have high unemployment rates, exceeding 30 percent in Swaziland and approaching that level in South Africa. Because inflation has been consistently higher in Swaziland (averaging 8 percent during the 1998–2001 period, compared to 5.5 percent in South Africa), by some measures bilateral competitiveness relative to South Africa has suffered.[45] As noted above, this has been compensated by the depreciation of the rand against major currencies, helping to sustain Swaziland's exports to third countries. If the strength of the rand that prevailed in 2003 persisted for an extended period, however, the advisability of the link of the lilangeni (Swaziland's monetary unit) to the rand might be called into question. South Africa has shown increased attention to the concerns of its partners in the CMA, and the quarterly meetings of the SARB's monetary policy committee since 2002 are preceded by meetings of the governors of the member countries. However, there are clearly limits to South Africa's willingness to move to a multilateral monetary union. SARB governor Tito Mboweni is quoted as telling the South African parliament's finance committee, "We have agreed we will do some research on what the feasibility is of a common central bank for South Africa, Lesotho, Swazi-

44. Cohen (2000).
45. However, the relative CPIs may not be a good measure of competitiveness, since they include the price of nontraded goods, which evolves differently from either traded goods' prices or labor costs.

land, and Namibia. It is not a bad idea, but I don't think it will fly politically—it's a dead duck."[46]

Botswana

Botswana, almost a decade after achieving independence in 1966, created its
own currency and central bank and, unlike its neighbors, decided to break
the exchange rate link with the rand.[47] Botswana has strong trade links with
South Africa, though linkages are somewhat lower than for the CMA countries (Lesotho, Namibia, and Swaziland) that retained the one-to-one parity
(see table 4-9). As noted above, the gravity model does a good job in bracket-
ing the extent of trade between Botswana and South Africa, with the model
without the currency variable giving the more accurate prediction. As is true
of its neighbors, Botswana also has a relatively high correlation between its
terms of trade and those of South Africa. Botswana's mining sector accounts
for about 35 percent of GDP, and diamonds (also important for South
Africa) account for about three-quarters of total exports.[48] In contrast, South
Africa is much more dependent on manufacturing exports.

The objectives of Botswana's exchange rate policy are to maintain exchange
rate stability and achieve low inflation. Exports of diamonds, because they are
priced in dollars, are not sensitive to the exchange rate of the pula, but the
authorities fear the effects of the so-called Dutch disease, namely, that diamond exports would crowd out the development of other export sectors. The
pula is pegged to a basket, with the peg adjusted from time to time. By keep-

46. Reuters North American Securities News, "South Africa's Mboweni: Regional Cbank
Idea 'Dead Duck,'" June 24, 2003.
47. The Bank of Botswana commenced operations on July 1, 1975, and the new currency, the
pula, was introduced in 1976. The background to the decision to introduce the pula (whose name
means rain or blessings) is described by the Bank of Botswana's first governor in Hermans (1997).
The governor notes that the IMF strongly warned against creating a separate currency because
holding the necessary reserves would be too costly, given Botswana's "poor long-term economic
prospects" (Hermans, 1997, p. 180). Fears that the population would not be willing to exchange
their rand for a new, untested currency proved groundless, and by the end of 1976 the Bank of
Botswana had a comfortable cushion of reserves, as a result of foreign currency credited to the
new central bank by the Reserve Bank of South Africa in exchange for the rand currency with-
drawn from circulation (Hermans, 1997, p. 187). The reserve position was strong enough that
the Botswana authorities could revalue the currency in 1977 by 5 percent against the U.S. dollar
(to which the rand was also pegged). As the then-governor described, "The revaluation was
greeted with disbelief in South Africa. The governor of the SARB, Dr. T. De Jongh, who had
advised so strongly against Botswana's withdrawal from the rand monetary area, was speechless
when he was informed, as a courtesy, by the then governor of the Bank of Botswana. The IMF
also expressed surprise when it was officially informed of the change" (Hermans, 1997, p. 208).
48. OECD (2002).

ing the nominal effective exchange rate roughly constant and keeping the rate of inflation equal to that of trading partners, the authorities hope to keep the REER constant, thus helping to insulate the rest of the economy from movements in the price and volume of diamond exports. A further benefit of the adjustable peg is that it diminishes the impact on the pula of rand volatility against other currencies. Accordingly, Botswana introduced a peg to a basket consisting of the SDR and the rand in June 1980.[49] Since then the pula has been revalued and devalued several times against the basket. By the end of 2002, however, the pula had appreciated by about 60 percent against the rand.

Botswana has been very successful in achieving growth (indeed it was the fastest-growing country in the world in the two decades after independence), and though its inflation rate on average has exceeded that of its main trading partners, it has been roughly the same as South Africa's in recent years (table 4-7). Unlike many other central banks in Africa with independent currencies, the Bank of Botswana has not resorted to accelerating monetary expansion and continual depreciation. Its success in resisting that vicious circle has been due to the fact that the government has run persistent budget surpluses, making it unnecessary for the bank to provide monetary financing. On the contrary, Botswana has used the adjustable peg to maintain international competitiveness on average while keeping monetary growth moderate.[50] The country's president, who has responsibility for setting the framework for how the external value of the pula is determined, has typically followed the advice of the Bank of Botswana and the minister of finance (whom the president is required to consult).[51] These developments have not led to speculative attacks (or strong pressures to revalue), probably because the economy does not have well-developed financial markets, in particular, instruments that would allow investors to take positions with respect to the currency or domestic assets.[52] The credibility of the peg has been enhanced by large foreign exchange reserves, which are a multiple of the domestic money supply (M2).

Because of persistent budget surpluses, capital inflows have not been able to take advantage of a large or deep market for government debt. Moreover, the short-term monetary instrument that is used to mop up liquidity, the Bank of Botswana Certificate, cannot be acquired by nonresidents. Sterilization of foreign exchange reserves also has been facilitated by the fact that government

49. The weights in the basket are undisclosed but roughly reflect trade weights. They are reviewed when circumstances make it desirable to do so.

50. Estimated interest rate reaction functions show that official rates respond positively to domestic inflation, but not to the real exchange rate (Bleaney and Lisenda, 2001).

51. Hermans (1997, p. 197).

52. See IMF Country Report 02/244.

deposits with the central bank have grown hand in hand with reserves. The increase in government deposits corresponds in large part to government revenues from diamond sales, which, due to budget surpluses, have not all had to be spent domestically; a portion has been saved. Given its large fiscal surpluses and foreign exchange earnings, Botswana is unlikely to be a model for other sub-Saharan African countries, which face greater demands on limited resources.

As financial markets become more developed and open to outside investors and the strong growth in diamond revenues levels off, Botswana may be led to consider alternatives to a strict basket peg. In such an environment, strong pressures to revalue or devalue the pula might develop. Exchange rate regimes with more flexibility or even greater commitment to a fixed parity would be better able to contain such pressures. The two likeliest alternatives would be an inflation target associated with a free or managed float, or a move to a monetary or exchange rate union with neighbors, in the context of the SADC or CMA.

Conclusion

The experience of the CFA and the CMA is varied, but it seems difficult to conclude that the existence of a monetary union per se has been associated with a dramatic increase in regional trade and policy coordination. In the CFA zone, monetary union in the first three decades after independence was accompanied by relatively little coordination of other policies. Free trade areas did not take hold, and there was no attempt at regional surveillance over fiscal policies or common banking supervision. It took the severe crisis of the late 1980s and early 1990s to spur a major effort at regional integration, leading to new supranational institutions and greater intergovernmental cooperation. Even here, despite being governed by the same monetary arrangements, the two regions of the CFA franc zone evolved somewhat differently, with greater progress made in WAEMU than CAEMC. Similarly, the extent of intraregional trade differs substantially in the two regions, with the former trading more than predicted by the basic gravity model and the latter about the same as predicted.

The CMA (with its predecessors) constitutes an even older monetary arrangement that ties the smaller countries to the rand, with asymmetry in size giving South Africa the power to set the monetary policy for the region. Lesotho, Namibia, and Swaziland thus delegate their monetary policy, even if they have their own currencies. Aside from the monetary arrangements, there is no other macroeconomic coordination, though there is close policy consultation in a number of areas (including as concerns the customs union).

Explicit limits on fiscal deficits have not been necessary because the smaller CMA countries do not have access to SARB monetary financing. Given the asymmetry of the relationship among the CMA countries, this lack of access has been clear and unambiguous. Thus an exchange rate or monetary union does not inevitably lead to, or require, regional macroeconomic surveillance.

The continued existence of both unions is due to special political circumstances as much as to economic imperatives. Without France's active encouragement of its former colonies to remain in the CFA franc zone (and sanctions on noncompliers), it is likely that the monetary unions in West and Central Africa would have dissolved, like those in the former British colonies. In southern Africa, sharing the currency of an important neighbor with a credible monetary policy made economic sense. Given the importance of their trade with South Africa and restricted domain for the circulation of their currencies, losing the possibility of an independent monetary policy was not a great loss for Lesotho, Namibia, and Swaziland. However, it is likely that even that monetary union might not have survived without the willingness of South Africa to adapt the arrangements to the needs of its neighbors.

It may be difficult, given the existence of relatively few monetary unions and the special features of each, to resolve conclusively the question of whether creating a monetary union elsewhere in Africa can be expected to stimulate trade significantly. WAEMU and the CMA, on the one hand, and CAEMC, on the other, provide opposing indications. In any case, based on the predictions of the gravity model, intraregional trade cannot be expected (even in favorable circumstances) to be as large as trade with Europe. Thus stimulating regional trade probably should not be a preponderant argument in favor of creating currency unions in Africa.

5

Experiences of Countries in Managing Independent Currencies

What are the individual country experiences with independent currency regimes? We focus in this chapter on those sub-Saharan African nations that are not currently members of a monetary union (either the CFA franc or CMA zone), covering the period from the 1970s to the beginning of the current decade. Countries are grouped into two broad categories: those that have moved to some form of flexible exchange rate system (the majority) and those with continued unilateral pegged (fixed or adjustable) exchange rate regimes. The objective of the chapter's analysis is twofold. First, and most important, countries currently involved in proposals either to form or join existing monetary unions have to evaluate the potential desirability of such arrangements against the costs and benefits of the alternative, which is continued use of independent currencies, in either flexible or fixed rate systems. Specifically, countries planning to form WAMZ and revitalize the EAC would all be changing from currently flexible rate regimes. Also, a potential COMESA or SADC monetary union would involve new monetary union status for both some currently flexible and some currently pegged rate countries. Second, by highlighting periods or situations during which exchange rate management became a key macroeconomic issue, we draw out some key areas or potential fault lines that exchange rate regimes, including monetary unions, would need to be designed or prepared to deal with.[1]

Note that our flexible and fixed exchange rate groupings use official classifications published by the IMF, which are de jure or based on countries' self-reporting of their regime. Alternative de facto classifications based on actual behavior (see chapter 2) show that a number of countries officially classified as managed or independent floaters actually behave more like intermediate regimes (very dirty floats or crawling pegs or bands).[2] The same is true (where data are available) for the smaller number of official unilateral pegs.

Appendix B presents a set of country vignettes in which experiences with flexible exchange rates are assessed. The vignettes highlight periods during which exchange rate policies were a key macroeconomic issue.[3]

What are the summary lessons we distill relating to the necessary conditions for successful management of independent currencies in Africa? We conclude that underdeveloped financial markets and inadequate fiscal discipline, particularly following external shocks, limit African countries' ability to successfully operate flexible exchange rate regimes; and that in some cases, "fear of floating"[4] appears justified. Often, however, adjustable peg regimes have also not been managed well due to losses of fiscal control and a resistance to devaluations.

Preliberalization Regimes

Many postindependence governments sought to promote development by establishing import-substitution industries. The primary policy instruments were a protectionist trade regime (restricting imports through increasingly cumbersome systems of tariffs, quotas, exchange controls, and licensing) and state-owned enterprises. At the root of many of the problems during the 1970s and 1980s were high government deficits, financed by money creation, which led to high inflation. In combination with fixed exchange rates that were not adjusted, real exchange rates became increasingly overvalued. Excessive domestic credit creation and the overvalued exchange rates also spilled over into high import demand.

1. The experience of African monetary unions discussed in chapter 4 should also inform understanding of these issues.

2. Alternative classifications are discussed later in this chapter.

3. By focusing on periods when exchange rate management became an important issue or problem, we risk overplaying the downsides of flexible rates relative to their potential benefits. Some additional positive effects are mentioned in the conclusion.

4. Calvo and Reinhart (2002).

Devaluations were considered politically dangerous to incumbents, so countries reacted to balance of payments difficulties by tightening exchange and trade restrictions, leading to large parallel premiums for foreign exchange. Asset motives also generated demand for parallel market foreign exchange, as extremely high financial sector taxation, high inflation, and controlled low nominal interest rates reduced the attractiveness of saving in domestic currency. At some point the authorities began to lose control of a vicious circle. Money financed deficits and foreign exchange controls led to an increase of smuggled or misinvoiced goods (both exports and imports), resulting in declining trade tax revenues that further worsened the deficit and started the cycle again.[5]

The controlled and rationed economy describes the extreme form of these regimes—some African countries exhibited less severe controls, for example, in goods markets. In other regimes, while foreign exchange controls existed, the dominant characteristic of the regime was rather the currency printing press where any shocks, fiscal or external, were met with passive monetary accommodation (Zaïre, Sierra Leone, and Zambia during certain periods).[6] As these systems lacked any nominal anchor, macroeconomic shocks led to almost automatic responses of prices and the exchange rate.

An attempt to change these systems began anywhere from the mid-1980s for some pioneering countries to the mid- or late 1990s for others. Reforms were often brought about by the presence of a new government (and some-times a new political ideology), an external crisis, or the combination of an unsustainable balance of payments position and conditionalities from the IMF or World Bank accompanying new adjustment loan programs.[7] Movement toward more market-determined, flexible exchange rate systems became a cen-terpiece of reform programs in many countries. The reform process has varied substantially across countries, from extremely gradualist to big-bang liberaliza-tions. Many countries began with a megadevaluation and continued with peri-odic devaluations, or managed crawls, gradually liberalizing export surrender requirements as well as other trade and exchange control regulations, while

5. These rationed economies in Africa have been examined in the literature. One type of analysis contrasts dynamically unstable systems where market interventions and fiscal require-ments are not mutually compatible (which eventually must change radically or implode, for example, in Tanzania and Ghana) with systems that, while grossly suboptimal, display policies that lead to a sustainable equilibrium (for example, in Kenya). (Bevan, Collier, and Gunning, 1990). Another approach focuses on the rents generated by rationing that lead to the develop-ment of parallel markets with market-clearing prices for credit, goods, and foreign exchange (Agénor and Ul Haque, 1996; Montiel, Agénor, and Ul Haque, 1993).

6. Honohan and O'Connell (1997).

7. Early success stories, such as that of Ghana, also inspired other countries to undertake difficult reforms previously viewed as politically dangerous and not likely to work.

introducing additional flexible exchange markets, such as foreign exchange auctions or interbank markets, together with foreign exchange bureaus. Reforms often culminated with the unification of the parallel market and flexible exchange rate, that is, the shrinking of the spread to very small levels. Even in countries where reforms were sustained, however, sizable parallel premiums often reemerged later during periods of macroeconomic instability or increasing effective market segmentation.

The dates when countries adopted flexible exchange rate regimes (managed or independently floating) according to the IMF de jure classification often correspond to their initiation of a comprehensive liberalization program (see table 5-1).[8] Table 5-1 shows dates when countries accepted the current account convertibility associated with Article VIII status under the IMF's Articles of Agreement. Most, but not all, of these flexible rate countries also have current account convertibility.

Country Experiences with Flexible Exchange Rates

Our examination of the experience of sub-Saharan African countries with flexible exchange rate systems groups the countries into three problem issues: underdeveloped financial sectors, poor management of fiscal policies and large external shocks, and fear of floating (see appendix B).

Flexible Rate Operating Problems Due to Financial Sector Weakness

While flexible exchange rate systems have been associated with favorable macroeconomic effects in a number of countries, the efficient operation of the foreign exchange market continues to be hindered by limited competition and large structural problems in the financial sector.[9] The system in many countries operates through an interbank market. Vignettes of country experiences in the Gambia and Guinea, for example, illustrate that the efficiency of interbank markets is limited when structural problems in the financial sector and a lack of information inhibit banks dealing with one another, or the market is highly segmented to include only a few large banks or other players. These problems led Guinea to change to an auction market, an arrangement that relies less on well-functioning financial markets but is subject to other difficulties. For example, generalized excess demand for foreign exchange on official markets may lead authorities to manipulate institutional arrangements to ease depreciation pres-

---

8. Most of these regimes are still in existence; footnotes in table 5-1 indicate where this is not the case. Also, the footnotes indicate periods of earlier, unsuccessful attempts at flexible regimes.

9. Problems include small market size, limited competition among banks, government involvement with or management of banks, limited financial instruments, and solvency and liquidity problems.

Table 5-1. *Currently Flexible Exchange Rate Regimes*

Country	Most recent and sustained flexible exchange rate regime[a]	Accepted IMF Article VIII
Angola	1998	. . .
Burundi	1999	. . .
Dem. Rep. of the Congo	1983	. . .
Ethiopia	1993	. . .
Gambia, the	1986	1993
Ghana	1986	1994
Guinea	1986	1995
Guinea-Bissau	1983	1997
Kenya	1993	1994
Liberia	1997	. . .
Madagascar	1994	1996
Malawi	1994	1995
Mauritania	1995	1999
Mauritius	1994	1993
Mozambique	1992	. . .
Nigeria	1998	. . .
Rwanda	1995	1998
São Tomé and Principe	1991	. . .
Sierra Leone	1990	1995
Somalia	1990	. . .
South Africa	1979	1973
Sudan	1992	. . .
Tanzania	1993	1996
Uganda	1992	1994
Zambia	1992	. . .
Zimbabwe	1994	1995

Source: IMF, Annual Report on Exchange Arrangements and Exchange Restrictions (2002).

a. Regimes officially classified as managed or independently floating are designated as flexible. Prior period in flexible exchange rate: Angola, 1994–95; Democratic Republic of the Congo, 1978; Mauritania, 1987–91; Nigeria, 1975–93; Sierra Leone, 1982 and 1986; Uganda, 1981–85; Zambia, 1985–86. Most recent year that a country went off flexible rate: Namibia, 1992; Guinea-Bissau, 1997; Zimbabwe, 1999.

sure. Foreign exchange auctions can also impose uncertainty about pricing and delivery of foreign exchange to participants. In the Gambia, because of institutional and informational problems, at times of pressures or turbulence in the foreign exchange market, spreads of 10 percent or so often emerge for a period as the parallel market adjusts much more quickly than the interbank market.

The most extreme constraint on operating a notionally flexible rate system exists in such countries as Ethiopia, where the financial sector is still dominated by a single state bank. The institutional structure of the exchange market was changed to an interbank market in 1999, but there has not been much activity. Clearly, it is difficult to have a genuine market when a single state bank heavily dominates the financial sector. In addition, it is hard to have a flexible exchange rate system when continued tight trade and payments restrictions and controlled financial markets largely prevent the emergence of domestic assets other than local currency. Demand for foreign exchange for trade and asset motives will continue to encourage the parallel market.

In addition to financial market underdevelopment, other structural conditions make efficient operation of flexible exchange rate systems difficult in sub-Saharan Africa. Export structures dominated by a few commodities lead to extreme seasonality or lumpiness of foreign exchange receipts, providing motivation for extensive intervention to smooth predictable exchange rate cycles. Another contributing factor is that a few big players often dominate the foreign exchange market: large companies or marketing boards on the export side and aid agencies and large trading companies on the import side. The lack of private speculators engaging purely in foreign currency trading also creates difficulties.

Poor Management of Fiscal Policies and Large External Shocks

Policymakers perceive that there are conflicts involved in trying to both control inflation and maintain a competitive real exchange rate, particularly when the terms of trade are deteriorating. The experience of Ghana and Zambia in the 1990s illustrates these policy dilemmas. Although cognizant of the need to allow the exchange rate to depreciate in response to market forces (including changes in the terms of trade) so that the REER is maintained at a competitive level, policymakers are often concerned that rapid nominal depreciation will ignite inflation. The root causes of losses of control over inflation, however, do not stem from the various forms of monetary nominal anchors, but rather from the inability to shield the central bank from weak fiscal discipline. In particular, losses of fiscal discipline in the face of external shocks can contribute to accelerating inflation and macroeconomic volatility, such as Ghana experienced in the late 1990s.

Liberalization of the exchange market in the Democratic Republic of the Congo, Angola, Sudan, and Nigeria has been limited and stop-start in nature in the face of continued severe macroeconomic instability. These country cases illustrate that when monetary, and particularly fiscal, policies are excessively expansionary, attempts to liberalize and make the exchange rate regime more flexible will usually be unsuccessful. Conditions during hyperinflation are merely the most extreme example. In addition, stop-start or extremely gradual liberalizations, where the real objectives of policymakers are unclear, are less likely to be successful, as it appears that the public loses confidence in the credibility of the reform.

Fear of Floating

There appears to be some "fear of floating,"[10] including (in different sub-Saharan African countries and at different times) fear of depreciation and appreciation.[11]

Fear of depreciation often relates to concerns that rapid nominal depreciation will ignite inflation. The higher costs of servicing external debt are another factor, although much less so given large debt relief. There is often no effective domestic lobby for depreciation to ensure competitiveness, as export sectors are often comprised of enclaves or rural smallholder producers. Urban consumers and import-substituting manufacturing sectors, in contrast, can be vocal lobbies for cheap, imported, final and intermediate goods.

Fear of appreciation often stems from government concerns about competitiveness of the export sector, both traditional commodity exports and sometimes nontraditional exports. In countries facing rapid increases in aid, such as Uganda, Tanzania, and Mozambique from the late 1990s through 2002, fear of appreciation often limits use of foreign exchange sterilization (through the sale of foreign exchange to the private sector, that is, by letting the exchange rate float). Difficulties with domestic bond sterilization, however, can lead to high and volatile interest rates, budgetary pressures, and changes in policy direction that make it difficult for the market to determine the objectives of foreign exchange and interest rate policy. Uncertainty about the underlying demand for money complicates determining whether limited sterilization, or a policy of letting the aid inflows increase the money base, will be inflationary.

As for the divergent views of the IMF and country authorities on this issue, to date evidence on the ground is mixed. In Tanzania and Uganda (but not Mozambique), inflation has remained low despite instances of rapid growth in reserve money, suggesting that the countries' preferred strategy of limited sterilization is appropriate.[12] Under particular assumptions, Buffie and others

10. Calvo and Reinhart (2002).

11. Although figures 2-2 and 2-3 indicate that as of 2001, exchange rate volatility against the dollar and the euro was substantial for many countries.

12. Appendix B also discusses the experiences of Zimbabwe and Kenya in managing large surges in private capital inflows. The case of Zimbabwe showed that attempts at targeting the real exchange rate and controlling inflation in the face of significant capital inflows can lead to crises, particularly if the underlying problem (the large budget deficit) is not controlled. Trying to target the real interest rate below its equilibrium value can also contribute to loss of confidence in monetary policy. In Kenya's case, the high interest rates associated with sterilization policies led to significant treasury bill holdings by the bank and nonbank sectors. This further complicated budgetary financing as the willingness to hold treasury bills was sensitive to expectations about the appropriateness of the governments' macroeconomic policies.

show that a heavily managed float is the most attractive approach to managing a large and persistent aid inflow when the policymakers are credibly committed to low inflation.[13] Further work is needed, however, to explore whether fear of floating makes sense in more general conditions, particularly for countries facing large terms of trade shocks and volatile aid inflows. The exchange rate and monetary management of large aid and external shocks clearly pose difficult challenges for policymakers in flexible rate systems.

Performance in Preflexible and Flexible Periods

How have the countries that have moved to flexible exchange rate systems performed in terms of key macroeconomic indicators? Table 5-2 summarizes average performance across these countries during their flexible periods as well as two preflexible periods: the five and ten years before changing to a flexible rate system.[14] War-torn countries are excluded as economic performance is heavily dependent on the effects of the conflict, and this exclusion significantly affects the overall averages. First, following Calvo and Reinhart, an exchange rate flexibility index is calculated, as the ratio of the variance of monthly percent changes in the exchange rate to the sum of variances of monthly percent changes in the exchange rate and reserves.[15] According to this index, exchange rate regimes in these countries indeed have become more flexible in the de jure declared flexible periods, although the size of change in the average index is not large.

We look next at a number of macroeconomic indicators. The idea is not to argue for causal relationships. In examining unconditional changes across periods, clearly factors other than changes in the exchange regime could be driving differential performance. In general, macroeconomic indicators have improved in the more recent flexible exchange rate period for these countries. Growth in both real GDP and real GDP per capita is higher on average, while inflation and black market premiums are generally lower. There is a significant degree of variance across the countries, however. The average black market premium in flexible periods would be substantially lower if Nigeria were excluded, and inflation falls more when excluding Sudan and Zambia, two very high inflation countries.[16]

13. Buffie and others (2004).

14. Countries included in table 5-2 are those covered in the vignettes (Ethiopia, Ghana, Guinea, Kenya, Madagascar, Mauritius, Mozambique, Nigeria, South Africa, Sudan, Tanzania, the Gambia, Uganda, Zambia, and Zimbabwe) as well as additional flexible rate countries (Guinea-Bissau, Malawi, Mauritania, and São Tomé and Principe) but excluding war-torn countries (Angola, Burundi, Democratic Republic of the Congo, Liberia, Rwanda, Sierra Leone, Somalia).

15. Calvo and Reinhart (2001).

16. Note that by 1997–2000, however, Sudan's inflation fell significantly, reaching single digits in 2000.

Table 5-2. *Average Performance of Flexible Exchange Rate Regime Countries in Preflexible and Flexible Periods*[a]

Performance indicator	Ten-year period before adopting flexible rate	Five-year period before adopting flexible rate	Flexible period
Exchange rate			
Flexibility index	16.20	17.29	18.81
Volatility	0.05	0.06	0.05
Real GDP			
Growth	2.1	2.6	3.4
Per capita growth	−0.4	0.1	0.6
Percent change in			
Terms of trade	−0.3	−1.0	−0.1
REER	−2.1	−5.1	−4.4
Inflation	34.2	35.0	26.9
Black market premium	162.6	203.4	62.6
Fiscal deficit as percent of GDP			
Including grants	−5.7	−5.6	−5.6
Excluding grants	−8.6	−9.2	−10.5

Sources: Figures for exchange rate flexibility index and volatility, real GDP and GDP per capita growth, and inflation are from authors' calculations and IMF, International Financial Statistics database (2003). Percent change in terms of trade from Cashin, McDermott, and Pattillo (2004). Black market premium from Reinhart and Rogoff (2002). The REERs from IMF, Information Notice System database (2003). Fiscal deficits from World Bank, African Development Indicators database (2003).

a. IMF classification used to identify flexible exchange rate periods. Regimes classified as managed floating or independently floating are termed *flexible.*

Averages over the following countries with flexible exchange rate periods (up to 2000) in parentheses: Ethiopia (1993–2000), Ghana (1986–2000), Guinea (1986–2000), Guinea-Bissau (1983–96), Kenya (1993–2000), Madagascar (1994–2000), Malawi (1994–2000), Mauritania (1995–2000), Mauritius (1994–2000), Mozambique (1992–2000), Nigeria (1998–2000), São Tomé and Principe (1991–2000), South Africa (1979–2000), Sudan (1992–2000), Tanzania (1993–2000), the Gambia (1986–2000), Uganda (1992–2000), Zambia (1992–2000), and Zimbabwe (1994–98).

Periods over which averages are calculated are country specific, depending on the year the flexible exchange rate was adopted. Any subsequent periods where countries were not on a flexible regime are omitted from averages (although earlier abandoned flexible rate periods are included in preflexible period averages).

Excludes war-torn countries with flexible rates: Angola, Burundi, Democratic Republic of the Congo, Liberia, Rwanda, Sierra Leone, and Somalia.

Table 5-2 also indicates that the REERs have depreciated on average during these countries' flexible periods, after appreciating during the preflexible periods. Figure 5-1 graphs the country-specific REERs, with a vertical bar in each panel indicating the year of movement to a flexible regime. One of the most important fundamentals associated with the real exchange rate, a real commodity

Figure 5-1. *REER and Real Commodity Prices, 1979–2001*[a]

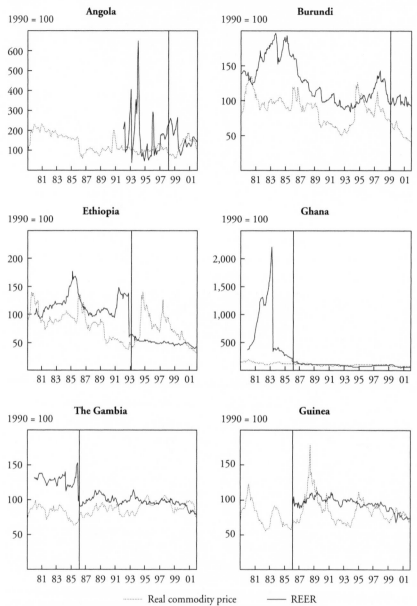

a. Vertical bars indicate the year in which countries adopted flexible exchange rate regimes.

Figure 5-1. *REER and Real Commodity Prices, 1979–2001*[a] *(Continued)*

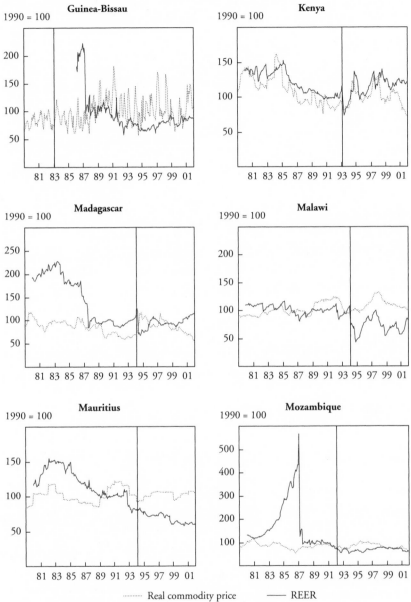

.... Real commodity price — REER

a. Vertical bars indicate the year in which countries adopted flexible exchange rate regimes.

Figure 5-1. *REER and Real Commodity Prices, 1979–2001*[a] *(Continued)*

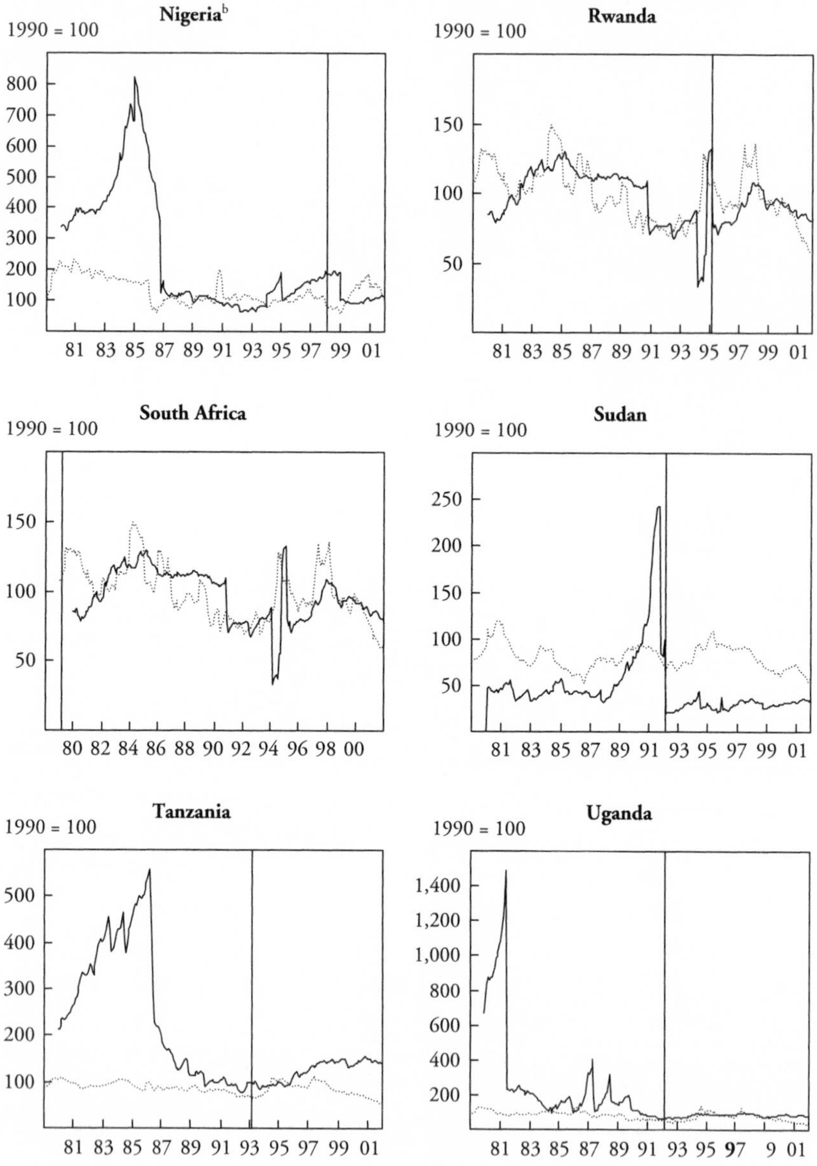

Real commodity price —— REER

a. Vertical bars indicate the year in which countries adopted flexible exchange rate regimes.

b. Flexible exchange rate for entire period except 1994–97.

Figure 5-1. *REER and Real Commodity Prices, 1979–2001[a] (Continued)*

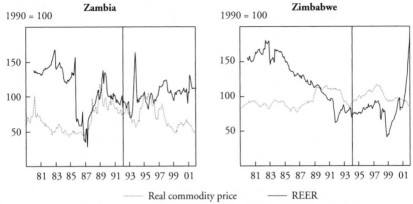

a. Vertical bars indicate the year in which countries adopted flexible exchange rate regimes.

price index,[17] is also shown in figure 5-1 to illustrate the extent to which movements in the REER are influenced by commodity prices in the preflexible and postflexible periods. For most of the countries, the graphs show that the movement to a flexible exchange regime was accompanied by a large depreciation of the REER. On average, the REERs remain more depreciated in the flexible period and, for a number of countries, exhibit a continual depreciating trend after the adoption of flexible rates. In viewing the graphs, however, it is important to note again that official announcements of movement to a flexible regime may not always correspond to rates that appear flexible in practice. For example, while the de jure classification shows Mozambique changing to a flexible rate system in 1992, an alternative classification based on observed behavior suggests that the system fluctuated between a dirty float or crawling peg and a fixed rate before moving to a flexible rate in 1998.[18]

Finally, the last column in table 5-2 shows that fiscal deficits on average are very similar during these countries' preflexible and flexible exchange rate periods. Thus we have little evidence on whether fixed or flexible rates are associated with greater fiscal discipline. In any case, causality is an important question here. It could be that progress on fiscal discipline contributes to the ability to maintain some degree of fixed or flexible rates or that fixed or flexible regimes help support fiscal discipline.

17. See Cashin, Céspedes, and Sahay (2002) for an analysis of the extent to which real exchange rates of commodity-exporting countries and their real commodity prices move together over time.

18. Levy-Yeyati and Sturzenegger (2002); classification from Reinhart and Rogoff (2002) is not available for Mozambique.

Table 5-2 is based on de jure classifications of exchange rate regimes. For comparison we analyze differences in growth performance in all sub-Saharan African countries across different exchange rate regimes, using Reinhart and Rogoff's "natural classification" based on observed behavior.[19] For this analysis, we use data and specifications from Rogoff and others that examine the relationship between exchange rate regimes and economic performance from 1970 to 1999, after controlling for other variables that may also influence performance.[20]

Figure 5-2 shows how per capita growth performance differs across sub-Saharan African countries using the IMF's de jure classification, sub-Saharan African countries using the natural classification, and all developing countries using the natural classification.

The figure shows the coefficients on dummy, or categorical, variables representing the exchange rate regime, and should be interpreted as a regime's performance relative to the pegged regime excluded from the regression, conditional on other variables.[21] Using the de jure classification, the results indicate that growth in pegged regimes in sub-Saharan Africa is about 2.76 percent per year higher than for countries with intermediate flexibility, while the difference between growth in pegs and floating regimes is not statistically significant. While the natural classification showed that for all developing countries growth appears to decline with increased flexibility (but the effects were not significant), for the sub-Saharan Africa subsample, there is a statistically significant 3.7 percent per year lower growth in limited flexibility regimes compared to pegs. The difference between growth in pegs and either managed or freely floating regimes is not significant. Thus using either the de jure or natural classification, growth is higher in pegged regimes relative to intermediate regimes, while the growth differences between pegs and flexible regimes are not significant.

Country Experiences with Fixed or Adjustable Pegs

The alternatives for countries that are not currently members of currency unions (CFA franc zone or the CMA) are to continue their existing flexible or fixed exchange rate systems, or to form or join monetary unions. We complete

19. Reinhart and Rogoff (2002). The classification distinguishes regimes that are freely falling (notionally floating but with severe macroeconomic stress evidenced by high inflation) as a separate category and uses parallel market rates (when they differ substantially from official rates) to classify regimes. De facto regimes are divided into five categories: fixed, limited flexibility, managed, floating, and freely falling.

20. Rogoff and others (2003).

21. The regressions control for factor accumulation (investment ratio, education, population level, and growth), trade openness, terms of trade growth, tax ratio, government balance, and conditional convergence as well as country-specific fixed effects and year dummies. Detailed results available upon request.

Figure 5-2. *Growth Performance across Regimes*[a]

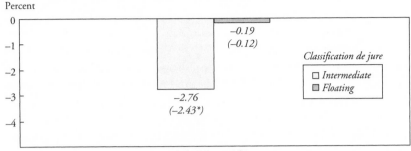

Sub–Saharan Africa

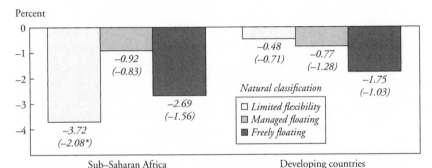

Sub–Saharan Africa   Developing countries

Sources: Authors' calculations. Data and regression specifications are from Rogoff and others (2003).

a. The bars represent differences in per capita growth relative to pegged exchange rate regimes, conditional on other variables. They show the coefficients on dummy variables representing the exchange rate regimes in regressions controlling for investment ratio, education, population level and growth, trade openness, terms of trade growth, tax ratio, government balance, and conditional convergence as well as country-specific fixed effects and year dummies.

Figures in parentheses are *t*-statistics.

*Significance at 10 percent level.

the description of experience with existing regimes by considering countries (outside the CFA franc or CMA zones) with fixed rate systems: single currency or basket pegs, both fixed and adjustable.[22] By 2002, there were actually very few countries with such arrangements. A number of these countries are considering joining various monetary union projects.

Unfortunately, since several of these countries were also war torn for significant periods (for example, Burundi, Eritrea, and Liberia), economic performance was dominated by the wars and not exchange rate or other policies. It is also difficult to generalize from Zimbabwe's case, which moved back from a

22. Vignettes of these countries' experiences are also presented in appendix B.

flexible to a fixed rate system (notionally adjustable, but very rarely changed) in 1999, since that country has been in the midst of a severe, general politico-economic crisis and large contraction, accompanied by a cutoff in external assistance and capital flows. The four other sub-Saharan African countries currently with some form of peg (as of 2001) are Botswana along with three small islands or city-states, which are more dependent on services (Djibouti), tourism and maritime activities (Seychelles), or remittances (Cape Verde) rather than the commodity exports that dominate most African countries' structures. However, these three countries' experiences are also instructive to some extent. The limited experience of the nonwar or crisis countries with fixed or adjustable peg systems suggests the following lessons.

Adjustable pegs have contributed to low or moderate inflation and periods of strong growth. However, when concerns have arisen about the sustainability of pegs, the underlying problem usually has been overly expansionary fiscal policies. The scope for macropolicies is constrained by very high degrees of openness, the fixed exchange rate, and free flows of capital. Demand management must rely heavily on budgetary policy and, in some cases, particularly on government wage policies. This situation is most stark in the case of Djibouti's currency board but is also true for the other countries. Independence of the central bank from pressures to monetize large fiscal deficits is also important in these regimes in order to maintain adequate reserve cover and the viability of the peg.

Close relations with an industrial country can help in critical situations but have downsides also. For example, while Cape Verde's drawing on its credit line with Portugal in 2000 (even though it was officially blocked because of previous noncompliance with the rules) helped sustain the peg at that time, the expectation of future bailouts may not contribute to maintenance of fiscal discipline.

When the authorities respond to balance of payments pressures with trade and foreign exchange restrictions (preventing pressures from affecting the exchange rate), macroimbalances continue to build, and competitiveness and efficiency decline precipitously as the real exchange rate becomes overvalued. Ongoing adjustments of the peg are important to prevent the emergence of large misalignments. When delayed such that a megadevaluation is probably warranted, countries resist, concerned about potential costs.

In contrast to the three countries above, Botswana has successfully managed its basket peg system generally to maintain competitiveness and support growth. An important part of that success has been maintenance of fiscal discipline, a liberalized exchange control system, some degree of central bank independence, and occasional adjustment of the exchange rate.

Conclusion

Countries contemplating joining or forming monetary unions must compare the costs and benefits against the alternative of continued use of independent currencies in either flexible or fixed rate systems. Currently, de jure flexible rate systems are much more prevalent in sub-Saharan Africa (outside the CFA and CMA zones). Historically, the move of many of these countries to flexible rates was an important part of the liberalization and reform process of the 1980s and 1990s. Collier and Gunning argue that it would have been extremely difficult for a liberalizing government to be credible if it had maintained a fixed exchange rate regime, as the overvalued fixed rate system had been at the center of the control regime (foreign exchange rationing, import licensing, price controls), with its associated corruption and inefficiencies.[23] Also, flexibility was important to help determine the appropriate level of the exchange rate—a difficult process during periods of transition.

Currently, what is the relevance to sub-Saharan Africa of exchange rate flexibility? For Latin America, some have argued that exchange rate flexibility and independent monetary policies have been misused and have typically just produced inflation.[24] Is the same true for Africa? Flexible exchange rate regimes in Africa have successfully reduced corruption and inefficiencies associated with nonmarket allocation of foreign exchange; dramatically lowered or eliminated parallel market spreads; reduced large, initial, real exchange rate overvaluations; and, by allowing some adjustment to terms of trade shocks, cushioned some of the negative effects on output.[25] The designation of some of these regimes as flexible, however, is questionable, as rates are often heavily managed. Moreover, exchange rate management has sometimes not been disciplined, which has resulted in high inflation and exchange rate instability.

It is clear from our review of country experiences that successful use of independent currencies requires fiscal discipline, which, although improving, is still a major issue in many countries. Preventing losses of fiscal control following shocks, such as terms of trade shocks, is extremely important for the viability of

23. Collier and Gunning (1999).
24. Hausman, Panizza, and Stein (2001).
25. The question of whether the REERs in developing countries adjust more to terms of trade shocks under flexible rates is not settled in the literature. Broda's (2001) evidence says yes, while Calvo and Reinhart (2002) suggest no. For sub-Saharan Africa, Hoffmaister, Roldos, and Wickham (1998) find, paradoxically, that the REERs in CFA countries respond more to terms of trade shocks than in non-CFA countries. Cashin, Céspedes, and Sahay (2002) find a long-run relationship between real commodity prices and the REER in a number of countries, and they find that both some fixed and some flexible exchange rate sub-Saharan African countries can be designated as commodity currencies.

flexible rates in African countries that face substantial external volatility. Central bank independence, particularly from pressures to monetize large deficits, is another major pillar for having independent currencies. Except for South Africa, the degree of central bank independence in sub-Saharan Africa is extremely low.

In addition, as our country reviews indicate, operating truly flexible exchange rate regimes requires efficient financial markets. However, structural problems and underdevelopment plague financial markets in most African countries.

From the experience of the small number of nonwar or crisis countries with fixed or adjustable pegged regimes, however, it is clear that neither the fixed nor flexible system option is without pitfalls. Adjustable fixed rate systems have contributed to low to moderate inflation, macroeconomic stability, and periods of strong growth. Botswana, in particular, has been well served by its adjustable basket peg. In other cases, however, losses of fiscal control and restoration of exchange controls have led throughout the 1990s to deteriorating competitiveness and severe concerns over the viability of the peg.

These costs and benefits of current regimes will need to be weighed against potential outcomes with monetary unions, discussed in later chapters. The current experience with flexible and unilateral fixed rates has highlighted important issues that any future monetary and exchange rate systems will likely confront. These include the crucial requirement to maintain fiscal discipline, the development of efficient financial systems (for operating flexible rates and facilitating domestic bond markets), and the challenge of the monetary and exchange rate management of large aid inflows and terms of trade shocks.

6

Proposed Single Currency for West Africa

On April 20, 2000, in Accra, Ghana, the leaders of six West African countries declared their intention to proceed, by January 2003, to a monetary union to be known as WAMZ.[1] This would be a first step toward a wider monetary union in 2004, which would include all ECOWAS countries. The leaders committed themselves to lowering central bank financing of budget deficits to 10 percent of the previous year's government revenue, reducing budget deficits to 4 percent of GDP by 2003, creating a convergence council to help coordinate macroeconomic policies, and setting up a common central bank. The declaration states that "member states recognize the need for strong political commitment and undertake to pursue all such national policies as would facilitate the regional monetary integration process."

The goal of a monetary union in ECOWAS has long been an objective of the organization, going back to its formation in 1975, and is intended to accompany a broader integration process that would include enhanced regional trade and common institutions. Although there have been attempts

1. The meeting was attended by three heads of state—Presidents Olusegun Obasanjo of Nigeria, Jerry Rawlings of Ghana, and Lansana Conté of Guinea—as well as representatives from Liberia, Sierra Leone, and the Gambia. Cape Verde, the remaining non-CFA ECOWAS member, has a currency peg to the euro with the support of Portugal and was not a signatory of the Accra Declaration on a Second Monetary Zone. Liberia has not actively participated in subsequent preparations for the WAMZ.

to advance the agenda of ECOWAS monetary cooperation, political problems and other economic priorities in several of the region's countries to date have inhibited progress. The initiative to create a second monetary zone was bolstered by the 1999 election of a democratic government and leader committed to regional integration in Nigeria, the largest economy of the region, raising the hopes that the long-delayed project could be revived. Since 2000, however, it has become clear that the timetable was too ambitious, and countries have made little progress in achieving macroeconomic convergence.[2] Therefore, ECOWAS heads of state in December 2002 decided to postpone the introduction of a single currency for the WAMZ until July 2005, while the target date for a merger with WAEMU has not been set.

The plan to create a second monetary union (in addition to that constituted by WAEMU), as well as the plan for a full ECOWAS monetary union, raises questions about the advantages and disadvantages of various alternative arrangements and strategies. There is clearly an important political dimension behind the recent initiative, but this should not lead one to ignore the economic benefits and costs. We quantify the net benefits using the model introduced in chapter 3 and calibrated there to Africa-wide data. In considering the possible net economic benefits of monetary union, the model uses data on the strength of trade linkages and on the degree of symmetry in terms of trade shocks and fiscal policies of potential members. In fact, there are major differences among the West African economies. In particular, Nigeria, a major oil exporter, faces a very different pattern of terms of trade shocks from the other economies of the region. It has also had relatively undisciplined fiscal policies. Moreover, existing trade among the region's countries is quite low, although there is no doubt considerable informal trade that is not recorded. Of course, one of the reasons for proceeding to monetary union quickly is to promote improvement in macroeconomic policies and enhance prospects for other aspects of regional integration, including regional trade. As discussed in chapter 4, the empirical literature suggests some boost to the trade among members of a monetary union.

In addition to the advisability of a monetary union, important institutional issues must be faced. The first choice is that of a central bank for the monetary union. Unfortunately, none of the WAMZ countries has a central bank with a track record of currency stability and low inflation. Nigeria, which accounts for more than half the population of ECOWAS and 75 percent of the GDP of the six countries proposing an initial monetary union, would be a natural candidate to provide the nucleus of a regional central

2. As argued, for instance, by Masson and Pattillo (2001).

bank, but Nigeria has a history of high inflation, and the Nigerian currency is inconvertible.

The second stage also raises the issues of whether the French Treasury's guarantee of convertibility of the CFA franc to the euro, at a fixed parity, would continue and, if not, what would guide the region's monetary policy. A second choice associated with a full monetary union, therefore, is whether the region's common currencies should have an external exchange rate anchor, such as a peg to the euro. A peg to the euro would provide exchange rate stability with the twelve-member euro area and neighboring six-member Central African CFA zone (CAEMC). Such a peg, however, would not have the credibility of the WAEMU peg in the absence of the French guarantee. Choosing instead to peg to a basket rather than to a single currency would permit some insulation from the fluctuations among major currencies, in particular, the dollar and the euro. An alternative monetary framework would be to forsake an external target and to key monetary policy onto a domestic objective, such as inflation.

West African Countries: Linkages and Asymmetries

An important advantage of a single currency is the saving of transactions costs involved in regional trade. However, as table 6-1 shows, the trade among WAMZ countries is much lower than among WAEMU countries, despite the fact that the GDP of the former is greater than that of the latter. WAEMU trade in fact is greater than can be explained by a traditional gravity model, suggesting that there may have been a boost to WAEMU trade as a result of decades of economic cooperation and sharing of the same currency. Therefore the low level of WAMZ trade may not be a bar to considering a monetary union among those countries. The second stage, a full ECOWAS monetary union, would internalize a greater fraction of the region's trade than is the case for WAEMU, even without allowing for the possibility that trade might increase endogenously in response to the creation of a monetary union. Hence WAMZ might make sense as a means to an end—the ECOWAS monetary union.

A second important factor influencing net benefits is the degree of symmetry of the shocks that affect the region's economies. Table 6-2 indicates that there is a major problem of asymmetry as concerns Nigeria, a country facing terms of trade shocks that are negatively correlated with those of some of the other economies of the region. This applies both to WAEMU and Nigeria's potential WAMZ partners. The source of this asymmetry is clear: Nigeria's exports are mainly crude oil, while other countries of the region are

Table 6-1. *ECOWAS: Patterns of Trade, 2002*
Percent of regional exports or imports

	Exports	Imports
ECOWAS		
ECOWAS	11.0	10.1
European Union	35.1	40.4
Rest of the world	53.9	49.5
WAEMU		
WAEMU	12.7	8.9
WAMZ	7.6	9.7
European Union	45.1	42.8
Rest of the world	34.6	38.6
WAMZ		
WAMZ	3.6	4.6
WAEMU	4.2	3.4
European Union	28.0	42.2
Rest of the world	64.2	49.8

Source: IMF, Direction of Trade Statistics database (2003).

oil importers. While the other countries also typically export primary commodities, the prices of the latter do not move together with the world oil price. Thus the terms of trade of Nigeria and the other ECOWAS countries behave quite differently. Moreover, not only are the correlations low or negative but also the variability of Nigeria's terms of trade shocks is large (the standard deviation of yearly changes in its terms of trade equals 21.5 percentage points, higher than that of any of the other countries in the region), making it an unstable partner whose size might induce undesirable movements in the region's real exchange rate. In contrast, as is evident from table 6-2, the correlations of terms of trade shocks are higher among WAEMU countries than between them and WAMZ countries, or among WAMZ countries, suggesting that WAEMU forms a more desirable currency area. Forming a larger currency area might dilute WAEMU's advantage in that regard.

Third, an important aspect of asymmetry that can interfere with the success of a monetary union when a central bank is not insulated from fiscal pressures is the degree of fiscal (in)discipline. A key aspect of the model discussed in chapter 3 lies in the extent to which government-financing requirements differ across countries. Of course, goals are generally unobservable. However, reasonable estimates of the cross-country differences in financing requirements can be obtained by looking at the determinants of political dis-

Table 6-2. Openness, Standard Deviation, and Correlation of Terms of Trade Shocks[a]

Country	Openness[b] Percent	Standard deviation of terms of trade shocks		Correlation of terms of trade shocks											
		Unscaled	Scaled[c]	Benin	Burkina Faso	Côte d'Ivoire	Mali	Niger	Senegal	Togo	Gambia, the	Ghana	Guinea	Nigeria	Sierra Leone
Benin	61	0.178	0.109												
Burkina Faso	43	0.072	0.031	**0.56**											
Côte d'Ivoire	82	0.063	0.052	0.22	0.06										
Mali	63	0.051	0.032	0.43	**0.94**	-0.01									
Niger	47	0.064	0.030	-0.03	-0.02	-0.40	-0.06								
Senegal	67	0.065	0.043	0.46	**0.57**	**0.59**	0.48	**-0.57**							
Togo	76	0.081	0.062	0.28	0.11	**0.52**	0.07	-0.41	0.49						
Gambia, the	154	0.186	0.286	0.14	0.37	**0.75**	0.26	-0.31	**0.62**	0.03					
Ghana	62	0.111	0.069	0.33	0.16	-0.16	0.08	0.05	0.28	0.14	0.17				
Guinea	39	0.073	0.029	-0.19	0.26	-0.16	0.32	-0.13	0.33	0.07	**0.54**	-0.41			
Nigeria	71	0.215	0.152	0.07	0.02	-0.23	0.01	-0.17	0.09	0.27	0.06	**-0.54**	**0.59**		
Sierra Leone	45	0.063	0.028	0.19	0.06	**0.65**	-0.05	0.06	0.15	0.26	0.17	**0.62**	-0.44	-0.38	
Average all				0.19	0.24	0.18	0.19	-0.15	0.27	0.14	0.19	0.13	0.06	-0.02	0.10
Average WAEMU				0.32	0.37	0.16	0.31	-0.25	0.34	0.17	0.21	0.26	0.07	0.01	0.19
Average non-WAEMU				0.08	0.13	0.20	0.09	-0.07	0.21	0.11	0.16	-0.03	0.05	-0.05	0.00

Source: Terms of trade index (1987 = 100, U.S. dollar–based), World Bank, World Tables, 2001.

a. Correlations in bold exceed 0.5 and are significant at the 5 percent level.

b. Calculated as the sum of exports and imports as a percent of GDP. From IMF, Balance of Payments Yearbook (2001); IMF, Direction of Trade Statistics database (2001); and Masson and Pattillo (2001).

c. Scaled by openness.

Table 6-3. *Corruption and Institutional Quality Indexes*

Country	Corruption[a]	ICRG Institutional Quality Index[b]
Gambia, the	−0.02	5.62
Ghana	−0.30	5.56
Guinea	−0.85	4.59
Nigeria	−0.95	4.20
Sierra Leone	−0.02	2.98
WAMZ average	−0.43	4.59
Benin	−0.78	
Burkina Faso	−0.37	4.31
Côte d'Ivoire	−0.08	5.53
Mali	−0.48	3.42
Niger	−1.57	3.96
Senegal	−0.24	5.27
Togo	−0.24	3.41
WAEMU average	−0.54	4.32
Sub-Saharan Africa	−0.48	4.68

Sources: Corruption scores from Kaufmann, Kraay, and Zoido-Lobaton (1999); International Country Risk Guide (ICRG) from PRS Group (www.icrgonline.com).

a. Scores range from −2.5 to 2.5, with higher numbers indicating less corruption.

b. The ICRG index is an average of scores for measures of democratic accountability, corruption, government stability, bureaucratic quality, and rule of law. Scores range from zero to ten, with higher numbers indicating better institutions.

tortions. From white elephants to pervasive inefficiencies in the provision of priority services like health and education, socially wasteful outlays often are associated with corruption. Table 6-3 compares corruption measures for the ECOWAS countries with the average for the rest of sub-Saharan Africa, as well as a global sample whose average is 0. African countries perform significantly worse than other regions. Most important for our analysis, there are also large differences in the scores across the ECOWAS countries, with Niger and Nigeria emerging as the most affected by corruption while the Gambia is very close to the world average.

Other aspects of a country's institutional environment may distort expenditure policies. Using International Country Risk Guide (ICRG) data, we calculated an institutional quality index, which combines equally weighted indexes of democratic accountability, corruption, government stability, bureaucratic quality, and rule of law.[3] This broader index is similar to those

3. A score of ten is the maximum and indicates the highest institutional quality.

used in the literature on institutions and growth.[4] Table 6-3 shows that the average institutional quality index for both WAEMU and WAMZ member states is lower than the average for sub-Saharan Africa. The Gambia, Ghana, Côte d'Ivoire, and Senegal have the highest indexes for the countries considered, while Sierra Leone, Togo, and Mali are at the low end of the scale.

Using the methodology described in appendix A, we find that estimated diversion wedges vary substantially across the region, ranging from 21.5 percent of actual expenditures in Côte d'Ivoire and Senegal to more than 70 percent in Nigeria (see table 6-4). We need to make a further calculation to obtain financing needs. In particular, we note that actual spending may vary because of other reasons related to the extent of development: countries with higher per capita incomes also have a higher tax capacity, which permits them to offer greater social services to their citizens. While doing so may have ancillary costs, such as the reduced incentives to work associated with higher taxes, nevertheless this choice is quite separate from issues of corruption or of pressures on central banks to finance deficit spending. Thus as described in appendix A, we remove the systematic effect of per capita income on both expenditure and revenues (as ratios to GDP) and only consider spending evaluated at the average level of per capita income for Africa plus the government spending residual (that is, the extent that countries spend more than predicted by their level of income). We then add this to a fraction (half) of the diversion wedge described above[5] to get the estimate of the component of financing needs that is likely to put pressure on the central bank to monetize deficit spending. These figures, which are reported in table 6-4 for ECOWAS countries, indicate higher financing needs for Nigeria, Ghana, and Sierra Leone than for the remaining ECOWAS countries.[6] WAEMU countries all have lower ratios, though Burkina Faso and Mali have considerably higher values than Senegal and Côte d'Ivoire.

Model Evaluations of Monetary Unions' Net Benefits

We first consider whether the existing WAEMU is better than floating exchange rates for the countries concerned, with results of this exercise appearing in table 6-5.[7] To help in understanding the results, the various

4. See, for example, Hall and Jones (1999), or Easterly and Levine (2003).
5. Only a fraction is added to allow for diversion of spending as well as a higher spending target. We have no firm evidence of their relative importance, so we choose equal proportions.
6. A more complete set of data is in appendix A.
7. Guinea-Bissau was not included because of data problems as well as the fact that it has been a member of WAEMU only since 1997.

Table 6-4. *Selected Indicators for ECOWAS Countries, Averages, 1995–2000*[a]

Percent of GDP unless noted otherwise

Country	Government revenue[b]	Government spending	Overall surplus/ deficit[b]	Inflation (percent)	GDP per capita (current U.S. dollars)	Government spending at average income	Diversion	Financing need[c]
WAEMU								
Benin[d]	19.08	19.48	-0.40	5.6	370	29.09	34.57	46.37
Burkina Faso	21.82	25.12	-3.29	3.1	222	36.16	42.21	57.26
Côte d'Ivoire	21.64	23.58	-1.94	3.9	711	30.18	21.51	40.93
Mali	21.77	24.88	-3.11	3.4	246	35.69	38.16	54.77
Niger	12.95	15.78	-2.83	4.0	195	27.10	49.94	52.07
Senegal	20.21	20.11	0.10	2.6	511	28.43	21.61	39.23
Togo	16.38	20.19	-3.81	4.7	317	30.31	33.99	47.30
WAMZ								
Gambia, the	20.53	25.33	-4.80	2.6	343	35.19	29.33	49.85
Ghana	22.50	28.60	-6.10	31.8	374	38.17	47.70	62.02
Guinea	13.99	16.60	-2.61	4.5	512	24.90	35.71	42.75
Nigeria	25.90	25.00	0.90	22.4	290	35.37	70.57	70.65
Sierra Leone	11.41	19.73	-8.32	22.1	167	31.33	57.61	60.13

Sources: World Bank, African Development Indicators database (2002); and authors' calculations (see table A-3).

a. Excluding Cape Verde, Liberia, and Guinea-Bissau.

b. Including grants.

c. Government spending at average income plus half of diversion.

d. Diversion estimate for Benin is calculated as the average for the other WAEMU countries.

Table 6-5. *Costs and Benefits of WAEMU*

Country	Country shares of GDP of the union	Net welfare gain or loss	Correlation of shocks[a]	Ratio of average to own financing needs
Benin	0.0824	0.0827	0.6911	0.9377
Burkina Faso	0.0985	0.1543	0.6009	0.7920
Côte d'Ivoire	0.4137	0.0192	0.7737	1.1080
Mali	0.0987	0.1373	0.4905	0.8282
Niger	0.0729	0.1159	−0.3161	0.8711
Senegal	0.1816	0.0020	0.8331	1.1561
Togo	0.0521	0.0778	0.5628	0.9588

Source: Authors' calculations.
a. The correlation of terms of trade shocks with the union's average shock.

columns of the table present respectively the country shares of the GDP of the union, the net welfare gain or loss (if negative) to the country, the correlation of its terms of trade shocks with the union's average shock, and the ratio of the average financing need to the country's own value. The table suggests that WAEMU indeed is beneficial for all countries, essentially for two reasons. First, the monetary union fixes the exchange rate for a substantial proportion of trade (within the region or to the euro zone or the rest of the CFA franc zone), and second, the asymmetries between countries, either due to low correlations of shocks or very different government spending targets, are not so large as to make the monetary union unsustainable. To be sure, there are differences across countries, and Côte d'Ivoire and Senegal are estimated to gain the least from membership because their financing needs (as ratios to GDP) are lower than those of other members.[8]

It is reassuring that the model simulations imply a net gain for all countries that are currently members of WAEMU. In the top panel of the table in box 6–1 on pages 106–07, we decompose those gains into three components. The first assumes that all countries are the same in other respects and calculates the gain from conducting trade at the single currency, rather than each country having its own currency and monetary policy. The gain here is substantial and by assumption equal for all countries. The second and third components introduce asymmetries across countries due to differences in fiscal discipline and terms of trade shocks, respectively. In the model, fiscal

8. The notion that these two countries are more disciplined flies in the face of the experience of WAEMU before the devaluation of 1994, when the two larger countries exploited the lax enforcement of rules on monetary financing of deficits (see Stasavage, 1997). It seems that the reinforced fiscal surveillance that emerged from the devaluation crisis has helped to produce greater fiscal discipline in these two countries.

Table 6-6. *Costs and Benefits of ECOWAS*

	Country shares of GDP of the union	Net welfare gain or loss[a]	Correlation of shocks	Ratio of average to own financing needs
Benin	0.0340	−0.0824	0.2677	1.1865
Burkina Faso	0.0406	−0.0662	0.1979	1.0022
Côte d'Ivoire	0.1706	−0.0957	0.0508	1.4021
Mali	0.0407	−0.0705	0.1523	1.0479
Niger	0.0301	−0.0752	−0.2465	1.1023
Senegal	0.0749	−0.0980	0.3455	1.4628
Togo	0.0215	−0.0831	0.4255	1.2133
Gambia, the	0.0061	0.0143	0.2277	1.1512
Ghana	0.1078	0.1220	−0.2748	0.9254
Guinea	0.0597	−0.0542	0.5914	1.3425
Nigeria	0.4037	0.1799	0.9429	0.8123
Sierra Leone	0.0104	0.1104	−0.1986	0.9545

Source: Authors' calculations.

a. Relative to retaining the existing WAEMU for WAEMU countries, relative to independent floating for others.

asymmetries can lead to gains or losses (if a country suffers from a lack of discipline, then it gains from linking itself to others that are more disciplined, and conversely, suffers from ties to those lacking discipline), while terms of trade asymmetries (due to less than perfect correlation of shocks) only lead to losses. For WAEMU countries, the third component is quite small, and the losses from the fiscal asymmetry for the more disciplined countries (Côte d'Ivoire, Senegal) are not so large that they offset the gains from the other components.

We then proceed to evaluate the proposal for a full monetary union among ECOWAS countries. At this stage, we do not call into question the link to the euro that is associated with the French guarantee of convertibility—though, as discussed below, that would be a major issue should WAEMU be expanded in that way or merged with another monetary union. Instead, we assume that monetary union would simply add to the trade that was internalized by the monetary union as well as change the monetary policy settings by modifying fiscal pressures and introducing new shock asymmetries.

Table 6-6 presents the result of creating a full ECOWAS monetary union.[9] For countries currently operating an independent (and at least partially floating) currency, monetary union is compared to a regime of monetary independence. For the WAEMU countries, however, the relevant comparison is not to floating but to their existing institutional framework, namely, a monetary union among themselves. Hence for those countries the welfare gain or loss is

9. Again, omitting Guinea-Bissau, Cape Verde, and Liberia.

calculated accordingly. Simulation results suggest that only the WAMZ countries would gain from an ECOWAS monetary union, and even among them not all would gain.[10] In particular, Guinea, with its low spending target, would not gain from a monetary union that included a large, undisciplined country like Nigeria.[11] Similarly, if WAEMU countries were allowed to choose between their current monetary union and a larger ECOWAS arrangement, they would clearly prefer the former. The advantage of the existing WAEMU is its membership composed of fairly homogeneous countries. In ECOWAS, the large size of Nigeria (assuming that it had a corresponding influence over the union's monetary policy) would produce higher inflation in response to Nigeria's higher spending target and its monetary policy would be affected by very different terms of trade shock, dominated by Nigeria's export dependence on oil. Correspondingly, the correlation between a country's terms of trade and the average for the monetary union gives a value near unity for Nigeria (since it is a large part of the average) but negative correlations for Ghana, Niger, and Sierra Leone, and only small positive correlations for many of the others (reported in table 6-6).

The lower panel of the table in box 6–1 presents a decomposition of net gains for ECOWAS into the same three components: it confirms the importance of the fiscal asymmetry (in particular, Nigeria's high financing needs) in the welfare calculations. The terms of trade asymmetry, as the model is calibrated, is relatively less important—despite the fact that Nigeria is very different from its neighbors. While this calibration depends on various assumptions that go into the parameter estimates, they are reasonably robust to different parameter values.[12]

Even if a full monetary union of all ECOWAS countries would not seem to be desirable for the WAEMU countries—at least on the purely economic grounds included here—one can consider a more limited extension of WAEMU through adding new members. Rather than examining all the combinations, we simply consider whether a single country would find it in its interest to join and, conversely, whether that country would be an attractive

---

10. Welfare gains and losses are stated in terms of proportional (log) changes in GDP. For instance, welfare would be lower in Benin by the equivalent of 8.24 percent of GDP in an ECOWAS monetary union than in the current WAEMU.

11. Guinea's loss is relatively modest, because the loss from fiscal asymmetry is partially offset by the lower incentive to stimulate output by causing inflation associated with a regional central bank. Recent sharp increases in Guinea's government spending suggest in any case that it may no longer be appropriate to characterize the country as fiscally disciplined.

12. In Debrun, Masson, and Pattillo (2002), we examined the sensitivity of the welfare calculations to different parameter values.

Box 6-1. *Decomposing Net Gains from Monetary Unions*

The accompanying table decomposes the gains into three components: those due to externalizing the monetary policy externality (that is, lowering the temptation to create monetary expansion to stimulate output), gains or losses due to fiscal asymmetries, and losses due to asymmetric terms of trade shocks (components do not sum exactly to the calculated net gains due to interaction effects). The monetary policy externality is the source of large gains, while fiscal asymmetries give large gains for the less-disciplined countries and substantial losses for the more-disciplined ones. In contrast, asymmetries of terms of trade shocks seem to have only small costs.

The lower panel of the table presents decomposition for an ECOWAS monetary union, where the welfare gain (or loss, if negative) is calculated relative to WAEMU or existing independent currencies (see table 6-6) depending on the country. The decomposition is more approximate for WAEMU countries (given that that they already form a monetary union). However, the qualitative results are suggestive. With Nigeria in the ECOWAS monetary union, the fiscal asymmetry is a large source of losses for all countries, except Nigeria itself, the Gambia, Ghana, and Sierra Leone. The monetary asymmetry is a less important source of gains for WAEMU than WAMZ countries, since the former already internalize a large proportion of their trade. As before, the asymmetry of shocks is negative but modest.

partner for the existing members of WAEMU. Barring any overriding political motive, a sustainable monetary union would have to be incentive-compatible from the point of view of all potential and current members—that is, it would not decrease welfare compared to their current arrangements.

Table 6-7 suggests that each of the WAMZ countries would want to join (including Guinea, contrary to the ECOWAS case) in order to benefit from the larger monetary area and a more disciplined monetary policy. However, only Guinea would be an attractive candidate from the point of view of existing WAEMU members because of the generally higher government financing needs of the WAMZ countries, which would lead to a more inflationary monetary policy than desired by WAEMU. Again, the problem is compounded in the case of Nigeria by very asymmetric terms of trade shocks. It should be noted that losses to WAEMU countries from the Gambia joining are negligible and much smaller than the gains to the Gambia itself.

	Net gain	Monetary externality	Fiscal asymmetry	Shock asymmetry
From WAEMU				
Benin	0.0827	0.0617	0.0303	−0.0053
Burkina Faso	0.1543	0.0617	0.1090	−0.0008
Côte d'Ivoire	0.0192	0.0617	−0.0479	−0.0004
Mali	0.1373	0.0617	0.0885	−0.0006
Niger	0.1159	0.0617	0.0650	−0.0020
Senegal	0.0020	0.0617	−0.0674	−0.0003
Togo	0.0778	0.0617	0.0198	−0.0011
From ECOWAS				
Benin	−0.0824	0.0299	−0.1323	−0.0021
Burkina Faso	−0.0662	0.0299	−0.1103	−0.0016
Côte d'Ivoire	−0.0957	0.0299	−0.1506	−0.0022
Mali	−0.0705	0.0299	−0.1164	−0.0015
Niger	−0.0752	0.0299	−0.1231	−0.0014
Senegal	−0.0980	0.0299	−0.1548	−0.0015
Togo	−0.0831	0.0299	−0.1349	−0.0009
Gambia, the	0.0143	0.0915	−0.0840	−0.0083
Ghana	0.1220	0.0915	0.0458	−0.0060
Guinea	−0.0542	0.0915	−0.1739	−0.0013
Nigeria	0.1799	0.0915	0.1195	−0.0045
Sierra Leone	0.1104	0.0915	0.0276	−0.0033

Endogenous Adjustment of Countries' Economic Structures

While the analysis discussed above has taken existing economic structures as given, there are reasons to believe that they might evolve over time. Such evolution might modify the negative conclusion concerning the scope for creating or extending incentive-compatible monetary unions. A first reason for being less pessimistic has been suggested in the context of European integration: monetary union may modify the correlation of fluctuations affecting economies, making them more similar. For instance, Frankel and Rose find evidence that business cycles tend to become more synchronized as trade increases.[13] Since the latter can be expected to rise with the creation of a monetary union, it may be misleading to look at the initial correlation of fluctuations to assess

13. Frankel and Rose (1998).

Table 6-7. *Net Benefits of Adding Countries Individually to WAEMU*

	Share of GDP	Net gain or loss[a]	Correlation of shocks	Ratio of average to own financing needs
Benin	0.0812	−0.0003	0.6808	0.9390
Burkina Faso	0.0971	−0.0002	0.6058	0.7932
Côte d'Ivoire	0.4077	−0.0004	0.7735	1.1096
Mali	0.0973	−0.0003	0.4921	0.8294
Niger	0.0719	−0.0003	−0.3251	0.8724
Senegal	0.1790	−0.0004	0.8459	1.1577
Togo	0.0513	−0.0004	0.5497	0.9602
Gambia, the	0.0145	0.0933	0.4915	0.9111
Benin	0.0653	−0.0244	0.6104	1.0090
Burkina Faso	0.0781	−0.0195	0.4780	0.8523
Côte d'Ivoire	0.3280	−0.0285	0.8416	1.1924
Mali	0.0783	−0.0209	0.3691	0.8912
Niger	0.0578	−0.0223	−0.1956	0.9374
Senegal	0.1440	−0.0298	0.6869	1.2441
Togo	0.0413	−0.0252	0.4436	1.0318
Ghana	0.2072	0.1665	0.8466	0.7870
Benin	0.0720	0.0027	0.6335	0.9308
Burkina Faso	0.0860	0.0025	0.6426	0.7863
Côte d'Ivoire	0.3614	0.0035	0.7206	1.1000
Mali	0.0862	0.0027	0.5478	0.8221
Niger	0.0637	0.0029	−0.3366	0.8648
Senegal	0.1587	0.0038	0.8844	1.1477
Togo	0.0455	0.0031	0.5644	0.9519
Guinea	0.1265	0.0394	0.2176	1.0533
Benin	0.0416	−0.0921	0.2246	1.1964
Burkina Faso	0.0498	−0.0744	0.1548	1.0106
Côte d'Ivoire	0.2090	−0.1070	−0.0539	1.4138
Mali	0.0499	−0.0791	0.1201	1.0567
Niger	0.0369	−0.0844	−0.2394	1.1115
Senegal	0.0918	−0.1094	0.2764	1.4751
Togo	0.0263	−0.0928	0.3939	1.2234
Nigeria	0.4947	0.1765	0.4947	0.8191
Benin	0.0804	−0.0040	0.6861	0.9452
Burkina Faso	0.0961	−0.0031	0.5931	0.7984
Côte d'Ivoire	0.4035	−0.0046	0.7825	1.1170
Mali	0.0963	−0.0033	0.4809	0.8348
Niger	0.0711	−0.0035	−0.3090	0.8781
Senegal	0.1771	−0.0048	0.8245	1.1654
Togo	0.0508	−0.0040	0.5622	0.9665
Sierra Leone	0.0247	0.1697	0.5075	0.7604

Source: Authors' calculations.

a. Relative to WAEMU for WAEMU countries, relative to independent floating for others.

the desirability of entering a union. Thus it is argued monetary union may be attractive to a wider set of countries than would appear from a static application of OCA criteria.

While this argument may have some validity for industrial countries, it is much less plausible for African countries, since their production is still heavily weighted toward primary commodities. This production structure is largely influenced by climate and resource endowments, and price shocks to the economies are largely exogenous—unlike the case of differentiated manufactured goods, where the exporting country is likely to have some market power. While over time a monetary union may allow development of manufacturing sectors to serve the larger regional market, this is unlikely to make a large difference to the economies' aggregate fluctuations or terms of trade shocks for a number of years. In West Africa's case, it is highly improbable that Nigeria will substantially reduce dependence on oil exports or that other countries will follow suit and begin exporting oil—as a result of membership in a monetary union.

A second reason for being less pessimistic concerns the prospects that regional surveillance may enhance fiscal discipline, so that membership in a monetary union would result in much lower government spending and a lower fiscal wedge due to inefficient tax collection for the initially undisciplined country joining. A careful analysis of the experience in Africa suggests that monetary unions per se are not "agencies of restraint"[14] over fiscal policies.[15] The CFA franc zones both ran into major banking crises and extended economic downturns in part because their fiscal policies were not disciplined—despite having benefited from a common monetary policy and an unchanged exchange rate peg for about forty years. Instead, that experience shows that some other mechanisms have to be put in place—such as institutions performing regional surveillance over fiscal policies—that are effective in enhancing discipline. While there is no silver bullet, it seems as though progress has been made along these lines since the 1994 devaluation in both WAEMU and CAEMC. Peer pressure operates to some extent to limit governments' tendencies to exceed the ceilings for government deficits and debt. However, it is clear that further reinforcement of the effectiveness of the process is needed, since countries face essentially no economic sanction if they miss their targets.

In the context of the WAMZ monetary union, similar (though looser) convergence criteria have been put in place. However, countries have made little progress in meeting their targets, starting from initial levels that were far

14. Collier (1991).
15. Masson and Pattillo (2002).

away from them. There seems to be little appreciation of the need to prepare the grounds for entering monetary union by achieving low inflation and fiscal discipline. What would be needed to make an ECOWAS monetary union sustainable (and desirable to WAEMU members) would be to design strict rules that included sanctions for noncompliance. Only then could the creation of monetary union hope to bring about the fiscal discipline that would be required, in particular by Nigeria, for an ECOWAS monetary union. Unless agreement was reached on such mechanisms before countries were given a chance to join the monetary union, its sustainability would be in doubt, since the incentives for countries to agree later would be absent. Countries need to be able to apply peer pressure in order to make adjustment a precondition for joining a monetary union. A mechanism for applying peer pressure has just been created—the APRM of NEPAD. Though still untested, it aims to produce the necessary improvement in governance that would help solve the fiscal problems.

If progress is made in producing fiscal discipline, then as shown in Debrun, Masson, and Pattillo, the prospects for a welfare-enhancing monetary union are much better.[16] For instance, one scenario in that paper assumes that Nigeria's financing need (as a percent of GDP) is brought down to the average level for the rest of ECOWAS. In that case, monetary union becomes attractive for all concerned, including the present WAEMU countries—despite a continued asymmetry in export composition and terms of trade shocks. The challenge will be to create the conditions that achieve such a result.

A third reason for being more sanguine about potential advantages from the creation of an ECOWAS monetary union would be if the regional central bank could be endowed with sufficient independence that it could credibly resist pressures to monetize government deficits. We have assumed that the bank would reflect the interests of its shareholders (the member governments) and hence would suffer from such pressures. Even creating a central bank whose statutes prohibited monetary financing in our view would not be sufficient to ensure it. As in Europe, a promising strategy would be to build on the credibility of an existing institution (the Bundesbank in Europe's case). The BCEAO, the central bank of WAEMU, has a track record of monetary stability, and over time other central banks in the region may also demonstrate a proven ability to deliver sound monetary policies. If a new regional institution could build on the credibility of existing institutions, then its chances for success would be much improved.

16. Debrun, Masson, and Pattillo (2002). The earlier paper calibrated the parameters using just West African data. Here (as described in appendix A), we use the full sample of African countries for which data were available.

Prospects for Evolution of the CFA Franc Zone

The project to create the ECOWAS monetary union calls into question the continued existence of WAEMU and hence of the CFA franc zone itself. Though the terms of the eventual merger between WAMZ and WAEMU have not been agreed to, the issue of the French guarantee of convertibility of the CFA franc issued by the central bank of the latter (BCEAO) would necessarily come up for reexamination. Indeed negotiations before the creation of the euro zone raised the question whether France's arrangement with the CFA franc zone constituted a monetary arrangement falling under the legal framework created by the Maastricht Treaty to be decided by common accord, or instead was a purely budgetary arrangement with (minor) implications only for France's commitment not to run excessive deficits.[17] Though the latter interpretation was generally accepted, nevertheless, France's EU partners insisted that any substantial modification of the arrangements with the CFA franc zone would require their accord. In particular, a decision of the Council of the EU of November 23, 1998, requires France to inform European institutions of the operation of the CFA franc zone and to submit for their approval any proposed changes that would modify the nature or scope of the arrangements. Any such changes would have to be then approved by the European Council, on recommendation of the EU Commission and after consultation with the ECB.

The addition of a single country, especially one of only moderate size, might well not raise objections from the EU, nor imply any major additional demands on the French Treasury. However, what is envisioned by WAMZ is a merger of equals with WAEMU, and the new ECOWAS union would have a combined GDP that was more than double that of WAEMU at present. Nigeria alone would constitute 40 percent of the ECOWAS monetary union's GDP (see table 6-6). It is unlikely that France would accept to continue to provide a convertibility guarantee for a monetary union of that size, especially given issues relating to monetary and fiscal discipline of the larger zone.

An alternative that might seem attractive to ECOWAS but is unlikely to be agreed to by the EU would be for EU institutions to take over from France in providing for the link to the euro, either through the EU budget or by intervention of the ECB. Currently, the EU has not provided assistance even to countries about to accede to EU membership for them to adopt the euro or to peg to it. The EU is unlikely to do so for ECOWAS countries with which political links are much looser.

If an ECOWAS monetary union went ahead, it would likely be as a result of WAEMU countries agreeing to break the existing link with the French

17. See Gnassou (1999) for a discussion of the legal issues and for details on the European Council's decision.

Treasury's operations account. Consequently, ECOWAS would ensure the convertibility of the currency by the central bank's own reserves. ECOWAS countries would have to decide, as well, what would be the exchange rate regime of their currency, whether it would be pegged to the euro, as is at present the case for the CFA franc; it would be pegged to some other currency (or basket of currencies); or it would float with or without intervention by the central bank. While these are distant issues, they are important for gauging the desirability of a monetary union. If fiscal discipline cannot be enhanced, then there is a great likelihood that the new currency, left to its own devices with the loss of French Treasury support, would share the experience of independent African currencies (described in chapter 5) and would be associated with bouts of high inflation and exchange market instability.

Conclusions

An ECOWAS monetary union is an ambitious project driven more by political than economic logic. While there may be some increase in trade resulting from sharing a common currency, asymmetries due to fiscal positions and export composition in the region are great, and the existing trade linkages are small, suggesting that economic net benefits to the countries concerned would on balance be negative. Indeed our simulations indicate that for WAEMU countries, enlargement to the rest of ECOWAS of their monetary union would not be desirable, and this might well lead WAEMU not to agree to such a union. Most of the WAMZ countries would gain, but they would gain even more from a union of which Nigeria was not a member. Nigeria would produce problems for other countries if it continued to exhibit a lack of fiscal discipline. However, if an effective disciplining device were put in place—for instance, through institutions of multilateral surveillance able to impose sanctions for noncompliance or an improvement of governance associated with NEPAD—and as a result Nigeria were able to achieve fiscal discipline on a par with its neighbors (or better), then monetary union might be desirable and sustainable for all concerned.

The creation of a new ECOWAS currency raises other issues related to the exchange rate regime, since the involvement of France in the operations of the WAEMU monetary union would probably cease. The ECOWAS central bank could itself commit to a peg to the euro, the dollar, or a basket of currencies, but this would require an adequate level of reserves and some restrictions on capital movements. While there would be potential advantages of greater flexibility, there would also be dangers that the central bank, subject to pressures by member governments, would not be able to deliver on price and exchange rate stability.

7

Regional Integration in SADC

S ADC, a grouping of countries in southern Africa, emerged from the Southern African Development Coordination Conference (SADCC). In existence from 1980 until 1992, SADCC excluded South Africa and aimed to contain the apartheid regime and minimize its unfavorable effects on neighboring countries. Following the formation of the African National Congress (ANC) government and its dismantling of apartheid, in 1994 South Africa joined a revamped organization whose purposes became to foster harmonization and rationalization of policies and strategies for sustainable development in the region, achieve peace and security, and evolve common political values, systems, institutions, and other links among the region's people. It has contributed importantly to political cooperation among member countries and helped to limit regional conflicts, but on the economic policy side SADC's main achievement to date has been agreement on a trade protocol, calling for an 85 percent reduction of internal trade barriers over eight years, starting from September 1, 2000. So far progress has been slow in implementing the trade protocol, and it is uncertain whether the protocol will be applied as agreed. SADC has also put in place the sharing of information, especially in the financial area, through the SADC Committee of Central Bank Governors, as well as mechanisms for harmonizing financial regulations and improving payments systems in the region.

Monetary union is not yet an objective with an explicit timetable for achievement, but it is an implicit objective, since the AU aims to build a monetary union for the entire continent in stages, starting with each of the subregions. Monetary integration in the wider sense has already received considerable attention within SADC. Until 2001, sectoral responsibilities were devolved to the member countries, and South Africa had responsibility for the finance and investment sector. South Africa also chaired the SADC Committee of Central Bank Governors, which is currently entrusted with various projects to develop a common database of monetary and financial statistics, develop payment systems in SADC countries, examine the impact of exchange controls, coordinate training, and analyze differences in legal and operational frameworks among central banks. The SADC governments have also agreed to a set of indicators that will allow monitoring of progress toward macroeconomic convergence, focusing in particular on reducing the rate of inflation to low and stable levels, which could lay the groundwork for an eventual common monetary policy.

Moreover, monetary integration is viewed as an important building block for the free trade area. For instance, SARB governor Tito Mboweni, who is not a proponent of a rapid monetary union, has noted "one cannot implement free trade in goods and services without having the proper financial systems in place."[1] In the same interview, Mboweni stressed that monetary union itself is, however, still a long way off. But politicians have the habit of overcoming the caution of central bankers when high profile political objectives are at stake, such as taking an important step toward regional integration. So the issue of a SADC monetary union needs to be analyzed carefully because it might at some point become an explicit commitment.

SADC Countries: Economic Disparities, Weak Linkages

SADC is composed of a range of countries, with a wide disparity in per capita incomes and levels of development (see table 7-1). In particular, South Africa has long been a middle-income developing country with many features in common with OECD countries. Mauritius, Seychelles, and, more recently, Botswana have surpassed South Africa in per capita income, albeit without creating a broad industrial base, while Namibia is also relatively wealthy.[2] In the Indian Ocean, both Mauritius and Seychelles have prospered from tourism and by the introduction of export processing zones. To the north of SACU, countries are typically much poorer. Malawi, Mozambique, and Tanzania have annual per capita incomes below $200; once prosperous Zimbabwe has faltered; and Angola and the Democratic Republic of the

---

1. William Dhlamini, "Single Currency Concept 'a Long Way Away for SADC,' " *Namibian*, August 24, 2000 (www.namibian.com.na/Netstories/2000/August/Marketplace/009C27F854.html).

2. The CMA is discussed in chapter 4.

Table 7-1. *SADC Social Indicators, Averages, 1995–2000*

Country	GDP per capita (constant 1995 U.S. dollars)	Life expectancy at birth (years)	Population with access to safe water (percent)	Literacy rate of population 15+ years (percent)
Angola	488	46	38	...
Botswana	3,653	46	...	75
Dem. Rep. of the Congo	119	47	45	58
Lesotho	539	48	91	82
Malawi	164	41	57	58
Mauritius	3,958	70	100	84
Mozambique	172	44	60	42
Namibia	2,307	54	77	80
Seychelles	7,054	72	...	...
South Africa	3,935	54	86	84
Swaziland	1,465	54	...	78
Tanzania	183	47	54	73
Zambia	393	42	64	76
Zimbabwe	656	45	85	87

Source: World Bank, African Development Indicators database (2002).

Congo have suffered from long periods of civil warfare that have contributed to their impoverishment. The exploitation of oil wealth in Angola has raised per capita GDP, though not appreciably reduced poverty.

Trade and capital flow linkages until recently have been very low between South Africa and the rest of SADC, except for South Africa's close neighbors in SACU. With the end of apartheid, that disjunction can be expected to gradually diminish, and South Africa's trade with its northern neighbors should expand over time. Indeed it will be favored by the SADC Free Trade Protocol. But concern that quick liberalization might benefit South Africa while harming the existing manufacturing sectors in the rest of SADC has led governments to agree to include a provision in the trade protocol that calls for faster liberalization by SACU than by the less-developed SADC members. Table 7-2 identifies the non-negligible trade flows between pairs of SADC countries, those that exceed 1 percent of each country's total exports or imports. Other SADC countries constitute only a small proportion of each SADC country's total exports, with a few exceptions. South Africa is an important destination for other countries' exports and source for their imports, as would be predicted by the gravity model, given the size of its GDP and GDP per capita. Exports to Botswana are a substantial proportion of South Africa's exports. Aside for these important linkages, the export shares constituted by bilateral trade between SADC countries seldom exceed 4 percent.

Table 7-2. *Significant Regional Trade Flows within SADC,*
Averages, 1995–2000[a]

Country 1	Percent of country 1's total exports to country 2		Percent of country 2's total imports from country 1	
Botswana	South Africa	13.77	. . .	
	Zimbabwe	3.19		
Dem. Rep. of			. . .	
the Congo	South Africa	2.15		
Lesotho	Namibia	2.03	Namibia	1.09
	South Africa	85.00	Swaziland	1.30
Malawi	South Africa	14.52	. . .	
	Zimbabwe	2.51		
Mauritius	South Africa	2.27	Seychelles	1.43
Mozambique	Malawi	3.50	Malawi	1.53
	South Africa	13.74	Swaziland	3.49
	Swaziland	1.13		
	Zimbabwe	8.97		
Namibia	South Africa	55.00	Lesotho	2.71
	Zimbabwe	1.18	South Africa	1.02
			Swaziland	3.16
Seychelles	South Africa	1.81	. . .	
South Africa	Botswana	5.63	Angola	10.24
	Lesotho	1.18	Botswana	66.33
	Mauritius	1.08	Dem. Rep. of	15.96
	Mozambique	1.97	the Congo	
	Namibia	2.34	Lesotho	36.72
	Swaziland	1.17	Malawi	37.88
	Zambia	1.62	Mauritius	12.10
	Zimbabwe	3.52	Mozambique	50.65
			Namibia	27.31
			Seychelles	9.95
			Swaziland	32.41
			Tanzania	9.56
			Zambia	44.12
			Zimbabwe	30.86
Swaziland	Mauritius	1.43	Lesotho	1.97
	Mozambique	3.13	Namibia	1.87
	Namibia	1.68		
	South Africa	70.00		
	Tanzania	3.12		
	Zambia	2.01		
	Zimbabwe	3.52		
Tanzania	Dem. Rep. of	1.04	Zambia	1.22
	the Congo			
	Zambia	1.63		

Table 7-2. *Significant Regional Trade Flows within SADC,*
*Averages, 1995–2000*ᵃ *(Continued)*

Country 1	Percent of Country 1's total exports to country 2		Percent of country 2's total imports from country 1	
Zambia	Dem. Rep. of the Congo	1.85	Dem. Rep. of the Congo	1.67
	Malawi	4.77	Malawi	7.45
	South Africa	6.12		
	Tanzania	1.78		
	Zimbabwe	2.61		
Zimbabwe	Botswana	3.01	Botswana	17.27
	Malawi	2.95	Malawi	11.29
	Mozambique	1.79	Mozambique	4.14
	South Africa	11.73	Namibia	6.05
	Zambia	3.83	Swaziland	1.41
			Zambia	9.39

Source: IMF, Direction of Trade Statistics database (2003).
a. Bilateral trade is calculated by averaging exports from 1 to 2 and imports of 2 from 1.

The two other exceptions in the table are Mozambique's exports to neighboring (and landlocked) Zimbabwe (9.0 percent of Mozambique's exports) and Zambia's exports to Malawi (4.8 percent of Zambia's exports). On the import side, imports from South Africa are important for most all of the other SADC countries, and imports from Zimbabwe are substantial for Botswana, Malawi, Mozambique, Namibia, and Zambia.

Table 7-3 presents the accumulated stock of South Africa's capital outflows toward SADC and inflows into South Africa from SADC, compared to South Africa's claims on and liabilities to the rest of Africa and the world at large. Since the capital flows among other SADC countries are likely to be considerably smaller, table 7-3 probably provides a significant part of bilateral claims within SADC. These cumulated flows are quite modest. South Africa's claims on the rest of SADC are concentrated in SACU countries plus Mauritius (the latter is the single largest recipient). Foreign investment into South Africa is chiefly from the four other SACU countries, which constitute 75.8 percent of the SADC total. Moreover, SADC as a whole, even if it provides a very large share of South Africa's cumulated capital flows (either as a source or destination) to and from Africa (more than 80 percent), is very small when compared to South Africa's total foreign claims and liabilities, which are no doubt overwhelming with respect to the world's developed economies. It needs to be recognized, however, that the destination of capital flows may not be adequately captured by the data, for instance, if South African subsidiaries abroad are intermediaries for holdings in other African countries. This would tend to

Table 7-3. *South Africa: Foreign Assets and Liabilities, December 31, 2000*
Millions of U.S. dollars

	Direct	Portfolio	Other	Total
Assets: foreign investment from South Africa into SADC and other countries				
Angola	3.1	1.4	2.9	7.4
Botswana	36.4	41.6	81.6	159.6
Dem. Rep. of the Congo	0.6	0	13.3	13.9
Lesotho	23.4	8.8	207.1	239.3
Malawi	24.6	0.4	16.4	41.4
Mauritius	357.8	66.5	553.4	977.8
Mozambique	505.8	0	73.8	579.6
Namibia	156.8	9.4	140.3	306.5
Swaziland	174.4	9.1	88.3	271.9
Tanzania	10.9	0	11.8	22.7
Zambia	1.8	0	53.6	55.4
Zimbabwe	43.3	2.8	108.1	154.1
Total SADC	1,339	140	1,351	2,830
Other Africa	378.1	6.9	169.3	554.3
Total Africa	1,717	147	1,520	3,384
Total foreign assets	34,251	48,141	18,900	101,292
Liabilities: foreign investment from SADC countries into South Africa				
Angola	1.3	0.3	79.1	80.6
Botswana	11.1	569.0	185.6	765.7
Dem. Rep. of the Congo	2.2	0	2.0	4.2
Lesotho	2.7	5.9	295.1	303.7
Malawi	3.6	2.2	32.9	38.8
Mauritius	156.9	30.4	481.7	669.1
Mozambique	2.7	0.7	47.6	51.0
Namibia	17.6	1,196.9	287.4	1,501.9
Swaziland	24.1	8.7	308.0	340.8
Tanzania	1.5	0.14	1.4	3.1
Zambia	2.2	0.56	5.2	8.0
Zimbabwe	16.8	8.7	51.4	76.9
Total SADC	243	1,823	1,777	3,844
Other Africa	76.3	10.4	228.3	315.0
Total Africa	319	1,834	2,006	4,159
Total foreign liabilities	46,040	38,743	23,540	108,323

Source: Unpublished data provided by the South African Reserve Bank and its *Quarterly Bulletin*, December 2002.

understate South Africa's direct investment in neighboring countries.[3] More-over, even this level of foreign direct investment causes resentment in some neighboring countries, given the financial clout of South Africa's economy.

The SADC countries differ considerably in their starting points with respect to the common convergence indicators adopted by their governments in a Memorandum of Understanding on Macroeconomic Convergence (agreed August 8, 2002, in Pretoria, South Africa). The primary focus of the regional surveillance over macroeconomic policies is to maintain a low rate of infla-tion. Other indicators are the ratio of the budget deficit to GDP, the ratio of public and publicly guaranteed debt to GDP, and the balance and structure of the current account. Reference values for the first two of these indicators, as well as two more specifically financial variables, have apparently been specified by the Committee of Central Bank Governors for two subperiods to prepare for a possible monetary union in 2013–15. The values for the subperiods are: for the 2004–08 period, inflation under 10 percent (versus under 5 percent for the 2009–12 period); budget deficit at no more than 5 percent of GDP (versus no more than 3 percent); central bank credit to government at no more than 10 percent of previous year's tax revenue (no more than 5 percent); and exter-nal reserves at three months of merchandise imports (versus six months).

Table A-3 provides average values over 1995–2000 for the two main macro-economic convergence indicators, inflation and the deficit. It was noted several years ago by Jenkins and Thomas that the distance from the macroeconomic convergence targets is widely different across SADC countries.[4] While SACU countries had inflation of about 10 percent in 2002 (lower in 2003 due to the appreciation of the rand) and Mauritius, Seychelles, and Tanzania had single-digit inflation, the remaining countries exhibited persistently high inflation rates. While budget deficit figures are perhaps less reliable or easily compared, the recent data for 2002–03 indicate considerably higher figures for Zim-babwe, Mozambique, and Malawi than for the other SADC countries.

Costs and Benefits of Various Configurations for Monetary Integration

The design of monetary integration will influence the extent that the mone-tary policy reflects the circumstances of each of the member countries. In one case, a single country may set monetary policy for the others. This would be

3. We are grateful to Charles Harvey for this point, which would seem to be increasingly relevant with the recent London Stock Exchange listings of major South African companies, such as De Beers and South African Breweries.
4. Jenkins and Thomas (1996).

the case where smaller countries adopt the currency of another, presumably larger, one; this is often called *dollarization,* but it also applies to the CMA, in which Lesotho, Namibia, and Swaziland issue their own currencies but align their monetary policies to those of South Africa and allow the rand to circulate within their economies (though it is not legal tender in Swaziland). In these cases, it is the fiscal discipline of the anchor country that helps to determine the monetary policy of the union, if the central bank is not independent of the treasury. Fiscal policies of other countries may influence their ability to maintain their place in the currency area but do not affect the fundamental properties of the anchor currency.[5] We term this an *asymmetric exchange rate,* or monetary union. For a country considering joining the union, the extent of fiscal discipline of the anchor country will be important for the stability properties of the currency. For this reason (and also the independence of the Bundesbank), the deutsche mark was an attractive currency on which to center the transition to monetary union in Europe, though with the creation of the euro zone there is now a symmetric monetary union in which monetary policy is based on conditions in the whole of the euro area. Similarly, the rand serves as the anchor of the CMA not only because of the size of South Africa but also because the rand has generally not suffered high inflation as a result of fiscal pressures.[6]

In contrast, in a symmetric monetary union all the countries have some influence over monetary policy. Hence if a country has fiscal objectives that cannot be matched by revenues, it may influence monetary policy in an expansionary direction. Thus the benefits and costs of a symmetric monetary union need to take into account the degree of fiscal discipline of all potential members.

Though the problem of governments putting pressure on weak central banks may be partially ameliorated by the existence of a supranational central bank that is in a stronger position relative to any single national government, it is not completely solved. A large country with weak fiscal discipline can adversely influence the actions of the central bank. The resulting monetary expansion and high inflation may make a monetary union unattractive for countries with a less pressing need for monetary financing of government deficits.

As we have argued in previous chapters, these fiscal issues need to be considered alongside the traditional criteria related to the OCAs, namely, the asymmetry of shocks. Thus countries that are very dissimilar because they face very different shocks may not find it optimal to share a common mone-

---

5. There are other externalities related to fiscal policy, even when central banks do not face direct pressures to finance public deficits, but these are likely to be of the second order.

6. The issue of formal independence of the central bank may also come into play, though it is unlikely that a central bank, even if formally independent, could succeed in the face of fiscal policies that generated continued large deficits.

tary policy. In the African context, where many countries rely on a few com-modity exports with prices determined in world markets, variations in the terms of trade are a potent source of shocks whose correlation (or lack thereof) is an important potential influence on the desirability of monetary integration. Again, one needs to contrast an asymmetric exchange rate union, where a potential entrant will be concerned only with similarity with the anchor country's shocks, with a symmetric union in which the correlation with the average shock across all countries will be important.

Table A-3 also reports estimates for government financing needs, corrected for different levels of per capita income, which include a measure of fiscal distortions.[7] Among SADC members, CMA countries (aside from Lesotho) and Mauritius have much lower estimates for government financing needs than the others. Tanzania and Botswana are somewhat higher, followed by Zambia, Malawi, Mozambique, and Zimbabwe, while at the top end of the range are Angola and the Democratic Republic of the Congo.

Correlations across countries of the percent changes in their terms of trade (to gauge the degree of asymmetry of the shocks that affect SADC economies) are shown in table 7-4. It can be seen that over the period 1987–99, which is the longest period for which data exist for all countries,[8] there are numerous negative correlations, indicating severe asymmetries. Some countries—for instance, Angola and Mauritius—have mostly negative correlations with other SADC countries. In contrast, South Africa is positively correlated with Botswana, Lesotho, and Namibia,[9] which is not surprising given their close links within SACU. South Africa is also positively correlated with the Demo-cratic Republic of the Congo, Seychelles, Tanzania, and Zambia, while being negatively correlated with Mauritius and Zimbabwe.

Simulations of Various Monetary Unions

To quantify whether the welfare costs of a monetary union due to asymme-tries in shocks and fiscal policies are offset by the gains due to limiting ten-dencies toward overexpansionary monetary policies (and a monetary union is more effective in reducing this tendency, the greater is the trade internalized in the monetary union), we draw on the theoretical model and its calibration described in appendix A.

7. Based on the methodology described in appendix A.

8. Excluding Swaziland, which had only two available observations.

9. The negative correlation with Swaziland should be ignored and is probably due to the data problems mentioned in the previous footnote.

Table 7-4. *SADC: Correlation of Percent Changes in Terms of Trade, 1987–99*[a]

	Angola	Botswana	Dem. Rep. of the Congo	Lesotho	Malawi	Mauritius
Angola	1.0					
Botswana	0.15	1.0				
Dem. Rep. of the Congo	−0.37	0.17	1.0			
Lesotho	−0.19	−0.21	0.11	1.0		
Malawi	0.43	0.28	0.03	−0.38	1.0	
Mauritius	−0.06	−0.36	−0.09	0.17	0.47	1.0
Mozambique	−0.20	**0.70**	0.48	−0.09	0.07	−0.16
Namibia	−0.15	0.08	**0.67**	0.40	−0.18	−0.11
Seychelles	−0.45	0.38	**0.72**	−0.11	0.02	−0.42
South Africa	0.01	**0.59**	**0.66**	0.17	0.11	−0.12
Swaziland	0.13	0.26	−0.04	−0.37	**0.72**	0.11
Tanzania	0.04	0.07	0.33	−0.19	0.04	−0.12
Zambia	−0.27	0.18	**0.84**	0.10	0.18	0.03
Zimbabwe	**−0.63**	−0.43	**0.57**	0.05	−0.07	0.06

Sources: World Bank, African Development Indicators database (2002); UNCTAD and World Bank. See Cashin, McDermott, and Pattillo (2004).

a. Correlations in bold exceed 0.5 and are significant at the 5 percent level.

Simulations of the calibrated model were first conducted for the existing asymmetric exchange rate union, the CMA, assuming that monetary policy is set by South Africa. In fact, the model results indicate that compared to independently floating currencies, the CMA is in the interest of all participants, given their close trade links and the generally large positive correlation of shocks. Each of the CMA countries—namely, Lesotho, Namibia, South Africa, and Swaziland—would prefer to be a member than to pursue its own, independent monetary policy (see table 7-5). This is true even though we have modeled the monetary policy decisionmaking as reflecting only South Africa's economic conditions. (It is assumed that South Africa does, however, internalize the fact that exchange rates are fixed vis-à-vis its trading partners, hence decreasing slightly the temptation for monetary expansion). If we modeled the CMA as sharing monetary policy responsibility on the basis of relative GDPs, there would be little difference in the results, since South Africa contributes 96 percent of the CMA's GDP. However, all the countries in fact would slightly prefer the current, asymmetric version, because South Africa has the lowest financing need (as a ratio to its GDP) and thus provides a better anchor.

We then consider whether adding other SADC countries individually to the CMA is incentive compatible, both for the new member and the countries that

Mozambique	Namibia	Seychelles	South Africa	Swaziland	Tanzania	Zambia	Zimbabwe
1.0							
0.33	1.0						
0.41	0.31	1.0					
0.65	**0.65**	0.36	1.0				
−0.23	−0.37	0.31	−0.12	1.0			
0.57	0.30	0.14	0.35	−0.42	1.0		
0.33	0.25	**0.68**	0.49	0.23	0.04	1.0	
−0.16	0.23	**0.62**	−0.06	0.20	0.09	**0.51**	1.0

form the existing CMA (see table 7-6). Again, we assume that the current asymmetric arrangement would continue, namely, that South Africa would continue to have sole responsibility over monetary policy. All countries except Mauritius would find joining the CMA in their interest on the basis of the economic criteria modeled here. Moreover, the existing CMA members would all gain, if any country (including Mauritius) joined. Mauritius, in contrast, has a sufficiently low government financing need (and the lowest inflation in our sample) that it would not gain by adopting South Africa's monetary policy.

Table 7-5. *Net Benefits from Membership in the CMA*

	Share of GDP	Correlation of shocks	Average/own financing need	Net gain relative to float	Net gain from symmetric CMA
Lesotho	0.0065	0.1730	0.5784	0.2088	−0.0013
Namibia	0.0242	0.2906	0.9312	0.0366	−0.0026
South Africa	0.9601	0.9965	1.0075	0.0080	−0.0027
Swaziland	0.0092	0.2174	0.9299	0.0373	−0.0026

Source: Authors' calculations.

Table 7-6. *Net Benefits of Adding Countries Individually to the CMA*

	Share of GDP	Net gain or loss[a]	Correlation of shocks	Average/own financing need
Angola	0.0459	0.2391	0.7749	0.4866
Lesotho	0.0062	0.0003	0.5632	0.6093
Namibia	0.0231	0.0008	0.8901	0.9810
South Africa	0.9160	0.0006	0.5267	1.0614
Swaziland	0.0088	0.0006	0.7176	0.9796
Botswana	0.0336	0.1195	0.4322	0.7628
Lesotho	0.0062	0.0028	0.1946	0.5847
Namibia	0.0234	0.0056	0.3090	0.9414
South Africa	0.9279	0.0059	0.9930	1.0185
Swaziland	0.0089	0.0056	0.2378	0.9401
Lesotho	0.0064	0.0005	0.0949	0.5823
Malawi	0.0133	0.1599	−0.3951	0.6671
Namibia	0.0239	0.0011	0.2519	0.9375
South Africa	0.9473	0.0011	0.9933	1.0144
Swaziland	0.0091	0.0011	0.1581	0.9362
Lesotho	0.0063	0.0005	0.1602	0.5758
Mauritius	0.0281	−0.0496	0.1292	1.1833
Namibia	0.0235	0.0010	0.2515	0.9271
South Africa	0.9332	0.0011	0.9921	1.0031
Swaziland	0.0090	0.0010	0.1916	0.9258
Lesotho	0.0063	0.0010	0.1244	0.5853
Namibia	0.0236	0.0020	0.2649	0.9424
Mozambique	0.0228	0.1653	0.5011	0.6639
South Africa	0.9382	0.0021	0.9877	1.0196
Swaziland	0.0090	0.0020	0.1813	0.9410
Lesotho	0.0064	0.0001	0.1904	0.5822
Namibia	0.0241	0.0001	0.2848	0.9374
Seychelles	0.0039	0.2475	−0.1057	0.3754
South Africa	0.9563	0.0001	0.9961	1.0142
Swaziland	0.0092	0.0001	0.2232	0.9361
Lesotho	0.0061	0.0001	0.0428	0.5840
Namibia	0.0230	0.0003	0.2017	0.9404
South Africa	0.9122	0.0003	0.9823	1.0174
Swaziland	0.0088	0.0003	0.1101	0.9391
Tanzania	0.0499	0.0768	0.7071	0.8438

Table 7-6. *Net Benefits of Adding Countries Individually to the CMA*
(Continued)

	Share of GDP	Net gain or loss[a]	Correlation of shocks	Average/own financing need
Lesotho	0.0063	0.0009	0.2858	0.5841
Namibia	0.0237	0.0017	0.3031	0.9405
South Africa	0.9385	0.0018	0.9478	1.0176
Swaziland	0.0090	0.0017	0.2822	0.9392
Zambia	0.0225	0.1412	0.5893	0.6996
Lesotho	0.0061	0.0021	0.1765	0.5961
Namibia	0.0230	0.0042	0.2885	0.9550
South Africa	0.9141	0.0045	0.9960	1.0333
Swaziland	0.0088	0.0042	0.2182	0.9537
Zimbabwe	0.0479	0.1700	0.0989	0.6687

Source: Authors' calculations.
a. Relative to the CMA for CMA countries. Relative to independent floating for others.

As an illustration of the forces at work, table 7-7 decomposes the net gains faced by CMA countries if either Mauritius or Zimbabwe were to join (and also the latter countries' net gains). Internalizing the monetary policy externality (that is, lowering the temptation to create monetary expansion by depreciating the rand against the Zimbabwe dollar) is a major source of gains for all countries, while in the case of Mauritius, the negative effect of lower fiscal discipline

Table 7-7. *Decomposition of Net Gains for Mauritius or Zimbabwe as a Result of Joining the CMA*[a]

	Net gain	Monetary externality	Fiscal asymmetry	Shock asymmetry
Lesotho	0.2063	0.0091	0.2021	−0.0000
Mauritius	−0.0496	0.0091	−0.0592	−0.0005
Namibia	0.0376	0.0091	0.0293	−0.0002
South Africa	0.0091	0.0091	0.0000	−0.0000
Swaziland	0.0384	0.0091	0.0299	−0.0000
Lesotho	0.2378	0.0125	0.2021	−0.0000
Namibia	0.0408	0.0125	0.0293	−0.0002
South Africa	0.0125	0.0125	0.0000	−0.0000
Swaziland	0.0415	0.0125	0.0299	−0.0000
Zimbabwe	0.1700	0.0125	0.1624	−0.0000

Source: Authors' calculations.
a. Relative to independent policies.

Table 7-8. *Net Gain from SADC Exchange Rate or Monetary Union (Symmetric or Asymmetric)*

	GDP share	Correlation of shocks	Average/own financing need	Net gain[a] Symmetric	Asymmetric
Angola	0.0373	0.7192	0.5258	0.2314	0.2409
Botswana	0.0270	0.5729	0.8589	0.0849	0.1266
Dem. Rep. of the Congo	0.0307	−0.0267	0.5822	0.2236	0.2411
Lesotho	0.0050	0.5220	0.6584	−0.0191	0.0071
Malawi	0.0105	−0.5195	0.7543	0.1338	0.1685
Mozambique	0.0181	0.2873	0.7468	0.1392	0.1732
Namibia	0.0188	0.8079	1.0600	−0.0368	0.0145
Seychelles	0.0031	0.0129	0.4245	0.2544	0.2440
South Africa	0.7448	0.5609	1.1469	−0.0392	0.0153
Swaziland	0.0072	0.6566	1.0586	−0.0369	0.0144
Tanzania	0.0407	0.0810	0.9512	0.0427	0.0893
Zambia	0.0179	0.4204	0.7885	0.1130	0.1501
Zimbabwe	0.0390	−0.1104	0.7422	0.1428	0.1765

Source: Authors' calculations.

a. Relative to floating for non-CMA countries, and relative to the CMA for CMA countries.

of the union offsets the other gains. In both cases, asymmetries of terms of trade shocks diminish the gains only slightly.

Given table 7-6's results, we simulate an exchange rate or monetary union between the CMA and all SADC countries except Mauritius (presented in table 7-8). However, a larger exchange rate union along the lines of the CMA but including most of the SADC countries would challenge the existence of a monetary policy made in South Africa, since the latter would not be so disproportionately larger than its partners. Would a symmetric system make monetary union more desirable to the non-CMA countries? Table 7-8 suggests that this is not the case. In fact, only for Seychelles are the net benefits larger in the symmetric than in the asymmetric case. Seychelles has a large financing need and would prefer a situation in which monetary policy was easier than that dictated by South Africa. For all the other countries, however, the fact that the SARB provided low inflation consistent with its disciplined fiscal policies would make it a more desirable anchor than a multilateral central bank reflecting the average spending target. Thus economic logic would suggest that the SARB continue to set monetary policy, meaning that a SADC exchange rate union would be essentially a rand zone.

Conclusions

It would seem that there should be the basis for at least some partial SADC exchange rate union, since an expanded CMA that retained the existing asymmetric structure would be in the economic interests of SADC's largest economy as well as most of the other potential members. However, the economic benefits run in the face of the political imperatives for a multilateral monetary union in which monetary policy would be decided in a symmetric framework (though presumably larger countries would have more weight). Indeed while an asymmetric exchange rate union with additional members would be desirable to the CMA countries, since it would internalize a larger proportion of their trade without adding to fiscal pressures on monetary policy, the same would not be true of a symmetric monetary union with the rest of SADC, which according to our results would be viewed negatively by the CMA and, in particular, by South Africa. However, a monetary union for most of SADC that left monetary policy in the hands of the SARB is likely to be unacceptable to South Africa's SADC partners.

This tension is likely to limit expansion of the CMA in the next decades. The impetus for creating a larger union would doubtless have to come from South Africa, since it is already at the center of a successful exchange rate union, the CMA. Monetary integration with other SADC members is likely to be on South Africa's terms, therefore, since its central bank is (with the exception of Botswana's, which has, however, a much more recent history of central banking) the only institution in the region able to provide the credibility and stability that would make a monetary union a success. Hence a limited expansion of the exchange rate union to include a few SADC countries, with a dominant weight retained by South Africa, and selectivity in the admission of members, seems the likeliest outcome if the CMA were to be expanded or transformed.

In the longer term, fiscal discipline, expanded trade, and greater development of financial systems in the northern countries of SADC could narrow differences and make a symmetric SADC monetary union attractive to all. Only in these circumstances would South Africa be willing to give up control over monetary policy. A common currency would then lead to further expansion of the market for South Africa's exports, without forcing South Africa to adopt an inferior currency. Indeed this was the strategy in Europe, to make the countries with larger budget deficits and higher inflation converge to the German level before monetary union. SADC thus rightly puts the emphasis on regional surveillance over inflation and fiscal policies as a precondition for monetary union. At the present time, the assessment made by Jenkins and Thomas of macroeconomic convergence in the mid-1990s and its implications for the feasibility of a SADC monetary union still seems as valid as when it was originally expressed:

> In conclusion, the apparent lack of convergence of the southern African economies over time and the current significant divergence of policy and stability indicators suggests that southern Africa is not yet ready for regional monetary integration. Premature attempts at monetary integration could have political costs, since a failed attempt at monetary integration can generate political disagreements and recriminations that weaken prospects for coordination in trade, infrastructural development, defense and law enforcement.[10]

10. Jenkins and Thomas (1996, p. 23).

8

EAC and COMESA

Overlapping membership of countries in a number of regional organizations complicates plans for monetary integration in East Africa and southern Africa. There is a project under way to revive economic cooperation in a small, three-country group, the EAC, but two of these countries are also members of a much larger, twenty-country group, COMESA, which stretches from Egypt in the north to Namibia in the south. COMESA has its own agenda for regional integration and is a rival to SADC in these initiatives. Further complicating the situation, there are nine countries with membership in both SADC and COMESA.

EAC

The treaty establishing the EAC, comprised of Kenya, Tanzania, and Uganda, was signed by the three member governments in November 1999. Formally launched in January 2001, the EAC succeeded a 1996 cooperation agreement to revive regional integration that had ended following the 1977 collapse of the original EAC. The 1999 treaty provides for the formation of a customs union by 2004, to be followed by a common market, subsequently a monetary union, and ultimately a political federation. A second EAC Development Strategy (2001–05), agreed to by the member governments, sets out an action plan for widening and deepening cooperation in a range of spheres, including political, economic, social, cultural, research and technology, defense, as well as legal and judicial affairs.[1] The declared vision for regional integration is to create wealth and enhance competitiveness through increased production, trade, and investment in the region.

Regarding the monetary union objective of the community, the treaty's Article 82 states that the partner states will "cooperate in monetary and financial matters and maintain the convertibility of their currencies as a basis for the establishment of a monetary union." The treaty elaborates that cooperation will be "in accordance with the approved macroeconomic policies harmonization programs and convergence framework of the community in order to establish monetary stability."[2]

Monetary union is seen as a rather distant goal, however, and specificities and timetables are not currently under discussion. To date, the priority for the community has been movement toward a customs union through a program of tariff harmonization, namely, establishment of a common external tariff and elimination of internal tariffs. Progress has been relatively slow. After years of discussion and four postponements, the agreement establishing a customs union was signed in March 2004. On monetary union, the strategy is to lay the groundwork by maintaining currency convertibility, harmonizing macroeconomic policies (particularly exchange rate, interest rate, monetary, and fiscal policies), and working toward closer macroeconomic convergence. In practice, progress has been made on currency convertibility and sharing of information through the synchronization of budget days in the three countries. But macropolicy coordination or convergence is currently not high on the priority list for policymakers in the region.

Revival of the Old EAC

The current EAC is a revival of the old EAC, which included, at some point, a customs and monetary union as well as the joint administration of taxes and many services. The member countries, which shared a common currency under Britain's colonial rule, issued separate currencies after independence. But the 1967 treaty, formally establishing the EAC community, specified free exchange at par. The link to sterling was broken following the 1967 sterling devaluation.

1. East African Community, "EAC Development Strategy: 2001–05" (www.eachq.org/Dev_Strategy/EACDEVESTRATEGY20012005.htm).

2. East African Community, "East African Community—the Treaty" (www.eachq.org/eac-TheTreaty.htm). The treaty was established in 1999.

Why did the old EAC collapse? The two major contributing factors, namely, differences relating to the distribution of benefits and ideological clashes, were not specific to the monetary integration aspect. Kenya, the more industrialized partner, ran a persistent trade surplus with Uganda and Tanzania. The latter two countries felt that Kenya benefited more from the arrangement through trade and fostering industrial development and were disappointed that compensating mechanisms (subsidies, concessions from Kenya, or redistribution through the East African Development Bank) did not work.[3] Politically, Tanzania (under President Julius Nyerere) and Uganda (under President Milton Obote) pursued socialist-oriented strategies, while Kenya was more capitalistic. Tanzania did not recognize the Idi Amin government that took power in a 1971 coup in Uganda, which precluded summit meetings and contributed to the eventual collapse of the community. Ideological and economic factors also resulted in all three governments extending exchange controls to each other's currencies, culminating in the 1977 collapse of the union.[4] Another contributing factor on the monetary front was the erosion of regional controls on national monetary creation, undermining monetary discipline.[5]

The three countries agreed to relaunch the EAC in the early 1990s and set up the EAC Secretariat in 1996. An important step was taken when the agreement was signed as a treaty in November 1999. Since its inception, the new EAC has achieved a number of its objectives. In the area of monetary and fiscal policy coordination, for example, there is full convertibility of the three currencies in each of the countries, and an agreement has been reached to liberalize capital accounts. Finance ministers hold prebudget and postbudget consultations, and the budget presentation days have been synchronized. Other notable achievements include establishment of an East African passport and reductions in border delays, harmonization of customs documentation, and execution of a tripartite agreement on avoidance of double taxation.[6]

The primary focus of high-level negotiations has been movement toward a customs union. Although an initial report on the strategy was adopted by the member states in 1999, its findings were not implemented: initially, negotiations toward removal of internal tariffs bore no fruit, and there was no agreement on a common external tariff.[7] Since then the EAC treaty has come into force (July 2000), the EAC was formally launched (January 2001), and agree-

3. Goldstein and Ndung'u (2001).
4. Cohen (1998).
5. Guillaume and Stasavage (2000).
6. Mkenda (2001); Bigsten and Kalinda Mkenda (2002).
7. Rajaram and others (1999).

ment on a protocol for establishment of a customs union was reached in 2004.[8] The agreement plans for operation of the customs union to begin in January 2005. The three countries are starting from a position where although significant progress on trade liberalization was made in the 1990s, tariffs are still high, and bureaucratic application of rules and regulations still continues to act as nontariff barriers. Limited progress in reducing internal tariffs has been achieved recently under both COMESA and the EAC. Tanzania's continued low level of trade with regional partners has contributed to its negative view on regionalism, its withdrawal from COMESA, and its insistence that cooperation under the EAC should be based on the principle of asymmetry, or ensuring that more-developed partners open their markets faster than others.[9]

After a long period of negotiations, in June 2003 the presidents of the EAC countries agreed on a common external tariff structure of zero for primary goods, 10 percent for intermediate goods, and 25 percent for final goods.[10] Negotiations dragged, however, on the detailed categorization of products, particularly on a set of sensitive items representing about 20 percent of EAC imports. Even at the time the customs union protocol was finally signed by the heads of state in March 2004, about 300 items remained unclassified, and the countries had not agreed on what additional surcharges would apply to a select list of sensitive items. As Uganda and Tanzania were reluctant to give up protection against Kenyan imports, the 2004 agreement stipulates that these two countries will phase out internal tariffs on selected Kenyan imports over a five-year period. The customs union will thus be incomplete during the first phase of implementation.

The agreed common external tariff will result in a decline in simple average tariff rates in Kenya and Tanzania, but an increase in Uganda, suggesting that only the former two countries will benefit from lower import prices.[11] What is the projected impact of the planned customs union on revenue and trade? Recent studies have shown that implementation of the customs union would lead to only modest declines in customs revenue, of roughly 1 percent of total EAC tax revenue during the first phase of implementation.[12] The same source

8. Burundi and Rwanda have also expressed interest in joining the EAC, but this will probably not take place for some time. See East African Community Secretariat, "East African Community: From Co-operation to Community (1996–2001)," 2000 (www.eachq.org/About EAC/from co-op to community.htm).

9. Ng'eno (2002).

10. The 1999 report adopted by the EAC Secretariat recommended that the EAC countries adopt the Uganda (0, 7, 15) percent structure, but this was unacceptable to Kenya and Tanzania.

11. World Bank (2003).

12. World Bank (2003).

estimates that there will be almost no expansion of regional trade flows during the first phase, and only very modest increases in the medium run. The World Bank is also recommending that the current plan for customs union implementation should be simplified, as the large number of exceptions implies that the trade regime will remain complicated and difficult to administer, negating some of the expected benefits.[13] Going forward, there is need for further work on mechanisms for sharing costs and benefits of regional integration and on the appropriate application of asymmetry, if the new EAC is to avoid the problems faced by the old EAC.

It is, of course, extremely difficult to judge prospects for success in forming a customs union, common market, monetary union, and ultimately a political federation as envisioned. The key factor is the always-unknowable amount of political will. On the customs union, the difficult issue of distribution of benefits is raised in a recent paper by Venables, who uses the old EAC as an example of a regional integration agreement likely to fail because it promoted income divergence.[14] Slow progress in moving from the cooperation stage to formal negotiations for a customs union protocol is also not a good sign. Institutionally, the political weakness of the EAC Secretariat has hampered timely implementation of agreed measures. Limited institutional capacity also may be spread thin as the treaty specifies cooperation in such a broad range of areas.

To date, high-level discussions on the steps toward or the ultimate form of monetary union do not seem to have taken place. The EAC Development Strategy for 2001–05, agreed to by the heads of state, discusses cooperation in macroeconomic policy as the precursor to plans for monetary union. The importance of maintaining convertibility of currencies is stressed.[15] Macroeconomic convergence indicators are also specified, covering real GDP growth rates, inflation, current account deficits, fiscal deficits, reserve ratios, domestic savings, and the ratios of external debt to revenue. While written down on paper, it does not seem, however, that EAC and government officials in the three countries are actually aware of, or committed to, these convergence goals. It is also not clear what specific progress or plans for capital account liberalization are associated with EAC cooperation efforts. On capital market development, while goals include the establishment of a regional stock

13. World Bank (2003).

14. Venables (2000).

15. While the IMF's *Annual Report on Exchange Arrangements and Restrictions* (2002) notes that currencies are freely convertible and that excess holdings of partner country shillings are repatriated to the respective central banks for immediate credit in dollars, it is not completely clear how convertibility is operating on the ground.

Table 8-1. *EAC Social Indicators, Averages, 1995–2000*

	GDP per capita (constant 1995 U.S. dollars)	Life expectancy at birth (years)	Population with access to safe water (percent)	Literacy rate of population 15+ years (percent)
Kenya	338.5	49.2	49	79.7
Tanzania	183.1	46.4	54	72.1
Uganda	327.0	42.6	50	64.5

Sources: World Bank, World Development Indicators database (2002) and African Development Indicators database (2002).

exchange and standardized banking regulations (with little to no progress to date), there is no plan for a mechanism for regional banking supervision.

The objective of monetary cooperation is to have an East African single currency in place by 2010. No official statements have been made about the form of the exchange rate regime, although some documents do mention the desire to maintain market-determined exchange rates and acceptable levels of reserves. The Monetary Affairs Committee of the EAC has proposed that a monetary institute be set up to develop and monitor realistic convergence targets, to make plans for monetary union, and to follow up on implementation of agreements in this area.[16] It does not seem, however, that this proposal is being seriously discussed.

EAC Countries: Fair Degree of Linkages

Economic disparities across the three countries have narrowed since the second half of the 1990s, as Tanzania and Uganda have pursued macroeconomic and structural reform programs, spurring strong real GDP growth, while Kenya has lagged.[17] During 1995–2000, real GDP growth averaged 4 percent in Tanzania and 7 percent in Uganda, compared to 2 percent in Kenya, which is still generally ahead of the other two countries in terms of social indicators (see table 8-1).

As discussed in chapter 3, the benefits of a fixed rate between countries in a monetary union tend to be greater if countries have substantial intraregional trade and more symmetric shocks (which is more likely if economic structures are similar).

Internal trade within the region is relatively small, averaging 7 percent of exports and imports (see table 8-2). Still, this is close to the level of trade in ECOWAS (much higher than for the non-WAEMU countries) and higher in

16. USAID, "East African Community: Non-trade Policy, Economic Analysis Paper #2" (www.usaid.or.ug/econ%20papers/eac%20non-trade%20polic.doc [March 2003]).

17. Related also to the suspension of donor aid in 2000 because of concerns about corruption.

Table 8-2. *EAC Bilateral Trade Flows, Averages, 1995–2000*[a]

Country 1	Percent of country 1's total exports to:		
	Kenya	Tanzania	Uganda
Kenya	0	8.46	16.59
Tanzania	4.33	0	2.08
Uganda	0.68	1.03	0

Country 1	Percent of total imports from country 1		
	Kenya	Tanzania	Uganda
Kenya	0	10.06	38.19
Tanzania	0.92	0	1.65
Uganda	0.10	0.29	0

Source: IMF, Direction of Trade Statistics database (2003).
a. Bilateral trade is calculated by averaging exports from 1 to 2 and imports of 2 from 1.

general than internal trade in SADC, except for South Africa's very high trade with other SACU countries. The pattern of trade is quite uneven, however. For Kenya, the EAC (and COMESA) is an important and growing export market. Uganda and Tanzania, on the other hand, export very little to their EAC partners (although Tanzania's exports to Kenya are growing). Kenya's imports from the rest of the EAC are insignificant, part of its trend of declining imports from other African countries overall. For Uganda, Kenya is its most important import source, followed by Asia and the EU. In contrast, Tanzania's imports from the rest of the EAC are quite low.[18]

Unofficial cross-border trade, although difficult to quantify, is thought to be considerable. One set of surveys done in the mid-1990s estimated unofficial cross-border trade as highest between Kenya and Uganda, at 49 percent of official trade, followed by Tanzania and Uganda trade at 45 percent of official trade, and Tanzania and Kenya cross-border trade of about 12 percent.[19] In our simulations of a currency union, as for the other regions, we increase bilateral flows by 25 percent to account for informal trade.

Terms of trade shocks are the most important source of shocks for primary commodity-exporting countries. The correlations of changes in the terms of trade calculated in table 8-3 show that the average of correlations between countries (0.67) is higher than those for the existing monetary unions, WAEMU (0.20), and the CMA (0.37). Coffee is the primary export for both Tanzania and Uganda, which have the highest correlation of terms of trade shocks in the

18. Ng'eno (2002).
19. See references in Mkenda (2001).

Table 8-3. *EAC: Correlation of Percent Changes in Terms of Trade, 1987–99*

	Kenya	Tanzania	Uganda
Kenya	1.00		
Tanzania	0.56	1.00	
Uganda	0.64	0.80	1.00

Sources: World Bank, African Development Indicators database (2002); UNCTAD and World Bank. See Cashin, McDermott, and Pattillo (2004).

EAC. Following tea, coffee is also the second largest export for Kenya, whose shocks are relatively highly correlated with those in Uganda and Tanzania.

Macroeconomic convergence indicators and their specific target values do not appear to be firmly agreed to by the authorities. Table 8-4 indicates where countries stand relative to indicators specified in the EAC Development Strategy 2001–05 document. Performance on the GDP growth, inflation, and current account deficit indicators appears reasonable, except for Kenya's anemic growth figures. It is not clear whether the 5 percent targets for fiscal and current account deficits as a share of GDP are including or excluding grants. Assuming that the current account target includes grants and the fiscal deficit excludes grants, Uganda is still far off on the fiscal target. Performance is more mixed on the indicators for reserves, domestic savings, and debt service to revenues.

Net Benefits from Monetary Union

Appendix A discusses calibration of a model of the economic costs and benefits of a monetary union using data on the broadest set of African countries available. As with other planned or existing monetary unions, we use the common

Table 8-4. *EAC Macroeconomic Convergence Indicators and Performance, 2001*
Percent, unless otherwise indicated

Indicator	Target	Kenya	Tanzania	Uganda
Real GDP growth	7	1.1	5.9	5.0
Inflation	5	5.8	5.1	5.0
Current account deficit to GDP[a]	5	3.2/2.4	9.8/2.6	13.1/4.5
Fiscal deficit to GDP[a]	5	3.8/2.6	4.5/1.2	11.5/1.6
Reserves (months of imports of goods and nonfactor services)	6	3.6	5.1	4.9
Domestic savings/GDP	...	11.0	15.3	14.0
Debt service/revenues	15	20.1	27.0	12.8

Sources: Real GDP growth, inflation, current account and fiscal deficits, and reserves from IMF Staff Country Reports. Domestic savings and debt service/revenues from the IMF, World Economic Outlook database.

a. Excluding grants/including grants.

Table 8-5. *Net Gains from EAC Monetary Union*

	Kenya	Tanzania	Uganda
Share of GDP	0.4247	0.3156	0.2597
Correlation of shocks	0.8995	0.8362	0.8889
Average/own financing need	0.9496	1.0465	1.0339
Net gain	0.0378	−0.0060	−0.0006
Decomposition of net gains relative to independent policies			
Monetary externality	0.0145	0.0145	0.0145
Fiscal asymmetry	0.0241	−0.0211	−0.0155
Shock asymmetry	−0.0001	−0.0001	−0.0001

Source: Authors' calculations.

parameters and some region-specific parameters to calibrate the model for the EAC. Recall that the model implies that for any country, the net gains from joining a monetary union depend on differences in fiscal policy distortions, on the negative effect of inflation surprises in one country on neighboring countries' output operating through the strength of trade linkages, and on the correlation of shocks. Given the relatively strong (compared to other regions) trade linkages and shock correlation, we might expect a monetary union among the three countries to be mutually beneficial. On the other hand, however, Kenya (the country with the largest GDP weight, which in the model implies the largest weight in the common central bank's monetary policy) has the least fiscal discipline, as evidenced by a high government financing need (as well as actual government spending as a percentage of GDP).

In fact, table 8-5 indicates that participation in a monetary union is better than independent monetary policies (and separate currencies) only for Kenya among the EAC member countries. In contrast, both Tanzania and Uganda have small net losses. Their magnitudes are well under 1 percent of GDP, however, and they could well be offset by other factors (including political ones) that we have not modeled.

The second panel of table 8-5 decomposes the net gains for each country. Internalizing the monetary policy externality (the reduced incentive to boost output through unexpected inflation, or competitive devaluations) provides a substantial gain, following from the reasonable degree of interregional trade. Kenya, with a higher government financing need than the other two countries, gains from a central bank that is more disciplined, while Tanzania and Uganda, with more conservative government spending, show losses from the excessive monetary financing. Asymmetry of shocks leads to losses, although extremely small ones.

Thus the model simulations indicate that an EAC monetary union may run into the same asymmetry of net gains that contributed to the demise of the old

EAC.[20] What are the prospects for successful movement toward monetary integration? East Africa's long history of attempts at forging regional cooperation can either be viewed as a bad legacy of failures that are difficult to overcome or as a greater experience at regionalism than most other regions in the continent.

The prospects of moving forward depend on whether the first step of forming a customs union proves to be successful. Here, the distribution of trade benefits will clearly be an issue: Tanzania and Uganda continue to be concerned that Kenya will benefit disproportionately. Manufacturers in Kenya have protested that the common external tariff would leave them unable to compete with import products.[21] The EAC is considering installation of a compensatory mechanism for either countries or sectors that suffer losses from the customs union, an important outstanding issue in the negotiations. However, the likelihood of a compensation mechanism actually being implemented would appear slim. Finally, overlapping membership in other regional organizations (discussed below) both creates difficulties for negotiating common external tariff rates (considerably slowing the decision process) and could provide the EAC countries with exit options should the integration process falter.

On the positive side, there appears to be some political momentum to the process. Factors such as a common language, significant donor interest in the project, attention to involvement of the private sector, and a new government in Kenya in 2003 (where prospects appear brighter for economic reforms and donor aid is resuming) all also augur well for progress on regional integration.

COMESA

In addition to membership in the EAC, Kenya and Uganda are also members of COMESA. Tanzania, concerned about potential harm to its industrial development from a planned zero internal tariff, withdrew from COMESA in 2000 but is reported to be considering reentry. Tanzania is also a member of SADC.[22] As the overlapping membership and similarity of some integration objectives affect incentives and prospects for monetary union in the EAC, a brief review of the main objectives and monetary integration plans of COMESA is in order.

20. In contrast, Mkenda (2001) concludes that the EAC forms an OCA, based on a method that finds cointegration of real exchange rates.

21. Kraus (2003).

22. Implementing the EAC customs union may be further complicated by negotiations of economic partnership agreements for trade liberalization between the EU and various regional organizations in sub-Saharan Africa. Tanzania has decided to negotiate as a part of SADC, while Kenya and Uganda will be represented in COMESA (World Bank, 2003).

COMESA was established in 1994 as a strengthened successor to the Preferential Trade Area (PTA) for eastern and southern Africa, which was founded in 1981. COMESA is made up of twenty countries: Angola, Burundi, Comoros, Democratic Republic of the Congo, Djibouti, Egypt, Eritrea, Ethiopia, Kenya, Madagascar, Malawi, Mauritius, Namibia, Rwanda, Seychelles, Sudan, Swaziland, Uganda, Zambia, and Zimbabwe. Its broad strategy is that in order to attract private investment into the region, the small countries that make up its membership must be able to offer a large single market, leading to a focus on liberalization of the trade and investment environment.[23] Specific objectives include a full, free trade area; a customs union (by 2004); free movement of capital and investment; establishment of a monetary union with a common currency; and free movement of citizens, including right of establishment (freedom to set up businesses in any member state) by 2025. COMESA's most important achievement has been the formation in 2000 by nine member countries of a free trade area that eliminated tariffs and quotas on goods that conform to COMESA rules of origin.[24] Two additional countries, Burundi and Rwanda, joined in 2003. Other COMESA countries not yet part of the free trade area have reduced tariffs between 60 and 80 percent on COMESA-originating goods. Member states are still negotiating over the structure of the proposed common external tariff.

Monetary integration planning has been on the books for some time. A monetary harmonization program was prepared in 1990 for the then PTA, and this program was later endorsed in the treaty establishing COMESA.[25] The program envisaged a gradualist approach with several stages: full utilization of the clearing house's payments mechanism (1992–96); limited currency convertibility and an informal exchange rate union (1997–2000); fixed exchange rates fluctuating within a given margin (2000–24); central banks remain independent but monetary policy coordinated by a common monetary institution (2000–24); and the common monetary authority issues a common currency (2025 and onward). A 1995 review of the monetary harmonization program recommended a set of measurable macroeconomic and institutional targets. Progress toward these targets is reviewed below, although the extent of high-level official commitment is not clear.

A more recent review of the monetary harmonization program commissioned by the COMESA Secretariat in 2000 found that while some progress

23. Ngwenya (2000).
24. The free trade area members are Djibouti, Egypt, Kenya, Madagascar, Malawi, Mauritius, Sudan, Zambia, and Zimbabwe.
25. COMESA Finance and Economics, "Monetary and Fiscal Cooperation in Comesa" (www.comesa.int/finance/econmhp.htm [March 2003]).

had been made toward the policy and institutional targets, it was the result of individual country decisions or IMF or World Bank conditionality, and not steps taken in order to meet commitments made to COMESA.[26] The study argued that further progress would require stricter macroeconomic targets. It recommended that countries proceed at their own speed and that individual countries that have achieved macroeconomic stability could gain credibility by establishing currency boards linked preferably to the euro.

While COMESA's strategy for monetary cooperation has not addressed capital market liberalization, significant effort has been made to establish a new regional payment and settlement system, potentially managed by commercial banks, that could reduce costs of exchanging currencies in intra-COMESA trade. In terms of financial market integration, since 1999 the heads of central bank banking supervision units have met annually, and a framework of harmonizing bank supervision and regulation in the region is currently under discussion.

COMESA Countries: Weak Linkages

Prospects for trade and monetary integration in the region are complicated by overlapping membership in regional organizations. Nine of the COMESA partner states are also members of SADC.[27] Of these nine states, Namibia and Swaziland are already members of the CMA, with currencies linked to the South African rand. Kenya and Uganda are members of both the EAC and COMESA and so have conflicting commitments to two different planned customs and monetary unions. Tanzania is the only EAC country that is also a member of SADC.

Similar to SADC, COMESA countries span a wide range of development levels and economic and political conditions.[28] Although promoting trade in the region was the objective of the precursor PTA and COMESA, internal trade remains quite low (see table 8-6, which lists bilateral trade between pairs

26. Botswana Institute for Development Policy Analysis (BIDPA) and Centre for the Study of African Economies (CSAE) (2001).

27. Angola, Democratic Republic of the Congo, Malawi, Mauritius, Namibia, Seychelles, Swaziland, Zambia, and Zimbabwe.

28. BIDPA and CSAE (2001) suggest that subgroups of COMESA could aim for policy convergence as an interim step toward monetary integration. Currently, however, they find no evidence of convergence within these groups: (1) northern: Egypt, Sudan, Djibouti, Ethiopia, Eritrea; (2) central: Kenya, Burundi, Comoros, Congo, Mauritius, Rwanda, Seychelles, Tanzania, Uganda; and (3) southern: Zimbabwe, Angola, Madagascar, Malawi, Namibia, Swaziland, Zambia.

Table 8-6. *Significant Regional Trade Flows within COMESA,*
Averages, 1995–2000[a]

Country 1	Percent of country 1's total exports to country 2		Percent of country 2's total imports from country 1	
Burundi	Kenya	2.97	...	
	Rwanda	2.29		
Dem. Rep. of the Congo			Rwanda	1.62
Djibouti	Ethiopia	10.99	...	
Egypt			Sudan	1.45
Eritrea	Kenya	1.06	...	
Ethiopia	Djibouti	9.23	Djibouti	9.28
	Egypt	2.55		
Kenya	Dem. Rep. of the Congo	1.92	Burundi	4.51
	Egypt	3.83	Comoros	3.81
	Ethiopia	1.52	Dem. Rep. of the Congo	3.75
	Rwanda	2.49	Ethiopia	2.14
	Sudan	2.02	Rwanda	16.85
	Uganda	16.59	Sudan	2.70
			Uganda	38.19
Madagascar	Mauritius	6.17	Comoros	1.72
Malawi	Egypt	2.47	...	
	Zimbabwe	2.51		
Mauritius	Madagascar	2.10	Comoros	1.36
			Madagascar	6.13
			Seychelles	1.43
Namibia	Zimbabwe	1.18	Swaziland	3.16
Sudan	Egypt	3.10	...	
Swaziland	Mauritius	1.43	Namibia	1.87
	Zambia	2.01	Rwanda	1.72
	Zimbabwe	3.52		
Zambia	Dem. Rep. of the Congo	1.85	Burundi	4.23
	Malawi	4.77	Dem. Rep. of the Congo	1.67
	Zimbabwe	2.61	Malawi	7.45
			Rwanda	1.33
Zimbabwe	Malawi	2.95	Burundi	1.32
	Zambia	3.83	Malawi	11.29
			Namibia	6.05
			Swaziland	1.41
			Zambia	9.39

Source: IMF, Direction of Trade Statistics database (2003).
a. Bilateral trade is calculated by averaging exports from 1 to 2 and imports of 2 from 1.

Table 8-7. *COMESA Correlation of Percent Changes in Terms of Trade, 1987–99*[a]

	Angola	Burundi	Comoros	Dem. Rep. of the Congo	Djibouti	Egypt	Eritrea	Ethiopia	Kenya	Madagascar
Angola	1.0									
Burundi	−0.03	1.0								
Comoros	−0.27	0.45	1.0							
Dem. Rep. of the Congo	−0.37	−0.06	0.28	1.0						
Djibouti	−0.06	**−0.59**	−0.30	−0.05	1.0					
Egypt	**0.82**	−0.37	**−0.56**	−0.21	0.00	1.0				
Eritrea	0.14	−0.32	**−0.56**	−0.25	0.33	−0.29	1.0			
Ethiopia	−0.11	**0.77**	**0.75**	0.25	−0.26	−0.48	**−0.56**	1.0		
Kenya	0.14	**0.60**	**0.53**	−0.13	−0.17	−0.38	**0.72**	**0.63**	1.0	
Madagascar	−0.05	**0.88**	**0.64**	−0.07	−0.47	−0.43	**−0.58**	**0.87**	**0.56**	1.0
Malawi	0.43	0.37	−0.23	0.03	**−0.55**	0.54	**−0.89**	−0.04	−0.04	0.06
Mauritius	−0.06	0.38	0.27	−0.09	**−0.87**	0.03	**−0.65**	0.04	−0.11	0.35
Namibia	−0.15	0.06	0.38	**0.67**	−0.13	−0.33	0.28	0.34	0.37	0.10
Rwanda	−0.15	**0.71**	**0.54**	0.19	−0.21	−0.45	0.35	**0.84**	**0.64**	**0.70**
Seychelles	−0.45	−0.25	−0.03	**0.72**	0.35	−0.20	0.34	−0.03	−0.17	−0.44
Sudan	−0.11	0.24	0.01	**0.56**	−0.32	0.04	−0.21	0.26	0.11	0.03
Swaziland	0.13	−0.02	**−0.60**	−0.04	−0.09	0.40	0.31	**−0.50**	−0.31	−0.43
Uganda	−0.14	**0.89**	**0.75**	0.20	−0.47	**−0.51**	**−0.67**	**0.94**	**0.64**	**0.94**
Zambia	−0.27	−0.29	−0.03	**0.84**	−0.02	0.13	−0.42	−0.09	**−0.60**	−0.33
Zimbabwe	**−0.63**	0.06	0.40	**0.57**	0.03	**−0.53**	0.34	0.13	−0.09	−0.04

Sources: World Bank, African Development Indicators database (2002); UNCTAD and World Bank. See Cashin, McDermott, and Pattillo (2004).

a. Correlations in bold exceed 0.5 and are significant at the 5 percent level.

of countries that exceeds 1 percent of their imports or exports). Exports to other COMESA countries as a share of total exports are most important for Kenya. In fact, the largest intra-COMESA trade is Kenya's exports to Uganda. Egypt imports one of the highest shares from selected other COMESA countries, which would be expected given the very large size of its market, but the share is still very low. For most other countries, export or import shares constituted by bilateral trade between COMESA countries seldom exceed 4 percent of total exports. Exceptions include substantial trade among neighboring Djibouti and Ethiopia (11 percent of Djibouti's exports go to Ethiopia and 9 percent of Ethiopia's exports flow to Djibouti), and other neighbors: 6 percent of Madagascar's exports go to Mauritius, 5 percent of Zambia's exports go to Malawi, and 4 percent of Zimbabwe's exports go to Zambia.

Given the wide range of export commodities, it is to be expected that the countries in the region would face quite asymmetric terms of trade shocks (see

Malawi	*Mauritius*	*Namibia*	*Rwanda*	*Seychelles*	*Sudan*	*Swaziland*	*Uganda*	*Zambia*	*Zimbabwe*
1.0									
0.47	1.0								
−0.18	−0.11	1.0							
−0.01	−0.11	0.16	1.0						
0.02	−0.42	0.31	0.07	1.0					
0.47	0.04	0.32	0.43	**0.54**	1.0				
0.72	0.11	−0.37	−0.31	0.31	0.22	1.0			
0.13	0.30	0.32	**0.76**	−0.16	0.23	−0.36	1.0		
0.18	0.03	0.25	−0.12	**0.68**	0.45	0.23	−0.15	1.0	
−0.07	0.06	0.23	0.07	**0.62**	0.01	0.20	0.17	**0.51**	1.0

table 8-7). The average correlation of shocks, 0.12, is lower than that for all existing or potential monetary unions that we have considered. The correlation of shocks is negative for a number of country pairs; shocks are negatively correlated on average with the rest of COMESA countries for Angola, Djibouti, and Swaziland. Correlations are highest between pairs of countries that primarily export coffee, namely, Burundi, Uganda, Ethiopia, and Rwanda.

The degree of official commitment to the targets proposed in the monetary harmonization program is not clear, and the specific targets are currently under review. Table 8-8 shows that progress, measured by average levels of the indicators during 1995–2000 as well as the latest year available, is extremely varied across the countries. Performance is clearly worst in the countries involved in wars or severe political crises (Angola, Democratic Republic of the Congo, Eritrea, Zimbabwe). On the key indicators of inflation and budget deficits, nine of the twenty countries had average inflation (for the 1995–2000

Table 8-8. *COMESA Monetary Harmonization Program Indicators*

Percent

	Budget deficit to GDP (10% target)		Broad money growth (10% target)		Central bank financing of government spending[a] (<10% target)		Real lending and deposit rates (target positive)		Debt services as a percent of export earnings (20% target)		Inflation (10% target)	
	(1995–2000)	Latest	(1995–2000)	Latest	(1995–2000)	Latest	(1995–2000)	Latest	(1995–2000)	Latest	(1995–2000)	Latest
Angola	-12.8	4.9	1,015.0	160.6	543.2	1.1	-55.5	-13.9	23.5	26.5	1,271.4	344.4
Burundi	-4.3	-0.8	11.7	15.7	54.6	87.9	2.0	3.0	38.8	39.8	19.5	24.3
Comoros	-3.8	-1.9	3.1	46.7	36.6	37.6			3.6	3.6	4.0	2.6
Dem. Rep. of the Congo			121.1	1,829.4			-33.2	-63.7	1.9	1.7	373.4	550.0
Djibouti	-3.2	-1.8	-2.3	7.5	8.7	15.7		8.7	4.4	5.5	2.9	2.4
Egypt	-1.5	-3.3	9.9	13.2	141.3	212.8	7.6	9.1	10.9	8.9	5.5	2.8
Eritrea	-32.4	-48.2	116.9	222.1	272.1	411.5			0.7	2.0	10.6	19.9
Ethiopia	-6.2	-11.4	8.3	9.8	196.4	171.6	6.5	19.2	18.7	18.7	3.3	4.3
Kenya	-0.6	-3.0	13.7	2.5	46.6	24.6	16.5	7.6	24.4	15.4	6.6	7.8
Madagascar	-4.5	-2.8	15.9	23.8	118.4	70.5	13.4	14.9	14.2	43.3	16.9	11.9
Malawi	-5.0	-5.0	37.8	14.8	34.5	35.9	5.3	23.9	15.4	7.8	38.5	29.6
Mauritius	-5.1	-7.2	13.1	10.9	13.9	10.1	14.2	18.0	10.0	6.9	6.1	4.4
Namibia	-3.6	-2.9	17.1	4.5			9.1	4.9			8.5	9.3
Rwanda	-2.9	0.1	22.4	11.0	180.8	66.6	2.0	4.8	20.8	11.4	8.5	3.9
Seychelles	-11.5	-15.7	19.9	12.0	76.6	69.7	8.8	4.1	5.3	2.6	2.0	2.1
Sudan	-1.6	-0.8	44.4	24.7	145.7	123.9			4.7	2.3	60.7	8.0
Swaziland	-0.5	-1.4	10.3	10.7			5.4	4.5	2.6	2.7	8.7	12.2
Uganda	-1.8	-3.6	17.9	9.2	249.2	172.0	15.3	14.2	18.1	7.4	5.5	6.3
Zambia	-2.9	-6.8	40.4	13.6	496.5	449.5	13.3	17.6	46.3	11.7	30.6	30.1
Zimbabwe	-9.8	-21.4	36.0	128.5	157.2	46.9	9.7	-18.9	25.8	6.8	34.4	55.7

Sources: World Bank, World Development Indicators and African Development Indicators databases (2002); and IMF, International Financial Statistics database (2003).

a. As a percent of previous years' tax revenue.

Table 8-9. *Net Gains from COMESA Monetary Union*

Country	Share of GDP	Correlation of shocks	Average/own financing need	Net gain from monetary union
Angola	0.0483	0.7843	0.6446	0.1844
Egypt	0.5482	0.7616	1.0328	−0.0121
Ethiopia	0.0434	0.0702	0.8521	0.0849
Kenya	0.0708	0.0976	1.0582	−0.0251
Madagascar	0.0255	−0.0155	1.1087	−0.0485
Malawi	0.0135	0.7295	0.9247	0.0443
Mauritius	0.0290	0.0724	1.6584	−0.2406
Namibia	0.0243	0.0487	1.2996	−0.1278
Seychelles	0.0040	−0.0313	0.5203	0.2567
Sudan	0.0670	0.4991	0.9426	0.0269
Swaziland	0.0094	0.2923	1.2975	−0.1269
Uganda	0.0433	0.0426	1.1521	−0.0684
Zambia	0.0230	0.1645	0.9667	0.0181
Zimbabwe	0.0504	−0.4301	0.9098	0.0521

Source: Authors' calculations.

period) greater than 10 percent, while five had budget deficits (excluding grants) greater than 10 percent of GDP.

Table A-3 provides information on government revenue, spending, and other fiscal indicators utilized in the calibration of the model described in chapter 3. Although performance is again varied, one notable feature is that fiscal discipline is quite strong in Egypt, which with a 50 percent share in the GDP of the region would have a large weight in decisionmaking of a common central bank.

Net Benefits from a Monetary Union

Table 8-9, which presents the results of simulating a monetary union for COMESA, demonstrates that differences across countries (in particular, in our measure of fiscal discipline, the government financing need) are large enough so that a number of countries would not gain by being members compared to retaining their independent monetary policies. Interestingly, this includes Kenya and Uganda, whose overlapping project of an EAC currency was analyzed above. The largest economy of the region, Egypt, is also estimated to be a small net loser. The largest gainers are identified as those with the weakest fiscal discipline: Angola, Ethiopia, Malawi, Seychelles, Sudan, and Zimbabwe.

Unlike SADC, COMESA has no natural anchor country, so we do not simulate an asymmetric monetary union. While Egypt, the largest economy, has generally had low inflation and a stable currency, this was in the context of price controls and obstacles to capital mobility. Nor does Egypt's central bank have a tradition of independence that would lend credibility to a regional monetary policy. It would also appear that participation in a COMESA monetary union is not actually on the radar screen of Egyptian policymakers.

Conclusions

Of the two projects, a monetary union constituted by the countries of the EAC seems the more viable. First, it is in the context of a serious effort to achieve political and economic integration. Second, the countries have a long, if checkered, history of collaboration. Finally, the economic disparities between the countries are substantial but not as wide as are faced by COMESA, which virtually spans the continent from north to south and includes countries with very different levels of per capita income and financial development. However, prospects for the EAC depend critically on its ability to address the reason for the failure of the old EAC, namely, the perception that Kenya will gain most of the benefits of integration.

9

A Single Currency for Africa?

The creation of a common African currency has long been a pillar of African unity, a symbol of the strength that its backers hope will emerge from efforts to integrate the continent. A common currency was an objective of the OAU, created in 1963, and the AEC, established in 1991. The project is intimately associated with the newly formed AU, whose constitutive act (which was signed by twenty-seven governments at the OAU/AEC assembly of heads of state and government in Lomé, Togo, on July 11, 2000, and which entered into force on May 26, 2001) has superseded the OAU Charter and the AEC Treaty, which were the legal instruments underlying the OAU.

The 1991 Abuja Treaty establishing the AEC (which became effective in May 1994 after the required number of signatures) outlines six stages for achieving an integrated economic and monetary zone for Africa that were set to be completed by approximately 2028. The strategy for African integration is based on progressive integration of the activities of the RECs, which are regarded as building blocks for Africa. These are:[1]

—Stage 1. Strengthening existing RECs and creating new ones where needed (expected to take five years);

1. See South Africa Department of Foreign Affairs, "African Economic Community," May 28, 2001, www.dfa.gov.za/for-relations/multilateral/aec.htm.

—Stage 2. Stabilization of tariff and other barriers to regional trade and the strengthening of sectoral integration, particularly in the fields of trade, agriculture, finance, transport and communications, industry, and energy, as well as the coordination and harmonization of the activities of the RECs (expected to take eight years);

—Stage 3. Establishment of a free trade area and customs union at the level of each REC (expected to take ten years);

—Stage 4. Coordination and harmonization of tariff and nontariff systems among RECs, with a view to establishing a continental customs union (expected to take two years);

—Stage 5. Establishment of an African common market and the adoption of common policies (expected to take four years); and

—Stage 6. Integration of all sectors, establishment of an African central bank and a single African currency, setting up an African economic and monetary union, and creating and electing the first pan-African parliament (expected to take five years).

The proposed creation of the African common currency is left to the final stage, which was intended to occur during the period 2023–28. However, the September 1999 Sirte (Libya) Declaration proposing the establishment of the AU called for shorter implementation periods and the speedy establishment of the institutions provided for in the Abuja Treaty, in particular, the African financial institutions. Article 19 of the Constitutive Act of the AU calls for the creation of the African Central Bank, African Monetary Fund, and African Investment Bank, with each of these institution's responsibilities to be defined in subsequent protocols. While the time horizon for replacing national currencies by an African currency is still distant,[2] it seems that procedures for countries to bid to host the central bank are soon to be announced. Several countries, including Ghana and Botswana, have already expressed interest in hosting the central bank.

The existing RECs, which are viewed as building blocks for the AU, are AMU, COMESA, ECCAS, ECOWAS, and SADC (see figure 9-1 for a list of their members and geographical locations). Thus the creation of a single African currency relies on plans for creating regional monetary unions. These unions would be an intermediate stage, leading ultimately to the merger into a single African central bank and currency. It is unlikely, however, that all of the countries in the regional groupings would find it in their interests to form a

---

2. The Association of African Central Bank Governors at its August 2003 meeting in Kampala, Uganda, declared that the governors would work for a single currency and common central bank by 2021 (Agence France Presse, August 20, 2003).

Figure 9-1. *Membership in Regional Arrangements*

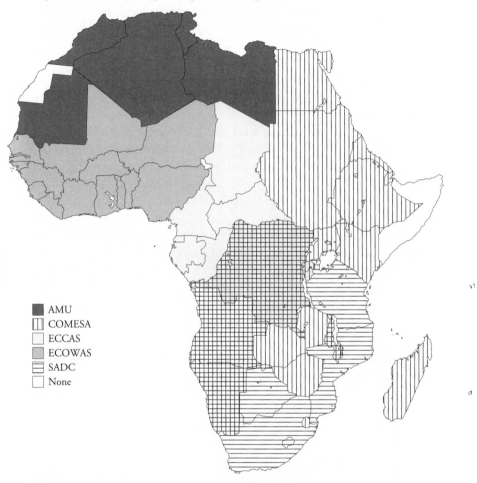

AMU
COMESA
ECCAS
ECOWAS
SADC
None

AMU
Algeria, Libya, Mauritania, Morocco, Tunisia

COMESA
Angola, Burundi, Comoros, Democratic Republic of the Congo, Djibouti, Egypt, Eritrea, Ethiopia, Kenya, Madagascar, Malawi, Mauritius, Namibia, Rwanda, Seychelles, Sudan, Swaziland, Uganda, Zambia, Zimbabwe

ECCAS
Burundi, Cameroon, Central African Republic, Chad, Democratic Republic of the Congo, Equatorial Guinea, Gabon, Republic of Congo, Rwanda, Sâo Tomé and Principe

ECOWAS
Benin, Burkina Faso, Cape Verde, Côte d'Ivoire, the Gambia, Ghana, Guinea, Guinea-Bissau, Liberia, Mali, Niger, Nigeria, Senegal, Sierra Leone, Togo

SADC
Angola, Botswana, Democratic Republic of the Congo, Lesotho, Malawi, Mauritius, Mozambique, Namibia, Seychelles, South Africa, Swaziland, Tanzania, Zambia, Zimbabwe

Source: Masson and Milkiewicz (2003).

regional currency. Another problem is that these RECs only partially overlap with existing monetary unions, and at least one proposed monetary union (for the EAC) overlaps with two RECs.[3] The two CFA franc zones, WAEMU and CAEMC, are important components of ECOWAS and ECCAS, respectively, but WAEMU makes up only about one-half of ECOWAS. CAEMC does not include Burundi, the Democratic Republic of the Congo, Rwanda, or São Tomé and Principe. South Africa and its CMA partners are only four of the fourteen current members of SADC.

Though the existing currency areas (the CFA franc zone and the CMA) could be expanded ad hoc and a modest new currency union created for the EAC, in our view such changes are unlikely to span the RECs defined above. Nevertheless, we consider in this chapter whether combining regional currencies in the five major geographical areas would make sense. Though the geographic areas may not themselves constitute desirable currency areas, we assume nevertheless that they have been formed. Assuming that they have, we look at whether all of the regions would find it incentive compatible to agree to share a single currency. As was the case within proposed currency areas, we find that there are asymmetries across the regions that would probably inhibit the creation, at a final stage, of a single African currency. In particular, corruption and a lack of fiscal discipline are likely to make many African countries poor partners in a monetary union project.

One theme of this book has been skepticism about the effectiveness of monetary solutions for nonmonetary problems. In particular, Africa has suffered from decades of decline and marginalization, as the early hopes of rapid development and enlightened government after independence were dashed by negative external shocks, poor economic policies, civil wars, and kleptocratic rulers. While Africa has received considerable amounts of bilateral and multilateral aid, this aid often has not been used wisely. Africa has also suffered from low world commodity prices and obstacles to its agricultural exports.[4]

The poor economic performance has led first to a reexamination of the effectiveness of aid by the major donor countries and, second, to a recognition by Africans that they need to take charge of their own destiny. Monetary union in itself would not solve these problems. Fortunately, a new initiative has emerged, NEPAD, which aims at improving economic and political governance by Africans and thus assuring donors (and private investors) that resource flows to Africa will not be wasted. NEPAD has the potential for correcting the funda-

3. Kenya and Uganda belong to COMESA, but not Tanzania, which is a member of SADC.
4. For instance, subsidies by advanced countries to their cotton farmers have artificially depressed prices on the free market. See Badiane, Goreux, and Masson (2002).

mental problems behind Africa's poor economic performance. If successful, it could create the conditions for African unity, including a single currency. However, it may well take its place among other failed African initiatives.[5] African leaders have yet to prove that they are willing to apply effective peer pressure, much less sanctions if peer pressure fails. And governments of rich countries may use a lack of progress on governance as a reason to reduce aid flows.

Why the Initiative to Form an African Monetary Union?

There are two principal reasons for the enthusiasm for monetary union in Africa. First, it is clear that the successful launch of the euro has stimulated interest in other regions. From Latin America to the Middle East and East Asia, monetary union is seen as a way of reinforcing regional cohesion and demonstrating a commitment to regional solidarity. However, it is sometimes forgotten just how long the road actually was to monetary union in Europe. The transition was fraught with obstacles and missteps, and even in official circles there were doubts until the ultimate day of the changeover in January 2002 whether the replacement of national currencies by euro notes and coins would go smoothly. Designing new institutions that were able to deliver stability-oriented monetary policy—particularly the European system of central banks—was complicated, as was creating the Stability and Growth Pact, which provides for regional coordination of fiscal policies. Despite the intense planning process, the institutions are still the object of considerable controversy and contention. In Africa fiscal problems are more severe and the credibility of monetary institutions is more fragile. If the process of creating an institution was so difficult for a set of rich countries with highly competent bureaucracies that have cooperated closely for more than fifty years, then realistically, the challenge for African countries must be considered enormous.

The second important motivation in Africa has been the desire to counteract perceived economic and political weakness by creating regional solidarity and cooperation, of which a common currency and monetary union would be potent symbols. Regional groupings would help Africa in negotiating favorable trading arrangements either globally (in the World Trade Organization context) or bilaterally (with the EU and United States). This objective of regional integration seems well founded, but it is unclear whether forming a monetary union would contribute greatly to it. A common currency may be the symbol of weakness, not strength, as was the case for the ruble in the dying days of the Soviet Union and during the creation of the Commonwealth of Independent

5. Helleiner (2002).

States. A currency that is ill managed and subject to continual depreciation is not likely to stimulate pride in the region or give the member countries any clout on the world stage. Moreover, as Nobel Prize winner Robert Mundell emphasizes, it is great countries (or regions) that make great currencies.[6] While the countries in the euro zone are important enough economically for the euro eventually to rival the dollar, that is not likely to be the case for an African currency even in the best circumstances. Africa's GDP is, and likely will remain, only a small fraction of that of Europe or the United States. In fact, at present the GDP of all of sub-Saharan Africa is no more than that of a medium-size EU country, such as Belgium or the Netherlands. These euro area countries, moreover, have much better communications and transportation links than do African countries, so Africa may not expect the same gains from economies of scale and reduction of transactions costs, even in proportion to its economic size, that are anticipated to result from Europe's monetary union.

Strategies for Achieving a Single African Currency

The strategy for forming an African currency relies on first creating currency unions in Africa's regions, then merging them into a single currency area.[7] Africa already has three examples of monetary integration, the two regions in the CFA franc zone and the CMA in southern Africa. In each case, the countries in these exchange rate or monetary unions are members of wider regional organizations that have plans to create their own monetary unions. These would subsume the existing monetary unions. In West Africa, ECOWAS would merge the West African CFA zone (WAEMU) with a projected second monetary zone. Doing so would most likely mean the end of the CFA zone. Similarly, SADC and COMESA's embryonic projects for monetary union envisage the creation of new central banks and a symmetric monetary union. If South Africa and the smaller CMA countries were to be a part of such a union, the rand area, with its considerable track record and credibility, would likely disappear.

The following summarizes the status of the projects for new regional monetary unions.

WAMZ is to be created by July 2005 and expected to lead to a merger with the West African part of the CFA franc zone to produce a single currency for ECOWAS. However, Nigeria will make a difficult partner for the rest of West Africa, given the country's much greater size, large budget deficit, generally

---

6. See Mundell (1999).

7. Article 44.2.(g) of the AEC Treaty states: "[member states shall] establish an African monetary union through the harmonization of regional monetary zones."

undisciplined fiscal policies, and its export of oil, in contrast to its neighbors, which export other primary commodities. Nigeria has the potential to influence monetary policies in ways that potential partners in a monetary union would find undesirable. Without an effective way of disciplining countries' fiscal policies and in the absence of similar shocks to the prices of countries' exports and imports (or terms of trade), a single currency for ECOWAS would not seem advisable.

In southern Africa, countries that are part of SADC intend to form a monetary union, though this is a much vaguer and more distant project. Many SADC members are, in any case, very far from macroeconomic stability. The southernmost countries, South Africa and the smaller members of SACU, are reasonably advanced and stable. However, their neighbors to the north include countries with recent or continuing problems of civil unrest or political and economic crisis (Angola, Democratic Republic of the Congo, and Zimbabwe) as well as some facing severe drought and poverty (Malawi and Zambia, for instance). Their financial systems are generally much less developed than those of the southernmost countries and the shares of manufactures in production and exports are low.

COMESA, a group of countries that cuts across two geographical regions, is also developing a monetary union project. Disparities among COMESA countries are about as important as those affecting SADC (and there is considerable overlap in memberships of the two organizations). But COMESA's drawback is that South Africa, the greatest pole of monetary stability in the region, is not one of its members. Three countries (Kenya, Tanzania, and Uganda, only two of which are in COMESA) also plan to revive the EAC, including the common currency area, that was dissolved in the decade following independence. These different projects illustrate a pervasive problem in Africa—overlapping commitments that are not necessarily consistent. Attempts to advance on too many fronts often result in inaction. Within the five main RECs associated with the AU (the three mentioned above along with AMU and ECCAS), ten countries belong to more than one regional grouping, with the Democratic Republic of the Congo holding three memberships (see figure 9-1).

A second, and potentially more promising, strategy, and an alternative to creating new, ambitious monetary and exchange rate unions based on the RECs, would be to build on the credibility of existing monetary or exchange rate unions (the CFA franc zone and the CMA) by adding to them countries that have demonstrated their commitment and ability to deliver sound economic policies by satisfying convergence criteria for a significant length of time. This strategy would not involve destroying existing monetary and exchange rate unions, which have generally contributed to regional stability.

Necessarily, however, the scope for expanding the CFA franc zone and the CMA would be limited, because not all potential members would be able to demonstrate sufficient convergence.

Unfortunately, the West African CFA franc zone has been hurt by unrest in Côte d'Ivoire, straining the cohesion of WAEMU and making consolidation of the monetary union essential before extending it. Its central African counterpart, CAEMC, is composed mainly of oil-producing countries with pronounced terms of trade swings. Extending the CMA, where South Africa is a fairly stable developed pole, may be a more attractive possibility in the short to medium run. Successful integration of Mozambique or Zimbabwe (should stability return to that troubled country), for instance, could provide significant gains to the region and impetus for further monetary integration. However, South Africa's SADC neighbors, with a few exceptions, are too far from the macroeconomic stability necessary to converge with the CMA and share the same currency, so many will not be candidates to join for decades. Thus this strategy, which is more likely to succeed and produce gains for the countries concerned than the de novo creation of a monetary union, would not lead to a continentwide currency. It would produce some modest gains in the use of the CFA franc and rand, but it would not prepare the ground for the adoption of a common currency in all regions.

Another disadvantage to hinging the goal of a single African currency on first creating new monetary unions spanning predefined regions is that the countries in each region may have little incentive to adapt their policies to some standard of best practice, since it is taken for granted that all countries will join. It will be very difficult for countries that have achieved a modicum of fiscal discipline to deny membership to those that have not. Thus there is a strong likelihood that an unstable and unattractive monetary union would be created. In contrast, adding countries to the existing monetary unions would give strong incentives for existing members to scrutinize potential members. Given the widespread problems of the lack of both fiscal discipline and stable macroeconomic policies, it is important to use the objective of monetary union to bring to bear pressures for greater discipline and better governance. Moreover, success breeds success. As the monetary union grows through adding countries with stable macroeconomic policies, it becomes more attractive for others to join. Thus the path chosen for creating monetary unions matters. It may be impossible to get all countries to agree to forming a currency union that spans the continent, but a partial monetary union could be feasible. If combined with stringent entrance criteria, it could provide a potent incentive for improved policies.

A third strategy for furthering monetary cooperation would be for African countries to have a common peg to an international currency and perhaps also a common regional currency board based on it.[8] Such a strategy would have the advantage of providing an external anchor for monetary policy (discussed in detail in chapter 10), and a peg to the euro would produce exchange rate stability vis-à-vis Africa's main trading partner.[9] It would further clearly place the onus on each country to follow appropriate policies to maintain the peg, since there can be no doubt where responsibility lies for doing so. However, the big drawback of such a proposal would be political: unilateral pegs, though they would produce stability between pairs of African currencies as a by-product, would not involve the African institution building and new currency creation that could serve as symbols of African solidarity. One suspects that they would not be durable either, unless institutions had been created to modify existing unsustainable fiscal policies. As Argentina's recent experience shows, even a supposedly irreversible commitment to a parity embodied in a currency board can succumb to high government indebtedness.

Is a Single African Currency a Good Thing?

The key factors influencing the benefits and costs from monetary union (importance of trade linkages in creating benefits and asymmetries in terms of trade shocks and in fiscal discipline in generating costs) also apply at a transcontinental level. But at the level of the whole continent, both benefits and costs are amplified as the potential size of a monetary union is increased. In particular, a monetary union that includes more countries is likely to internalize more trade (and in the limit of a single world currency, all trade becomes domestic trade), but it also tends to include a more heterogeneous group of countries.[10]

An important motivation for monetary union in Europe was to reduce the costs of changing money associated with trade and tourism. Trade within African regions tends to be a small proportion of total trade (an exception being the CMA), and the same is true even at the continentwide level. Intra-African trade is modest, so gains for a monetary union deriving from lower transactions costs would necessarily be much smaller than in Europe. Consistent with the gravity model, which posits that a country will trade more with

8. This has been advocated by Honohan and Lane (2000; see chapter 10 for detailed reference) and BIDPA and CSAE (2001).

9. Honohan and Lane (2000) point out that this advantage would be enhanced should the United Kingdom join the euro zone.

10. Thus Alesina and Barro (2002) show that in general neither a world where all countries have independent currencies nor a single world currency is optimal. See also Debrun (2003) for the factors that determine the equilibrium size of currency unions.

Figure 9-2. *Origin and Destination of Africa's Trade, 2000*

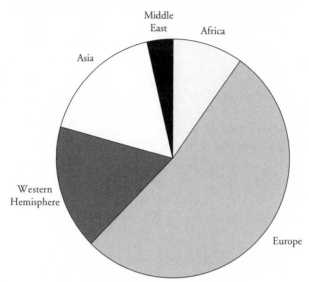

Source: Using exports plus imports from the IMF, Direction of Trade Statistics Yearbook (2002).

countries that have higher per capita incomes, most African trade is conducted with the richer countries of Europe, North America, and Asia and will remain so (see figure 9-2). Thus trade both within African regions and between them is small relative to their trade with the rest of the world (see table 9-1).

A second important reason to create a monetary union may be to improve on the monetary policies provided by national central banks, which have typically fallen prey to pressures to finance government deficits and hence have produced high inflation and depreciating currencies. There may be some advantage to delegating monetary policy to insulate it from pressures to finance governments. However, unless this occurs in the context of a large, stable anchor country (for example, South Africa) or existing multilateral institutions with a track record of independence and sound policies (for example, the West African CFA franc zone's central bank), new institutions are unlikely to provide a durable agency of restraint. Instead, large countries (whose governments exert an important influence over monetary policy actions) will continue to use the central bank as a printing press, directly or indirectly financing their spending. This was the experience before the CFA franc's 1994 devaluation in both western and central African CFA franc zones. Hopefully, reinforced fiscal surveillance and the recent agreement to eliminate completely central bank advances to governments have solved the prob-

Table 9-1. *Bilateral Trade Flows for Regional Economic Communities,*
Averages, 1995–2000[a]

Percent of group 1's total exports

Group 1	Group 2						
	AMU	COMESA	ECCAS	ECOWAS	SADC	EU	Rest of world
AMU	2.74	0.67	0.11	0.45	0.06	71.78	24.19
COMESA	0.77	5.47	0.74	0.19	5.94	41.25	45.64
ECCAS	0.61	0.67	1.89	0.68	0.95	43.76	51.45
ECOWAS	1.01	0.56	1.61	9.08	1.25	37.15	49.34
SADC	0.19	8.28	0.83	0.79	10.28	36.87	42.76

Percent of group 2's total imports

Group 1	Group 2						
	AMU	COMESA	ECCAS	ECOWAS	SADC	EU	Rest of world
AMU	3.00	0.73	0.74	0.69	0.38	1.29	0.26
COMESA	0.50	3.52	2.95	0.17	23.56	0.44	0.29
ECCAS	0.17	0.19	3.26	0.27	1.63	0.20	0.14
ECOWAS	0.77	0.43	7.46	9.62	5.80	0.46	0.36
SADC	0.22	9.77	6.00	1.32	74.72	0.72	0.49

Source: IMF, Direction of Trade Statistics database (2003).
a. Regional trade sums up member countries' bilateral trade (including trade internal to the region).

lem in the CFA franc zone. However, the mere creation of a regional central
bank will not ensure its independence from fiscal policy.[11]

Honohan and Lane provide two other reasons in support of the creation of
African monetary unions: as a bulwark against contagious speculation and a
way of achieving economies of scale in the financial sector. However, they
acknowledge that financial contagion has not been a problem to date because
African currencies do not appear on speculators' radar screens, and perversely
the creation of a common currency might attract more speculative attention.
As for financial sector economies of scale, the two CFA zones provide a mixed
example of this benefit, since even now there is very little cross-border banking
or activity on regional money markets. However, since the banking crisis and
devaluation of the early 1990s, each zone has created a supranational banking
supervisory agency, perhaps achieving some economies of scale in that activity
and distancing supervision from national political pressures.

We now turn to simulations of the strategy of creating a single currency for
Africa from regional monetary unions. Here, in order to rationalize the RECs,

---

11. Honohan and Lane (2000) acknowledge this point, though they argue that regional
monetary unions in principle can provide an agency of restraint.

Table 9-2. *Net Gains of RECs from Single African Countries to Full AU Monetary Union*

Regional entities	Average net gain	Government spending target	Trade with rest of African Union/GDP	Number gaining/ number in region
AMU	−0.0011	0.4420	0.0021	0/3
COMESA	0.0395	0.4848	0.0028	7/7
ECCAS	−0.0128	0.4309	0.0086	0/4
ECOWAS	0.1125	0.5920	0.0135	13/13
SADC	−0.0739	0.3948	0.0091	1/12

Source: Authors' calculations.

we remove overlap by assigning each of the thirty-nine countries in our sample to one or another group. In particular, AMU, ECCAS, and ECOWAS remain with their existing memberships. SADC is assumed to keep its current membership, except for the Democratic Republic of the Congo, which is assumed to be solely a member of ECCAS, and Tanzania, which we assign to COMESA to be with its EAC partners, Kenya and Uganda. The remaining countries are assumed to be members of COMESA.

In considering the formation of a larger monetary union from existing ones, it is natural to consider whether each member country in a REC would gain and also whether on average welfare in the community would increase.[12] If decisions require unanimity, the former would be most relevant, while the latter calculation, if positive, suggests that there may be scope for side payments that could induce the participation of all. Of course, the model, as described in chapter 3, excludes political considerations, which we have emphasized are likely to be important.

Table 9-2 shows the results of the simulations of a single currency for the AU, presenting the proportion of gainers in each REC, the average net welfare gain or loss, the average financing need for the community, correlations with the AU's terms of trade shock, and each community's trade with the rest of the AU as a ratio to REC GDP. Each of the REC monetary unions is assumed to be symmetric, but countries influence the community central bank's monetary policy in proportion to their share of regional GDP.[13] The same is assumed for the AU monetary union, where the region becomes the whole continent.

12. Another alternative would be to look at the situation of the median voter, that is, the country in the middle of the distribution. In practice, in our simulations the median country gains if (and only if) the average change of welfare across all countries in the region is positive (as can be seen from table 9-2, last column).

13. Neither the ECOWAS monetary union nor the others are assumed to benefit from a guaranteed peg to the euro.

The estimates of table 9-2 suggest that only two of the five RECs (ECOWAS and COMESA) in fact would gain on average from a single currency. These are the regions with the highest financing needs as proportions of their GDP. Even within these regions, there would be some losers as well as gainers. In contrast, the regions with more disciplined fiscal policies (AMU, SADC, and ECCAS) would not gain on average. Within SADC, in particular, South Africa (with its large share of the region's GDP) would face a significant welfare loss as a result of the common currency. For all the regions, trade with the rest of the AU is only a small fraction of GDP—typically less than 1 percent— suggesting that the gains from a common currency resulting from a reduction in the temptation for beggar-thy-neighbor depreciations would be very limited. In addition, absent improvements in fiscal discipline that would make the common central bank less subject to pressures to monetize deficits, the single African currency would not deliver low inflation and a stable exchange rate. Hence it would be inferior to some existing currencies, in particular, South Africa's rand.

NEPAD

Monetary arrangements cannot provide solutions to the profound development problems facing many African countries. At best, a monetary regime supported by fiscal discipline and good structural policies can provide a framework for low inflation and stable exchange rates. It cannot guarantee high growth. Thus monetary union should not be seen as a panacea or be driven by a grandiose political vision that hopes to find a symbol of unity and stability when the reality is quite different.

A parallel initiative to the ambitious monetary union project for Africa is NEPAD, whose goal is to promote economic growth and good governance. NEPAD emerged from the efforts of President Thabo Mbeki of South Africa (who proposed the Millennium Partnership for the African Recovery Program), President Abdoulaye Wade of Senegal (Plan Omega), Nigerian president Olusegun Obasanjo, and Algerian president Abdelaziz Bouteflika. The structure of NEPAD consists of an implementation committee of heads of state and government, a steering committee, and a secretariat to oversee the various programs. It starts from the recognition that governance problems are key and that each country must make changes to promote democracy, peace, and stability. Hence it is the responsibility of each African government to put its own house in order, but peer pressure within Africa can help in that process. NEPAD aims to create the conditions within Africa that would make the continent attractive to foreign investors, and it is hoped that the resulting inflows would help in producing sustained development. The NEPAD initiative has received the support of donor countries, and this support was reiterated at the June 2003 G-8 summit in Evian, France. NEPAD's objective to become a driving force for promoting economic growth and prosperity across the continent was emphasized at the July 2003 AU summit in Maputo, Mozambique.

There are four priority areas where actions by African countries are most essential:

—Stop regional conflicts through regional peacekeeping forces and by making concerted regional efforts to prevent armed involvement and material support of rebels by neighboring countries.

—Increase transportation and communication links to stimulate trade and competition as well as to exploit economies of scale.

—Adopt sustainable macroeconomic policies by making currencies convertible and monetary policies consistent with low inflation, reducing budget deficits, and eliminating central bank financing of government spending.

—Promote and attract investment in infrastructure, health, and education by convincing donors and private investors of the ability of African countries to provide a stable, noncorrupt environment based on the rule of law.

This is an ambitious agenda, and it is unrealistic to expect complete success in all four areas. However, NEPAD may contribute to developing a genuine domestic consensus in favor of sound policies in African countries. If so, Africa can get greater benefit from aid flows from donors and maybe increases in those flows. However, if African governments fail to improve governance, they risk getting lower aid flows than in the past, as donors, noting a history of aid ineffectiveness, pull back further.

The NEPAD process has just started. As of May 31, 2003, fifteen African countries had agreed to submit themselves to the APRM, a self-monitoring organization comprised of AU member states. The purpose of the peer review panel, which will have between five and seven members, is to promote the implementation of policies and standards that will lead to political stability, economic growth, development, and integration on a regional and continent-wide level. How the APRM will be applied, however, has yet to be seen. While signals from heads of state are thus far not promising, the appointment of distinguished and respected individuals to the peer review panel is a good sign. Reviews of individual countries are scheduled to begin with Ghana and South Africa.

Conclusions

Africa, like other regions of the world, is fixing its sights on creating a common currency. Already, there are projects for regional monetary unions, and the bidding process for an eventual African central bank is about to begin. Is it worth the effort, and will it provide an important solution to Africa's problems? Most observers judge that those problems are linked to civil conflicts, corruption, an absence of rule of law, undisciplined fiscal policies, poor infrastructure, and low investment—the last of which is due in part to foreign investors' mistrust of African governments. Addressing these problems should allow Africa to gain from globalization and the international trading system. The developed world must also help by opening markets for Africa's goods—in particular, by reducing the subsidies to their own farmers that effectively eliminate the comparative advantage that African farmers would have in production, for instance, of cotton and by providing financial assistance.

Monetary union, in fact, can address very few of Africa's fundamental ills. At best, it can produce low inflation, but it cannot guarantee growth. At worst, it can distract attention from essential issues. This is not to say that regional integration initiatives that aim to improve transportation and communications links, harmonize regulations, and exert peer pressure to improve economic policy and governance are not worthwhile. Improved governance and domestic policies would in turn facilitate regional economic integration, including monetary union. Absence of progress on these issues would almost certainly doom an African monetary union to failure.

10

Africa's Monetary Geography in the Coming Decades

I n the more than forty years since independence, Africa's monetary geography has been transformed. In part this is due to changes to the international environment, which make keeping fixed exchange rates against an external anchor more difficult for African nations (though the CFA franc is still rigidly fixed against the euro). In particular, the generalized move to floating currencies in the early 1970s has meant that now the major currencies (dollar, euro, and yen) fluctuate in value against each other. A peg to one of them means fluctuating against the others, which may make the peg fragile.

We conclude this book by drawing some lessons from the experience since independence and by presenting our views on how Africa's monetary geography may evolve in future decades, an exercise that is more akin to crystal ball gazing than scientific forecasting.

Though the current vogue for monetary union projects in Africa has been influenced by Europe, we have argued in previous chapters that the example of Europe is of limited relevance, as are the standard analytical tools used to assess the costs and benefits of monetary union. Hence we argued that the appropriate framework for considering monetary unions in Africa was one where, in addition to the OCA criteria of symmetry of shocks and factor mobility, the extent to which countries share similar financing needs and are not subject to pressures for spending diversion and corruption makes a big difference for the sustainability of a monetary union. While institutional design is important, it is unlikely that a newly created central bank would be able to assert its independence from fiscal policies. Instead, it would be a dependent central bank, even if not as dependent as a national central bank facing just one treasury. In these circumstances, including in a monetary union, a country with undisciplined fiscal policies (especially if that country were large) would not be attractive.

We used this analytical framework to assess the costs and benefits to countries of various proposed monetary unions, including a single currency for Africa. We concluded that these projects, assuming that they went ahead, would be unlikely to achieve their stated aim of including all countries in a region (or, ultimately, the whole continent). As asserted above, countries with poor fiscal policies make unattractive partners and, if admitted to a monetary union, could threaten its continued existence. Unfortunately, in most regions there are countries that fit this description. The idea that the mere membership in a monetary union would curb such fiscal indiscipline is implausible. More promising, however, is the use of union membership as a carrot to induce countries to rein in deficits and make fundamental structural adjustments. Such a use of peer pressure is consistent with the principles of NEPAD and could augment the effectiveness of the latter process. It is, however, inconsistent with the idea that creating an inclusive monetary union will induce countries to modify their behavior and, as is said, get religion. And strong use of the carrot of membership is almost sure to mean that some countries would not qualify.

If the current projects for monetary unions based on regional economic communities do not bear fruit, nor lead to a single currency by the target date of 2021, what will the monetary geography of Africa look like in twenty or so years? An important issue in this context is whether currencies (national or supranational) are fixed or float, or do something in between. This boils down to a choice between an external anchor and domestic target for monetary policy. We consider the international environment's important influence on this choice, as well as how the domestic context for policymaking may evolve.

International Environment

For the past thirty years, exchange rates of the major international currencies have fluctuated with respect to each other, generally without much intervention, despite occasional periods of coordination.[1] This has made it difficult for countries with trade that is diversified geographically to peg to a single international currency, since fluctuations of dollar, euro, and yen exchange rates have

---

1. Such as a result of the Plaza Agreement and Louvre Accord in 1985–87.

been substantial and have produced large fluctuations in competitiveness for countries with a single country peg. Basket pegs, with weights given to the various currencies that reflect the importance of trade linkages, are a possible solution to this problem but only an imperfect one: basket pegs are not very transparent and in practice are often changed, so that this regime tends to resemble more closely managed floating than a fixed peg.

It seems likely that this international environment of fluctuations among the major currencies will continue. These three currency blocs are closed enough that they do not suffer too much from exchange rate volatility (induced by speculative shifts, for instance), while they benefit from the possibility of varying their monetary policies to accord with different domestic economic fluctuations. In practice, the inflation pressures and business cycles affecting these economies have not been the same, and hence their central banks have appropriately moved interest rates in ways that have temporarily opened up differentials in favor of one or another bloc, and exchange rates have tended to fluctuate accordingly. Since average inflation has not been very different, however, there has been little trend to their exchange rates, at least over the last decade and a half.

This feature of the international monetary system argues for some flexibility of African currencies, at least for countries that do not have very strong economic linkages with one or another of the currency blocs. Though the regions in Africa trade most with Europe, that proportion is typically at most 50 percent or so, leaving them exposed to other currency fluctuations. While the creation of the euro and prospects for its expansion would make a euro peg an attractive proposition for some countries, this is not true for all. In particular, the oil-exporting countries (Angola, Gabon, and Nigeria, among others) would probably not want to peg to the euro but instead allow the value of their currencies to be influenced by the price of oil. South Africa, like other emerging market economies with a high level of financial development, will continue to benefit from flexibility with respect to all the major currencies.

A second important influence on the future evolution of African currency regimes concerns European attitudes toward the CFA franc zone and other pegs to the euro. At present, EU countries are reticent, not to say opposed, to committing resources to assist non-EU countries to peg to the euro. The main exception is France, which of course continues its involvement with the CFA franc zone.[2] However, if the ECOWAS monetary union goes ahead, then France would need to get the accord of its EU partners to continue to provide overdraft privileges and a convertibility guarantee—assuming that France wanted to do so. If instead a decision were taken by the EU to favor exchange

2. Portugal assists in the Cape Verde escudo's peg to the euro.

rate stability of African currencies against the euro, the EU institutions could take over from the French Treasury in this regard. Doing so, of course, would favor the continued fixed peg of the CFA franc to the euro and might also favor the creation of other monetary unions or currency boards with euro pegs.

On balance, this possibility does not seem very likely. Economic advantages to Europe seem small, since trade with Africa is only a small proportion of Europe's exports or imports. While the international use of Europe's currency would be increased somewhat, this is not generally viewed as an objective of policy. On the contrary, Germany and Japan have at times tried to discourage the international use of their currencies. It is also not clear whether any political benefits (for example, evidence of Europe's generosity or its larger sphere of influence) would offset political costs (charges of neocolonialism).

What would this mean for the CFA franc zone? It seems quite possible, in our view, that in twenty years the zone will no longer exist in its current form. While there may well be a currency union, perhaps with additional members, it seems more likely that the CFA franc will no longer be pegged to the euro with the help of France. This would then raise the issue of what would guide monetary policy in the CFA franc zones—a general issue of the exchange rate and monetary policy regime.

Hollowing out Exchange Rate Regimes

Advocates of the hollowing out hypothesis argue that the increase in capital mobility that has occurred as a result of liberalization and technological advances (and, by implication, will continue) would tend to make intermediate exchange rate regimes (for instance, adjustable pegs, bands, or dirty floating) disappear in favor of the polar cases of hard fixes (monetary unions or currency boards) or free floats.[3] They point out that industrial countries mainly have moved to the poles, as the result of speculative crises leading to the breakdown of the Bretton Woods regime of adjustable pegs or the European monetary system's narrow bands around central parities. These crises have shown the lack of credibility associated with such pegs, which are not viewed as irrevocable unless institutions are in place to make them extremely difficult to change. The example of Argentina shows that even currency boards may not be sufficiently hard, so that the elimination of one's currency by adopting another may be required in order to prove irrevocability.[4] While the EU countries have chosen the hard

3. Eichengreen (1994); Obstfeld and Rogoff (1995); Fischer (2001).
4. Even though the adoption of another currency might not be irrevocable, financial instruments would not be readily available to speculate against it.

pole, the other advanced countries have mainly chosen to float their currencies with little intervention. The hollowing out hypothesis, if true, would have important implications for the exchange rate regime choice of African countries. It might tend to reinforce the momentum in favor of monetary unions, especially if countries did not want to accept the volatility of freely floating exchange rates (which, as Calvo and Reinhart show, is evident in the behavior of most developing countries).[5]

However, the implications for Africa are not nearly that stark. First, as Frankel points out, while it is generally accepted that financial market integration, monetary independence, and pegged exchange rates are incompatible, it is still possible to trade off some monetary independence for some exchange rate flexibility without going to the polar cases.[6] Moreover, countries may choose not to fully integrate into world financial markets. In the presence of imperfect capital mobility, adjustable pegs and other intermediate exchange rate regimes are much easier to maintain. Many African countries, including the most financially developed, South Africa, maintain some sort of capital controls.[7] Speculative capital flows in sufficient volume to swamp countries' foreign exchange reserves require that financial instruments be available to take positions against the currency. Otherwise, capital mobility is limited. Many African countries have very little debt that is traded on financial markets that could be potentially held (and sold) by foreign investors, nor do foreign investors have the possibility of borrowing domestically or trading derivative instruments in the currency. Hence most African currencies (with the single exception of the rand) are not on investors' radar screens and have not been affected by the speculative crises affecting other developing countries.[8] Third, some intermediate regimes may be immune even if capital mobility is high, if they do not give one-way bets to speculators, for example, by guaranteeing a rate, come what may. For instance, dirty floating, smoothing of exchange rate fluctuations, or adjustable pegs and bands may not exacerbate speculative behavior if the monetary authorities show sufficient willingness to modify their targets for the rate. Of course, such regimes are also unlikely to deliver as much exchange rate stability.

5. They typically moderate exchange rate volatility through foreign exchange market intervention rather than floating freely. Calvo and Reinhart (2002).

6. Frankel (1999).

7. Though such controls were not sufficient in South Africa's case to prevent speculation and substantial depreciation of the rand. Consequently, the South African authorities have moved in the late 1990s to a more flexible system, and have also loosened capital controls recently, while the currency has strengthened.

8. Honohan and Lane (2000).

There is, in fact, little evidence for hollowing out in the data on exchange rate regimes of developing countries, even allowing for the fact that countries' official, or de jure, classification often differs from what they actually do.[9] While this may reflect much less advanced financial development than in the industrial countries, so that the changes seen in the latter will affect the former at some later date, it does not seem obvious that this is inevitable. Instead, choices among exchange rate regimes are likely to remain for African countries, at least for the next few decades.

Domestic versus External Anchors

We have ignored so far an important choice, both for countries with independent currencies and for monetary unions themselves, which is the choice of the target or anchor for monetary policies. While the CFA franc zone has maintained its external anchor, that is, its peg to the euro, other countries have, in parallel with moves to greater exchange rate flexibility, shifted to domestic monetary anchors, typically some monetary or credit aggregate (often in the context of IMF-supported programs). While it is beyond the scope of this book to review the use of domestic monetary or inflation anchors in Africa, the experience of other developing countries, as well as industrial countries, suggests that African countries may increasingly adopt inflation targeting. At present, South Africa is the only country that has adopted an explicit inflation-targeting regime for monetary policy, and moreover that adoption was recent and details of its implementation are still evolving (see chapter 4). It seems likely, nevertheless, that countries with developed financial markets, liberalized prices, and absence of fiscal dominance may want to follow suit.[10]

In the CFA franc zone, the peg to the French franc, and now the euro, has been maintained with the financial assistance of the French Treasury. If that assistance did not continue (for reasons that have been discussed in chapter 6, for instance), WAEMU, CAEMC, or both would have to consider the choice between maintaining the exchange rate peg to the euro by using their own reserves, moving to an intermediate arrangement where the euro peg (or other peg, for instance, to a basket) was one (but perhaps not the sole) variable guiding monetary policy, and, a domestic target.

Maintaining a rigid peg without other institutional changes might be difficult, even with comfortable reserve cover, as is currently the case for the

9. Masson (2001).

10. See Eichengreen and others (1999) for a discussion of the prerequisites for inflation targeting.

CFA franc zones. Capital mobility is likely to increase in the absence of explicit attempts to limit it, and a currency circulating in a wide area might well appear on the radar screens of speculators. An alternative to harden the peg would be to create an explicit currency board based on the euro, which would force automatic contraction or expansion of the money supply in response to reserve outflows and inflows. This would give some extra guarantee that monetary policy would be adjusted appropriately for the maintenance of the peg. The case of Argentina shows the limitations of this approach, however. Without support from other policies, the strain on the parity may be too great to bear.

Given a degree of independence of the central bank from fiscal authorities, as is the case to some extent for both the BCEAO (the central bank of WAEMU) and the BEAC (the central bank of CAEMC), a less constraining and more sustainable regime would be an intermediate regime where the value of the currency vis-à-vis a basket of international currencies guided monetary policy, but some weight was also given to domestic inflation and economic activity. A natural basket would give equal weights to the dollar and euro, and such a compromise would facilitate monetary cooperation within ECOWAS, given the extent of Nigeria's dollar-based trade. The commitment to the basket peg could be deliberately vague to remove the perception of one-way bets, and yet considerable attention could still be paid to the external value of the currency. Such a regime might either be a transition to an inflation-targeting regime (as in practice it proved to be in Israel and Chile)[11] or might instead be intended to be permanent.

Africa's Role in the Global Economy, 2025

To succeed with regional (and monetary) integration, Africa must succeed in stopping conflicts, promoting the rule of law, reducing corruption, and achieving sustainable macroeconomic policies. If so, one can imagine that Africa could develop around some dynamic regional economies—South Africa, Nigeria, Kenya, Algeria, and Cameroon, among others—and that regional integration would proceed to link countries within these regions in a way that exploited economies of scale. What will Africa's trade arrangements be with the rest of the world? It is plausible that, as in Asia at a similar stage of development, Africa in twenty years would still try to use trade barriers to protect domestic markets and develop a manufacturing sector. Nevertheless, many countries would likely use export-processing zones as tools for develop-

11. See the discussion in Eichengreen and others (1999).

ment, plugging themselves into the global economy without being fully exposed to its competitive winds.

What is likely to be the situation for Africa's currencies? In purely economic terms, Africa is unlikely to benefit from having its own, single currency rather than adopting a widely used international currency (the dollar or the euro). When the political enthusiasm for an African currency abates, different regions are likely to choose different solutions. North Africa may well peg to (or adopt) the euro, as ties with the EU will continue to strengthen. The CFA franc zone will probably not exist in its current form. The countries concerned may move to use the euro, or to be linked to it with EU support, but this will depend very much on Europe. The likelier alternative is a regional currency with a regime of managed floating against the euro or a basket of currencies. The difficult challenge will be to generate enough monetary discipline to ensure that such a currency is stable, as will also be true of East Africa, if a common currency is introduced there. In southern Africa, the area based on the rand, the continent's only floating hard currency, is likely to have expanded. But it will not form the nucleus for a pan-African currency, because Africa is too diverse in its export commodities and financial development. So African economic integration is likely to continue to fall far short of a continentwide monetary union. But this should not prevent progress in economic development and in the many other dimensions of cooperation among African countries.

A

Calibration of the Model

The main elements of the model used to evaluate monetary integration projects are:

—a Barro-Gordon supply equation or expectations-augmented Phillips curve extended to include international spillovers from neighbors' monetary policies;

—the government's budget constraint;

—and an assumed objective function for the government.[1]

In a country with its own currency, the government is assumed to exert control over the central bank, so that the former chooses both the monetary and fiscal policy instruments to maximize an objective function that depends linearly on output and depends negatively on squared deviations of inflation from a target that reflects supply shocks, of government spending from its target, and of tax rates from an implicit target of zero. In a monetary union, the central bank is assumed to maximize a weighted average of the member countries' objective functions (where weights reflect relative GDP levels), while each government of a member of the union chooses its own fiscal policy. In each

---

1. The model is described in more detail in Debrun, Masson, and Pattillo (2002, 2004). In that earlier work, which was specific to West Africa, we applied a different calibration and our estimates of resource diversion were also different. Here we are able to draw on a larger database of African countries. Nevertheless, conclusions concerning ECOWAS (see chapter 6) are similar to those we reached before.

case, governments satisfy a one-period budget constraint that forces spending to be financed either by taxes or by the country's share of seigniorage (again, in a monetary union this is assumed to be divided up using GDP shares).

The building blocks of the model are thus the following equations:

Supply equation:

$$y_i = c(\pi_i - \pi_i^e - \tau_i) - \sum_{k \neq i, k=1}^{n} \theta_{i,k} c(\pi_k - \pi_k^e) + \varepsilon_i, \, i = 1, \ldots, n \qquad (1)$$

where

y_i: output
τ_i: a tax rate
π_i: inflation
ε_i: a supply shock.

Government budget constraint:

$$g_i = \mu \pi_i + \tau_i - \delta_i, \qquad (2)$$

where

g_i: ratio of government spending to GDP
μ: the inflation tax base
δ_i: a distortion that shows up in increased government spending for nonproductive uses or reduced tax revenues, due to diversion.

Government objective function:

$$U_i^G = \frac{1}{2} \left\{ -a[\pi_i - \tilde{\pi}(\varepsilon_i)]^2 - b\tau_i^2 - \gamma(g_i - \tilde{g}_i)^2 \right\} + y_i \qquad (3)$$

where $\tilde{\pi}$ and $\tilde{g}$ are targets for inflation and government spending, respectively. Note that only nondistorted spending g_i affects utility, while the government's budget constraint reflects an additional drain on the budget due to diversion δ_i.

A monetary union affects the scope for monetary expansion to stimulate output, since one channel for its effect, namely, depreciation of the exchange rate, is limited because countries cannot depreciate against other members of the union. Thus the proportion of trade that is internalized by the monetary union is an important parameter: the greater it is, the lower is the incentive to stimulate output beyond its potential through monetary expansion. As in the Barro-Gordon model, this temptation is self-defeating since its systematic use produces needless inflation without stimulating output. However, we retain a stabilization role for monetary policy so that there is some value to retaining monetary policy discretion—it is not always better to tie the hands of the monetary authorities through membership in a monetary union. Specifically, we assume $\tilde{\pi}(\varepsilon) = -\eta\varepsilon$, that is, that the inflation target is proportional to the (negative of the) supply shock.

A key linkage in the model is the effect of spending targets on inflation and taxes, since higher spending needs to be financed in one way or the other. Membership in a monetary union moderates the influence of a country's spending target on inflation when compared to a regime with an independent currency. In reality, spending (as ratio to GDP) differs across countries for various reasons. Countries with higher per capita incomes can generally afford to offer more government services, as both revenues and spending rise in tandem, and this component causes no problem for inflation. Thus we estimate the relationship to per capita income of revenues and spending together, and evaluate spending at an average level of per capita GDP (across all African countries in our sample). However, governments may have spending targets greater than the average, and they may put pressure on inflation since tax revenues are unlikely to rise in tandem. Furthermore, there may be diversion of tax revenues and spending to favor government supporters due to weak institutions. This distortion is also unlikely to be matched by higher tax revenues so that it would put pressure on the central bank to generate higher inflation and seigniorage. We label the sum of target government spending (evaluated at average GDP) and the distortion δ the financing need (FN).

The model implies that inflation π and tax revenues τ (as a ratio to GDP) will be determined differently in countries with independent currencies compared to those that are members of a monetary union.

In particular, we can summarize the model as follows:

$$\pi_i = \frac{\gamma\mu b}{\Lambda} FN_{Ai} + \frac{\gamma(1+\mu)+b}{\Lambda} - \frac{b+\gamma}{\Lambda}\theta_{Ai} - \frac{\eta a(b+\gamma)}{\Lambda}\varepsilon_{Ai}, \quad (4)$$

$$\tau_i = \frac{a\gamma}{\Lambda} FN_i + \frac{\gamma^2\mu^2 b}{(b+\gamma)\Lambda}(FN_i - FN_{Ai}) - \frac{a+\gamma\mu(1+\mu)}{\Lambda}$$

$$+ \frac{\gamma\mu}{\Lambda}\theta_{Ai} + \frac{\eta\gamma\mu a}{\Lambda}\varepsilon_{Ai}, \quad (5)$$

where

FN_i: country i's financing need

FN_{Ai}: the average over the financing needs for the monetary union of which i is a member (or equal to FN_i for a country not in a monetary union)

θ_{Ai}: the proportion of trade internalized by the monetary union (or zero for a country not in a monetary union)

Table A-1. *Estimates of Spending and Revenue Ratios as Functions of per Capita Income*

	Coefficient	Standard error
g_0	.1774154	.0133362*
g_1	.1078046	.0243236*
g_2	−.0181573	.0062355*
$\log(\sigma_u)$	−2.956680	.1313506*
$\log(\sigma_v)$	−2.765808	.1313506*

Source: Authors' calculations.
*Significant at the 1 percent level.

ε_{Ai}: the average over the supply shocks in the monetary union (or the country's own shock, if not in a monetary union)

a, b, γ, μ, η: positive parameters

$\Lambda = a(b + \gamma) + \gamma\mu^2 b > 0$.

We use equations 4 and 5 above to derive the parameter values, noting that the third term in the inflation equation and the second and fourth terms in the tax equation are zero for countries that are not in a monetary union.

The first step requires an estimate for the spending targets. We note that spending and revenues tend to rise with per capita incomes. Since this part does not put financing pressures on the central bank, we remove its effect from both series by evaluating them at the average (weighted by GDP) per capita income across our sample of thirty-two countries for which we have complete data (which equaled $1,759 in 1995–2000).[2]

Estimating a quadratic function of per capita income confirms the positive relationship, which flattens out as income rises. Table A-1 gives maximum likelihood estimates of

$$\left(\frac{g_i}{\tau_i}\right) = g_0 + g_1 y_i + g_2 y_i^2 + \left(\frac{u_i}{v_i}\right). \qquad (6)$$

Spending and revenue ratios are decimal fractions, while per capita income is in thousands of dollars. The quadratic implies that the maximum tax or spending ratio is reached at a per capita income of about $3,000 (see figure A-1). We label the spending and tax ratios purged of the per capita income effect, that is, predicted values at average per capita income $\bar{y} = 1.759$ plus the residuals from the above equations, as $\bar{g}_i$ and $\bar{\tau}_i$, respectively:

2. Table A-2 includes data for thirty-four countries, but Angola and the Democratic Republic of the Congo have poor data resulting from high inflation and periods of civil war and were excluded from our calibration.

Figure A-1. *Government Spending and Revenues*

Percent of GDP

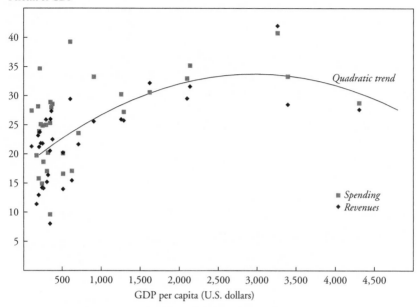

GDP per capita (U.S. dollars)

Source: World Bank, African Development Indicators database (2002).

$$\left(\frac{\bar{g}_i}{\tau_i}\right) = g_0 + g_1\bar{y} + g_2\bar{y}^2 + \left(\frac{u_i}{v_i}\right). \tag{7}$$

The next step concerns estimating the unobservable component of financing needs that corresponds to distortions leading to overspending and diversion of taxes. A practical difficulty here is that politically motivated outlays also divert resources from socially desirable projects rather than come on top of them. As a result, actual budget figures are more likely to reflect undercollection of taxes and underspending on such social priorities as health and education instead of overspending. To reconcile this feature of the data with the model's assumption, as in Debrun, Masson, and Pattillo, we assume a mapping from the extent of actual resource diversion (viewed as underspending on priority sectors) to the overspending bias affecting the model's unobservable financing needs.[3]

We proceed in five steps to assess spending distortions in each country. First, we estimate the impact of institutional quality on health and education outlays (socially desirable expenditure), using cross-sectional regressions

3. Debrun, Masson, and Pattillo (2004).

of the latter on indexes of institutional quality and corruption and control variables, including GDP per capita.[4] The corruption and institutional quality measures are taken from other studies.[5] Second, the estimated equations allow us to calculate hypothetical outlays one would observe in the absence of institutional imperfection, that is, in the case where institutional indexes would be at their maximum value. Third, any underspending bias is interpreted as the amount of resources diverted from socially desirable goals because of institutional failures. Fourth, we calculate a diversion wedge as the difference between actual and calculated outlays on priority sectors as a percentage of the hypothetical amounts. Fifth, we assume that this diversion wedge can be applied to all of GDP and add it to actual spending levels (evaluated at mean per capita income) to produce our estimate of financing needs, FN.

Table A-2 presents the estimates of diversion from health and education spending obtained using this methodology as well as the underlying data on institutional quality. To be conservative, we halve the percentage diversion and add this to the estimates of government spending evaluated at average per capita income calculated earlier (table A-1). This gives us our financing needs with systematic effects of per capita income removed, reported in table A-3, along with actual government revenue and expenditure data, rates of inflation, and the calculated values for $\bar{g}_i$ as defined in equation 7. We augment the set of thirty-four countries with diversion estimates for five additional countries, which will be important when studying monetary unions, based on figures for neighboring countries with similar rates of inflation.

The estimate of μ, which is the size of the inflation tax base, is important because it affects the ability to finance the government using seigniorage. The budget constraint each country faces is given by equation 2 above. The model assumes the same parameter for all countries, and we calculate it by a GDP-weighted sum over the thirty-two core countries in our sample in table A-3:

$$\hat{\mu} = \frac{\sum \omega_i (g_i - \tau_i)}{\sum \omega_i \pi_i} = 0.481. \tag{8}$$

Another important parameter is the trade that is internalized by the monetary union. The monetary unions that are present in our African data are the two CFA zones and the CMA. The CFA franc zones (CAEMC and WAEMU) have the particularity that their common parity is fixed in terms of the euro (fol-

---

4. See Gupta, Honjo, and Verhoeven (1997), and Gupta, Davoodi, and Tiong (2000).

5. International Country Risk Guide (ICRG), produced by PRS Group (www.icrgonline. com); Kaufmann, Kraay, and Zoido-Lobaton (1999).

Table A-2. *Expenditure on Priority Sectors: Estimates of the Diversion Effect, 1999*[a]

Country	ICRG institutional quality index	Health Actual	Health No diversion	Education Actual	Education No diversion	Diversion in percent of no diversion spending
Algeria	4.88	3.3	4.4	n.a.	n.a.	25.1
Angola	4.20	3.9	5.2	n.a.	n.a.	25.5
Botswana	6.51	2.4	3.3	4.0	4.6	18.3
Burkina Faso	4.31	1.2	2.6	2.0	2.9	42.2
Cameroon	5.09	1.0	2.4	n.a.	n.a.	57.6
Congo, Republic of the	4.23	1.8	3.0	6.1	7.0	20.9
Côte d'Ivoire	5.53	1.2	2.3	5.5	6.2	21.5
Democratic Republic of the Congo	1.96	1.2	3.3	n.a.	n.a.	63.4
Egypt	5.61	1.8	2.9	n.a.	n.a.	37.4
Ethiopia	3.56	1.4	2.9	2.7	3.7	37.9
Gabon	4.99	1.9	3.4	n.a.	n.a.	43.4
Gambia, the	5.62	1.6	2.6	2.6	3.2	29.3
Ghana	5.56	1.4	2.7	n.a.	n.a.	47.7
Guinea	4.59	2.1	3.3	1.6	2.4	35.7
Guinea-Bissau	2.59	1.1	2.9	n.a.	n.a.	62.7
Kenya	5.69	n.a.	3.5	n.a.	6.0	19.0
Madagascar	4.95	2.4	2.0	5.3	3.4	31.5
Malawi	4.13	n.a.	4.7	n.a.	3.3	28.9
Mali	3.42	1.1	3.4	2.6	3.2	38.2
Morocco	5.64	3.3	2.7	2.4	5.3	26.0
Mozambique	4.77	1.9	3.0	2.2	2.2	38.9
Namibia	7.07	1.3	4.8	4.6	8.3	9.3
Niger	3.96	1.8	2.8	1.4	n.a.	49.9
Nigeria	4.20	4.0	2.4	7.8	n.a.	70.6
Senegal	5.27	1.4	3.6	n.a.	4.3	21.6
Sierra Leone	2.98	0.7	2.7	n.a.	2.2	57.6
South Africa	7.07	2.6	3.8	3.6	6.8	9.1
Sudan	2.66	1	2.6	1.1	1.9	67.1
Tanzania	5.14	n.a.	2.3	n.a.	3.4	34.1
Togo	3.41	3.3	2.8	6.3	5.2	34.0
Tunisia	5.53	0.7	3.4	0.8	5.9	21.0
Uganda	4.06	1.1	3.3	2.6	4.4	32.1
Zambia	4.47	1.1	4.5	4.2	3.1	25.9
Zimbabwe	5.60	2.2	4.1	5.2	7.3	16.3

Source: World Bank, African Development Indicators database (2002); www.icrgonline.com (2003).

a. The health expenditure regression includes a constant, the log of GDP per capita at PPP (average, 1990–97), an index of institutional quality (simple average of ICRG indexes for political stability, democratic accountability, and corruption, ranging from 0 to 10, with higher numbers indicating better institutions), a dummy identifying countries with HIV/AIDS prevalence rate above 10 percent, life expectancy, and infant mortality. The sample consists of thirty-four African countries and estimates were obtained by ordinary least squares. The education expenditure regression includes a constant, the log of GDP per capita at PPP (average, 1984–98), illiteracy and an interaction variable between illiteracy and institutional quality (simple average of ICRG indexes for political stability, democratic accountability, corruption, rule of law, and bureaucratic quality). Here, the sample only consists of twenty-four African countries due to missing data.

n.a. = Not available.

Table A-3. *Selected Indicators, Averages, 1995–2000*

Percent of GDP, unless noted otherwise

Country	Government revenue[a]	Government spending	Overall surplus/deficit[a]	Inflation (percent)	GDP per capita (current U.S. dollars)	Government spending at average income	Diversion	Financing need[b]
Algeria	32.18	30.60	1.57	10.4	1,621	31.25	25.06	43.78
Angola	44.29	57.12	−12.83	1,271.4	586	64.77	25.50	77.52
Benin[c]	19.08	19.48	−0.40	5.6	370	29.09	34.57	46.37
Botswana	42.02	40.79	1.23	9.9	3,262	38.29	18.33	47.45
Burkina Faso	21.82	25.12	−3.29	3.1	222	36.16	42.21	57.26
Cameroon	15.45	17.09	−1.64	6.9	626	24.40	57.63	53.21
Côte d'Ivoire	21.64	23.58	−1.94	3.9	711	30.18	21.51	40.93
Democratic Republic of the Congo	25.60	33.24	−7.63	6.2	904	38.32	20.94	48.79
Egypt	25.78	27.24	−1.46	5.5	1,291	29.70	37.36	48.38
Ethiopia	21.28	27.44	−6.16	3.3	104	39.69	37.91	58.64
Gabon	27.67	28.80	−1.13	2.1	4,305	29.38	43.39	51.07
Gambia, the	20.53	25.33	−4.80	2.6	343	35.19	29.33	49.85
Ghana	22.50	28.60	−6.10	31.8	374	38.17	47.70	62.02
Guinea	13.99	16.60	−2.61	4.5	512	24.90	35.71	42.75
Guinea-Bissau	23.75	34.66	−10.91	27.6	210	45.83	62.68	77.17
Kenya	27.37	28.01	−0.65	6.6	359	37.72	19.00	47.22
Lesotho[d]	46.00	47.00	−1.00	7.8	459	55.78	12.26	61.91

Madagascar	14.11	18.64	−4.53	16.9	257	29.34	31.46	45.07
Malawi	23.17	28.18	−5.01	38.5	187	39.58	28.92	54.04
Mali	21.77	24.88	−3.11	3.4	246	35.69	38.16	54.77
Mauritius[d]	20.81	25.88	−5.07	6.1	3,620	24.00	12.26	30.13
Morocco	25.95	30.25	−4.30	2.6	1,256	32.92	25.98	45.91
Mozambique	21.18	23.89	−2.71	20.3	200	35.16	38.85	54.58
Namibia	31.58	35.18	−3.59	8.5	2,136	33.78	9.34	38.45
Niger	12.95	15.78	−2.83	4.0	195	27.10	49.94	52.07
Nigeria	25.90	25.00	0.90	22.4	290	35.37	70.57	70.65
Senegal	20.21	20.11	0.10	2.6	511	28.43	21.61	39.23
Seychelles[d]	45.11	56.64	−11.53	2.0	7,416	89.90	12.26	96.03
Sierra Leone	11.41	19.73	−8.32	22.1	167	31.33	57.61	60.13
South Africa	28.52	33.31	−4.78	7.0	3,393	30.98	9.12	35.54
Sudan	8.04	9.61	−1.57	60.7	342	19.48	67.06	53.01
Swaziland[d]	29.89	30.39	−0.50	8.7	1,370	32.38	12.26	38.51
Tanzania	14.22	14.91	−0.69	17.5	238	25.80	34.11	42.85
Togo	16.38	20.19	−3.81	4.7	317	30.31	33.99	47.30
Tunisia	29.54	32.97	−3.42	3.7	2,098	31.69	20.96	42.17
Uganda	15.19	17.03	−1.84	5.5	302	27.30	32.14	43.37
Zambia	26.00	28.91	−2.91	30.6	349	38.72	25.94	51.69
Zimbabwe	29.44	39.25	−9.81	34.4	604	46.75	16.34	54.92

Sources: World Bank, African Development Indicators database (2002); and calculations reported in table A-2.

a. Including grants.

b. Government spending at average income plus half of diversion.

c. Diversion estimate for Benin is calculated as the average for other WAEMU countries (excluding Guinea-Bissau).

d. Diversion estimate for Lesotho, Mauritius, Seychelles, and Swaziland is calculated as the average for Botswana, Namibia, and South Africa.

lowing the replacement of the French franc by the single European currency); this limits the scope for a monetary expansion by the BCEAO and the BEAC to stimulate output, since the exchange rate cannot depreciate against the euro.[6] Our parameterization is based on the amount of trade that is conducted at the CFA franc's fixed parity: the high value for the ratio of exports to both CFA franc zones and the euro zone as a ratio of the region's GDP, θ_A, implies limited scope for monetary independence. It can be seen that for both WAEMU and CAEMC, exports to CFA franc and euro zone countries divided by GDP exceed one-eighth. The CMA, in contrast, is based on a floating rand; therefore, its value for internalized trade is much lower. Estimates, based on 2000 data, are WAEMU, 0.1256; CAEMC, 0.1652; and the CMA, 0.0605.

With these preparations, we can use equations 4 and 5 above to estimate the other parameters. In particular, for the thirty-two countries for which we have spending targets, we estimate these two equations using the method of seemingly unrelated regression (or SUR). Estimates of coefficients accompanied by t-ratios, in brackets, are given below:

$$\pi_i = -0.2302 + 0.7985 FN_{\theta Ai} - 0.40326\theta_{Ai} + \varepsilon_{\pi i}. \tag{9}$$
$$(1.63) \quad (2.83) \quad\quad (2.04) \quad\quad\quad R - sq = 0.288$$

$$\bar{\tau}_i = 0.2005 + 0.2016 FN_i - 0.0897\theta_{Ai} + 0.0416(FN_i - FN_{Ai}) + \varepsilon_{\tau i}. \tag{10}$$
$$(3.48) \quad (1.75) \quad\quad (1.12) \quad\quad (0.26) \quad\quad R - sq = 0.146$$

Consistent with the model, financing needs (evaluated at mean per capita income and averaged over members of a monetary union) have a strong impact on inflation, while being a member of a monetary union significantly reduces inflation. Estimation of the tax equation, equation 10, also gives results that are consistent with theory (the constant terms in each case are dependent on normalization of revenues and spending and can have either sign): higher financing needs lead to higher taxes while within a monetary union the higher-financing-need countries relative to the average show an even higher tax rate. Because the monetary policy reflects the average financing need, inflation is lower than optimum for high-financing-need countries,

---

6. Our treatment here also differs from that in Debrun, Masson, and Pattillo (2002, 2004), where we ignored the fixed parity. It is still possible to have a different monetary policy in the CFA franc zone than in the euro zone, because capital mobility is not perfect, and moreover the French Treasury guarantees the parity through the potentially unlimited support provided by its operations account. In practice, the scope for monetary independence is clearly limited, and there are institutional checks on that independence when reserves of the CFA franc countries fall too low.

meaning that tax revenues there need to be increased further. The latter effect is not significant, however. The coefficient of θ_A, which theory says should be positive, in our estimates is negative.

We use the coefficients with the correct signs in the two equations to estimate the parameters a, b, and γ. In particular, if we call a_1, a_2, b_1, and b_3 the relevant coefficient estimates from equations 9 and 10, and equate them to the corresponding expressions in equations 4 and 5, we can derive

$$\hat{a} = \frac{\hat{\mu}a_1 b_1}{a_2 b_3}, \hat{b} = \frac{a_1^2}{a_2 b_3} \text{ and } \hat{\gamma} = \frac{a_1^2}{a_1 a_2 \hat{\mu} - a_2 b_3}.$$

The resulting estimates are given below:

Parameter	First estimate	Final estimate
a	4.620711	0.9569204
b	38.0491	7.87973
γ	4.617129	8.623756

The estimates of a and b are not well determined because the denominator is close to zero. If we increase the value of the coefficient b_3 by one standard error, then the denominator increases away from zero, yielding estimates that seem more sensible and much closer to that obtained in an earlier paper using a different methodology.[7] We adopt them as our final estimates here. In that paper, we also examined the sensitivity of evaluations of the net benefits of monetary union to changes in the parameters and concluded that those evaluations were reasonably robust to changes within the range of estimates given above.

Finally, the value of η captures the stabilization role for monetary policy. We normalize this parameter to unity, meaning that a negative supply shock (that is, terms of trade shock) leads to an equal percentage point increase in the target for inflation.

7. Debrun, Masson, and Pattillo (2002).

B

Country Vignettes

In lieu of comprehensive individualized coverage, this appendix describes several categories of countries that have undergone periods during which, for similar reasons, exchange rate policies were a key macroeconomic issue.[1] In a few cases, the country vignettes discuss differences of opinion between the IMF and country authorities on exchange rate policies. As the IMF is the primary international organization advising on exchange rates, these instances again highlight important (sometimes controversial) issues, including the appropriate degree of flexibility, sterilization of capital inflows, controls versus using other policies in addressing balance of payment pressures, and the appropriate level of the exchange rate for competitiveness.

Underdeveloped Financial Sectors: Problems Operating a Flexible Rate

Underdeveloped financial systems (of which state-dominated banking systems are the most extreme example) make it difficult for countries to efficiently operate flexible exchange rate systems.

1. The only flexible rate countries not covered are selected war-torn countries (Rwanda, Sierra Leone, and Somalia), as well as a few others (Guinea-Bissau, flexible from 1983 to 1997, when it joined WAEMU; Malawi; Mauritania; and São Tomé and Principe). South Africa was discussed in detail in chapters 2 and 4.

Financial Systems' Structural Weaknesses

The Gambian economy has had ups and downs since the beginning of the Economic Recovery Program in 1986, but the market-based flexible exchange rate is generally viewed as having served the economy well. However, while the system has had some favorable macroeconomic effects, as in many African countries an underdeveloped financial sector continues to limit efficient operation of the exchange market. Thus we use the Gambia to highlight the institutional difficulties of operating a flexible exchange rate system in a financial sector with limited competition and large structural problems. While the system operates through an interbank market, by the late 1990s activity in the market was still limited as authorized dealers avoided revealing their financial positions to each other and rarely dealt among themselves. Instead, dealers preferred to deal with the central bank or sometimes with the parallel market. (Some improvement was registered by 2002.) Spreads of 3 to 5 percent between the interbank and parallel market (the foreign exchange bureaus that transact mainly in cash) reflected limited competition in the interbank market and the efficiency of the informal market. Although the market has been liberalized, there is a prudential limit on the amount of foreign exchange that commercial banks can hold, which sometimes makes banks dependent on short-term credit from their overseas partners or parents in order to meet the demand for foreign exchange.[2] Foreign exchange transactions' costs are high, and banks are not allowed to accept foreign currency deposits, although that policy was under review in 2001. At times of pressures or turbulence in the foreign exchange market, spreads of 10 percent or so often emerge for a period as the parallel market adjusts much more quickly than the interbank market. For example, in 2000–01 the central bank attempted to meet pent-up demand for foreign exchange in the interbank market using competitive bids (rather than selling at prevailing rates) to reduce spreads that were more than 15 percent.[3]

Guinea's interbank market during the 1994–99 period illustrates similar institutional problems. Before September 1999, the foreign exchange market was highly segmented. An official market was dominated by state enterprises and donors (who operated through two large banks) and large importers. The rest of the transactions took place in a so-called parallel market of foreign exchange bureaus, many of which gained official status when licensing was introduced in 1997. The spread between the two rates was between 4 and 6 percent until mid-1998, at which time it started to widen as the authorities

2. IMF Country Report 99/71.
3. IMF Country Report 01/148.

began propping up the official rate. By early 1999 the parallel market accounted for about 60 to 70 percent of the foreign exchange market and the spread was 10 to 15 percent. Market segmentation became more pronounced (with shortages) while those with access to official rates earned substantial rents. The central bank introduced a weekly auction for foreign exchange in 1999, which helped to reduce the spread significantly.[4] Since then the spread has remained below 2 percent, although with periodic spikes during periods of central bank interventions to prop up the currency, as, for example, in the first quarter of 2000. The market is still quite segmented, however, between the auction market (commercial banks, authorized bureaus, and the central bank) and the unofficial parallel market (unauthorized agents transacting mainly in cash but also through offshore accounts). The parallel market is increasingly involved in transactions of the informal mining sector. There is a general shortage of foreign exchange on the official market, and given the banks' lack of confidence in each other, there are no interbank transactions between auctions (where the bidding does not appear to be purely competitive). In 2001 the central bank progressively lengthened the intervals between auctions in order to try and reduce pressure for depreciation on the exchange rate.[5]

State Bank–Dominated Financial Sector

After a socialist history of extensive controls, Ethiopia liberalized its foreign exchange markets with the 1994 introduction of an auction market. The first test of the system was the 1994–95 coffee boom, where the ability to control monetary and inflationary effects was limited by import restrictions and the maintenance of 100 percent export surrender requirements, so that exporters could not use foreign exchange to import capital goods, for example. Policy responses were generally in the right direction but relatively weak. For example, the amount allocated to the foreign exchange auction was increased, but not enough to prevent excess demand for imports and an inflationary increase in net foreign assets. Upward pressure on prices was a disincentive to keep wealth in local currency (birr)–denominated assets, but as there were no other assets besides foreign exchange, the parallel premium increased.[6]

After some first-generation liberalizations, the process stalled and regulations remained burdensome.[7] The nominal and real exchange rate were kept quite stable. The institutional structure of the exchange market was changed to an interbank market in 1999, but there has not been much activity since

4. IMF Country Report 00/33.
5. IMF Country Report 02/153.
6. IMF Country Report 96/52.
7. IMF Country Report 99/98.

then. Clearly, it is difficult to have a genuine market when a single state bank heavily dominates the financial sector.

Flexible Rate Difficulties When Macroeconomic Policy Is Undisciplined

Successful operation of flexible rate systems is not possible when macroeconomic policies, particularly fiscal policies, are undisciplined, or reforms are erratic.

Poor Management of Fiscal Policies and Large External Shocks

Ghana's 1983–91 reform program achieved initial successes in sharply turning around negative growth, triple-digit inflation and parallel market premiums, and a large part of economic activity in parallel markets.[8] Gradual liberalization of the exchange and trade system was the centerpiece of the reform program. Loss of fiscal control after 1992, however, led to high and variable inflation.[9]

In 1999 Ghana suffered a major terms of trade shock, as world prices for its main exports (cocoa and gold) plummeted and oil prices doubled. Neither fiscal nor monetary policies responded appropriately, however. The government maintained farm-level cocoa prices at levels that were too high. This severely compromised revenue from the cocoa sector and led to borrowing from the banking system to finance the resulting higher deficit. Fearing that rapid depreciation would further stoke inflation, the Bank of Ghana intervened in the foreign exchange market to slow nominal depreciation, resulting in continued real appreciation of the cedi. The central bank was finally forced to abandon this strategy in November 1999, when reserves were run down to dangerous levels.[10]

An initially very high real appreciation followed Zambia's move to a flexible exchange rate system in 1992, in the context of triple-digit inflation, high copper prices, and high interest rates that attracted some private capital flows. The introduction of a cash-budget rule in 1993 succeeded in ratcheting down inflation.[11]

The stability of the nominal exchange rate since 1996 and the dominant role of the Zambia Consolidated Copper Mines (ZCCM) in the foreign exchange market have raised questions about the true degree of exchange rate

8. Kapur and others (1991).
9. Pellechio and others (2001).
10. IMF Country Report 01/141.
11. Adam and Bevan (2000).

flexibility, but the authorities' view was that the ZCCM played a stabilizing role. The late 1990s illustrate the volatility Zambia faces. During 1998–99, both copper and agricultural production were depressed, the budget in larger deficit than planned, and the external position had weakened because of uncertainty regarding protracted delays in the ZCCM privatization, donors' withholding of aid, and inappropriate macroeconomic policies. The currency depreciated sharply and there was a large loss of reserves. The inflationary impact of the steep depreciation complicated anti-inflation policy, and the failure to tighten money contributed to continued currency weakness and creeping dollarization. Performance bounced back in 2000–01, given the recovery of the privatized mining sector as well as manufacturing and services. A sizable appreciation of the real exchange rate ensued. The situation was reversed again in 2002 with the withdrawal of Anglo American,[12] declining copper prices, and drought, which lowered growth and increased inflationary pressures. Although there has been volatility in the real exchange rate, this measure of competitiveness has remained broadly unchanged since the mid-1990s, despite a large deterioration in the terms of trade and persistently large current account deficits.

Continued Severe Macroeconomic Instability and Limited Liberalization

The most extreme example of this pattern is the Democratic Republic of the Congo, which uses what is technically classified as a floating exchange rate system since it first attempted to float the currency in the context of an interbank market in 1983 (see table 5-1). Although there was some success in narrowing the huge parallel market premium, the central bank came under intense political pressure to slow the speed of depreciation, and so a premium reemerged. The authorities tried floating again in 1991, but the policy was again complicated by antidepreciation pressure and a lack of bank notes, so a complicated multiple-rate system emerged instead. This was the start of the hyperinflation period of 1990–96, when the cumulative increase in prices was 6.3 billion percent. The primary cause of hyperinflation was the uncontrolled budget deficit financed by money creation, a deficit arising from the breakdown of public administration in the context of political instability, governance problems, civil strife, and war.[13] Hyperinflation created a vicious circle of a breakdown in financial intermediation—an uncontrolled spiral of parallel exchange rate depreciation and increased dollarization—that all fur-

12. In January 2002 Anglo American, the mining company which had acquired a large stake in the privatized ZCCM and was owner of the Konkola Copper Mines, announced they would withdraw and write off $350 million in Zambian assets.

13. Beaugrand (1997).

ther compounded the fall in fiscal revenue. Following a brief respite after 1996, resumption of the war in 1998 led to a similar cycle of budget monetization, high inflation, and depreciation, now under a fixed-rate system.[14] In an effort to conserve foreign exchange for official uses, the system was progressively tightened, leading to the January 1999 banning of domestic transactions in foreign exchange and culminating with the banning of domestic holding of foreign currencies. A floating rate was reintroduced in 2001, resulting in a large depreciation and reunification of multiple rates.

The pattern in Angola was similar in many respects. A first attempt at a flexible exchange rate system in 1994–95 made some initial progress in lowering the 9,000 percent parallel market premium, but the very small amounts of foreign exchange allocated to the flexible system, highly overexpansionary fiscal and monetary policies, and external pressures led to large, rapid depreciation. (Although abundant oil revenues could create a comfortable fiscal position, large-scale corruption meant that substantial revenues were siphoned off.) The exchange rate was refixed in 1996. Subsequently, a number of currency exchanges (introductions of new currencies involving changes in parity) took place. Another attempt at a float occurred in May 1999, but the very large depreciation (and intensification of the war) led back to triple-digit inflation in 2000.

Sudan has had a two-decade-long history of attempted exchange market reform. One of the main objectives of reforms in the 1980s was to increase the share of remittances (from the sizable community of nationals working abroad) brought into the country through legal channels. The authorities attempted to unify the exchange markets through discrete megadevaluations and gradual trade liberalization but failed, largely due to lack of fiscal reform.[15] From 1992 to 1996, the authorities again undertook several unsuccessful reform efforts, now in the context of an exchange rate system classified as flexible. However, attempts were often partial, significant market segmentation continued, and regulations were often changed. Again, the lack of supporting fiscal polices and foreign exchange reserves hampered reforms.[16] Another gradual reform achieved unification of exchange markets in 1998; exchange controls on current account transactions were gradually lifted. From 1999 to early 2002, however, the central bank pursued a de facto fixed regime, first intervening to maintain the rate and then dictating that the rate had to move within a narrow band. In 2003 the central bank formally adopted a managed float, abandoning the band and replacing the auction with an interbank market. Exchange rate

14. IMF Country Report 01/123.
15. Elbadawi (1997).
16. IMF Country Report 99/53.

management is now influenced by the broad money target, the international reserves target, and limits on intraday fluctuations.[17]

Nigeria began a structural reform program in 1986–90, but since then economic mismanagement and stop-and-go policies (particularly regarding the exchange rate) have contributed to high and variable inflation and a generally overvalued real exchange rate. In 1994 the government reimposed interest rate ceilings and eliminated the free market for foreign exchange, pegging the currency at an overvalued rate. Partial deregulation began again in 1995, with the liberalization of exchange rate controls, restoration of foreign exchange bureaus, and introduction of a dual exchange rate regime, with an administratively determined official rate and a flexible auction rate.[18] Relatively prudent fiscal and monetary policies during 1996–97, together with high oil prices, contributed to reducing inflation from a peak of 77 percent in 1994 to 10 percent in 1997 and to increasing average real GDP growth to 4 percent. Economic growth, however, continued to be hampered by fuel, power, and fertilizer shortages as well as political uncertainties.

By early 1998 Nigeria had a multiple exchange rate system: an artificially overvalued official rate for government and oil transactions; an autonomous foreign exchange market (AFEM) with a rate administratively determined in a managed float (with reference to the interbank and parallel rate) and supported by net infusions of foreign exchange from oil exports; plus foreign exchange bureaus and an active parallel market. Access to foreign exchange for current account transactions was quite liberal, although some restrictions remained. The Abdulsalami Abubakhar administration abolished the official exchange rate in 1998. Some progress on reforms was made in the face of sharp drops in petroleum revenues, but then large, extra-budgetary expenditures increased the budget deficit to more than 8 percent of GDP in the first half of 1999, financed by central bank credit. Although the government of President Olusegun Obasanjo, democratically elected in June 1999, registered some early policy improvements, by 2000 severe macroeconomic imbalances had increased as the deficit surged with pressures to deliver a democracy dividend: expenditures dissipated the large windfall oil gains, inflation accelerated to double digits, and instability dominated the foreign exchange market.[19] After abolition of the AFEM and successful introduction of the interbank market (Interbank Foreign Exchange Market, known as IFEM) in 1999, the central bank prohibited in 2000 the transfer between banks of foreign exchange purchased from the central bank, leading to the

17. IMF Country Reports 02/245, 03/390.
18. Moser and others (1997).
19. IMF Country Report 01/131.

segmentation of the IFEM with two distinct rates (one effectively a predetermined rate) and the widening of the parallel market premium. Macroeconomic instability continued, and by 2002, facing a rapid decline in international reserves, the authorities were forced to carry out a series of devaluations and later adopted a new Dutch auction system. The depreciation that occurred helped lower the premium and stabilize the market, although it still remains segmented and excessively regulated.[20]

Flexible Rates When There Is "Fear of Floating"

Before summarizing country cases in this category, we describe here a few common background features relevant to the experiences of Uganda, Tanzania, and Mozambique in managing large aid inflows during the late-1990s through 2002.[21]

Challenges in Monetary Management of Recent Large Aid Inflows

Each country implemented deep structural reforms, including exchange rate unification (Uganda in 1992, Tanzania in 1994, and Mozambique in 1993); achieved consistently tight fiscal positions; and experienced rapid growth during the late 1990s through 2002. All three countries emerged from their stabilization phases with very low levels of domestic money demand and domestic debt, as well as very thin markets in government securities.[22] Against a backdrop of already high aid inflows, there was a surge in new aid starting in the late 1990s. For instance, in 2000–01 net donor inflows amounted to 11 percent of GDP in Uganda. Given the strong nontradable bias in public expenditure, in all three countries net domestic liquidity injections from the government were large relative to the existing levels of debt and money. In addition to aid inflows, the countries have also experienced substantial increases in private capital flows.

Uganda's recent aid surge came at a time of a sharp deterioration in the terms of trade, given the slump in world coffee prices. Although the exchange rate was notionally flexible, the Bank of Uganda did not adhere to the strategy of sterilizing the liquidity through the sale of foreign exchange proceeds to the private sector (that is, by letting the exchange rate float) because of its unwillingness to let the exchange rate appreciate in the face of the term of trade deterioration. Instead, the bank initially attempted sterilization through

20. IMF Country Report 03/3.
21. This section draws extensively on Buffie and others (2004).
22. At the end of the 1990s, reserve money in each country averaged around 4 percent of GDP.

the domestic debt market, but given the required scale of the sterilization, this led to a rapid increase in domestic interest rates, debt stocks, and debt service costs. In fact, the increase was so rapid that the bank reversed its strategy in 2001, although initially without sterilizing through foreign exchange sales.[23] Reserve money grew much faster than programmed, and the IMF and Uganda's Ministry of Finance pressured the central bank to let the exchange rate float. The episode led to high volatility in interest rates and the exchange rate, but inflation still remained low, and the real exchange rate did not appreciate.

The Bank of Tanzania, motivated by a similar fear of real exchange rate appreciation as in Uganda, responded to the aid surge by, in effect, abandoning its flexible exchange rate and accumulating foreign exchange reserves in order to target the nominal exchange rate.[24] The Tanzanian shilling first depreciated against the U.S. dollar in 1999 and then was held constant for eighteen months before depreciating again in 2002. Initially sterilizing the liquidity through domestic debt sales, concerns over interest costs led the central bank to scale back bond sterilization. With both conventional sterilization instruments essentially pinned down, reserve money grew rapidly. Tensions emerged between the Bank of Tanzania (which argued that the economy was experiencing a structural shift in money demand, so that it was unnecessary and inappropriate to fully sterilize the growth in reserve money) and the IMF (which took the position that any increase in money demand was likely running its course and the strategy risked reigniting inflation).[25] As of February 2003, while the real exchange rate had appreciated, there was no evidence of a resurgence in inflation.

A surge in private capital inflows preceded the rapid aid increase in Mozambique. The reserve buildup was sterilized through the fiscal channel by decreases in net domestic assets as the government accumulated deposits. By late 1999 and early 2000, official aid flows had increased. The previously tight fiscal stance was loosened somewhat, partly due to reconstruction expenditures and lower revenues reflecting a massive flood crisis. Although the Bank of Mozambique was not attempting to offset an exchange rate appreciation, it was still reluctant to sterilize. As in Uganda, the bank argued that the increase in reserve money was noninflationary and reflected a recovery in money demand.[26] In this case, however, there was a sharp increase in inflation.

23. IMF Country Report 03/97.
24. IMF Country Report 03/2.
25. IMF Country Report 03/1.
26. IMF Country Report 01/17.

Private Capital Flows

Following a comprehensive liberalization program that began in 1991 (with foreign exchange liberalization completed by 1994), but failing to correct an underlying fiscal problem, the Zimbabwean authorities assigned too many objectives to monetary policy. These included controlling inflation, managing the exchange rate (attempting a constant real exchange rate rule), and stimulating real activity through interest rate policy.[27] High budget deficits resulted in rapid accumulation of domestic debt, high inflation, and correspondingly high interest rates. Private capital inflows from 1993 to mid-1996 put pressure on the real exchange rate. The authorities' response was nominal depreciation, accumulation of reserves, and partial sterilization through treasury bill sales. This led, however, to the classic cycle of higher interest rates, more inflows, and higher budgetary costs. By 1997 it became clear that the government had switched to money creation to finance the deficit, while trying to force interest rates lower. With classic signs of an impending crisis (excess money balances, overvaluation, declining reserves), the market looked for signs of a policy reversal in the government's budget for 1997. But the market saw the opposite and a currency crisis ensued.[28]

Following Kenya's exchange market unification in 1993, the policy focus was to keep reserve money on its targeted path while intervening in the foreign exchange market to minimize appreciation. Early capital inflows led to a similar scenario as in Zimbabwe. In 1995 the Central Bank of Kenya tried to bring down interest rates, but this led to a big redemption of treasury bills, capital outflow, and pressure for depreciation of the exchange rate. After a successful defense, the bank returned to a high interest rate policy to stabilize the exchange rate and build reserves.[29] Unlike Zimbabwe, there was not the huge underlying fiscal problem in Kenya. However, capital flows again put pressure on the exchange rate in 1996 and led to classic sterilization cycles. The nonbank public also shifted into holding government paper, which may have depressed money demand, and inflation increased. Tables turned, however, when the IMF suspended its program in 1997 because of governance problems, and other donors also pulled out. In an initial response, investors pulled out of government paper, reserves dropped, and the currency depreciated. Later, a fragile stability returned to the financial markets. In 1999 central bank intervention in the exchange market was limited to achieving the reserve target (replenishing the foreign exchange used to service the external

27. Ellyne (2000).
28. IMF Country Report 01/13.
29. Ndung'u and Ngugi (1999).

debt, while gradually building reserves), and fiscal steps became the key to avoid pressure on the exchange rate. In 2000–02 the nominal and real exchange rate remained relatively stable, despite a worsening of the terms of trade. However, the authorities' view was that exchange rate stability might have reduced currency risk premiums and interest rates over the period.[30]

Fixed-Rate Systems in War Countries

During the period from the 1980s through 1993, the Burundian franc was pegged to the Special Drawing Right (SDR), with the peg adjusted several times by the authorities in order to maintain competitiveness. The real exchange rate depreciated from 1985 to 1992. Burundi began a comprehensive reform program in 1991, but the government's priorities were soon dominated by the outbreak of civil conflict in 1993. The peg was changed to a weighted basket of principal trading partners' currencies and adjusted periodically, but the real exchange rate appreciated by 33 percent during 1993–97 and parallel market spreads of more than 50 percent began to emerge.[31] A fragile peace was achieved in 2000. The new government moved from a peg to a managed float, intervening in the exchange market to limit the spread between the official and parallel rates.[32]

Eritrea's record with a fixed-rate system is too short to analyze. For the record, we describe briefly how the country moved to a peg. The Ethiopian birr (flexible rate) was adopted starting from Eritrea's independence in 1993, originally with an official rate that applied to transactions between the two countries and a preferential rate for private imports and all exports. The two rates were unified in April 1997, and Eritrea introduced its own currency, the nafka, to replace the birr at a one-to-one parity in November 1997.[33] War between the two countries broke out in May 1998. Throughout the war, which ended in December 2000, Eritrea's exchange rate was market determined. With reserves nearly depleted and the authorities worried about the effect of rapid depreciation on inflation, exchange controls were implemented in July 2000 and the exchange rate fixed. Although the controls were later repealed in 2001, the rate had barely moved (the system is essentially a fixed rate, although notionally flexible) by the end of 2002. The essentially fixed rate, precarious reserve position, and extensive restrictions on current account payments have led to a parallel market premium of around 60 percent, encouraging rent seeking and fraud.[34]

30. IMF Country Report 02/85.
31. IMF Country Report 97/114.
32. IMF Country Report 02/242.
33. IMF Country Report 97/88.
34. IMF Country Report 03/165.

Liberia's case is interesting because of its long history as an independent country using the U.S. dollar and more recent experience with the circulation of competing currencies.[35] Starting in 1944, the U.S. dollar was legal tender, and the Liberian dollar was held at a fixed one-for-one parity. In August 1988 the rate became market determined. Liberia's economic situation began deteriorating in the early 1980s, following terms of trade declines, economic mismanagement, and mounting arrears that led to a breakdown of relations with creditors and donors. By the mid-1980s, the U.S. dollar–based financial system was near collapse. Although the traditionally circulating medium was both U.S. and Liberian dollars, starting in 1985 a parallel market for foreign exchange emerged, with the Liberian dollar trading at a discount, reaching Liberian $2.30 per U.S. dollar by 1989. The 1989–97 civil war brought most economic activity to a virtual standstill. When the war broke out, five-dollar banknotes with the portrait of J. J. Roberts (Liberia's first president) were issued in areas controlled by rebels led by Charles Taylor. In 1991 Liberty banknotes where issued in areas controlled by ECOWAS military forces, ECOMOG. The competing currencies were exchanged at various rates that differed from their official parity with the U.S. dollar. Following the end of the civil war and the election of Charles Taylor as president in 1997, the currency was once again unified. However, parity with the U.S. dollar was not reestablished, and the currency quickly depreciated to more than fifty Liberian dollars to the U.S. dollar.[36]

Other Fixed-Rate Systems as of 2001

Two-thirds of Djibouti's population live in the capital, and the rest lead a poor pastoral existence in the desert.[37] The economy was traditionally based on services for the substantial presence of the French military and dependents, off-shore banking, and the port. The Djibouti franc is freely convertible and has been pegged at an unchanged level to the U.S. dollar since 1973, although

35. Founded in 1821 as a colony to serve as a home for liberated American slaves, Liberia became independent in 1847. U.S. notes and coins circulated as currency from the first, while British West African pounds were also legal tender until 1944, at which time Liberia issued the Liberian dollar, which was linked at par to the U.S. dollar.

36. IMF Country Report 00/50.

37. Djibouti also has had an interesting monetary history. Djibouti, also known as French Somaliland, was a colony of France until 1946, when it became an overseas territory known as Afars and Issas. Upon independence in 1977, it became known as the Republic of Djibouti. From 1885 until 1943, Maria Theresa thalers, French francs, and Indian rupees all had legal tender status, though as of 1907 the Banque de l'Indochine also issued a franc note for Djibouti. Djibouti was part of the CFA franc zone at its formation in 1945, but in 1949 it left the zone and pegged its currency to the U.S. dollar.

most trade is conducted with Europe. The central bank operates a currency board, with francs in circulation covered by U.S. dollar deposits. Up until the early 1990s, the currency board and fixed exchange rate appeared to have contributed to Djibouti's development as a regional trade and financial center, although the external position was chronically weak. Even in the second half of the 1980s, however, economic performance had begun to weaken. Real GDP declined by 1 percent annually from 1984 to 1990, following the end of a real estate boom and drop in public investment, as well as deterioration in neighboring countries. In 1991 an ethnic-based conflict broke out. Deterioration of the fiscal position was the key economic issue throughout the 1990s. In the first half of the decade, budget deficits grew with the effect of conflict, unstable regional politics, declining aid, the heavy weight of the government wage bill, and poor fiscal discipline. IMF staff reports assessed that the sustainability of the exchange rate regime required substantial fiscal tightening. Although some on-again, off-again adjustment did take place in the second half of the decade under IMF programs, by the late 1990s, there was substantial concern about competitiveness and the strain on the exchange rate, also considering the real appreciation (about 55 percent over the decade) stemming from the U.S. dollar peg. IMF staff have argued that the deterioration in competitiveness, suggested by overvaluation and very high real wages, is a major factor behind sluggish growth and persistent balance of payments pressures and that an exchange rate devaluation should be seriously considered. The authorities also recognize that improvements in competitiveness are critical for growth.

Seychelles is a small open economy, dependent on tourism and maritime activities, with a traditionally large role of the public sector in economic activity and employment. The Seychelles rupee was pegged to the SDR until 1996, followed by a peg to a basket with changing weights.[38] Substantial social progress was recorded from independence in 1976, with per capita GDP rising from $800 to $7,000 in 1998. However, rising macroeconomic imbalances during the 1990s seriously affected efficiency and competitiveness, such that the average growth rate declined during this period. At the outset of that decade there were no exchange controls, but significant import and price controls existed. That system was disrupted by external difficulties during the Middle East crisis of 1991, and external payments restrictions and surrender requirements were reinstated, although they did not prevent accumulation of external arrears. A small parallel market was in existence by 1993, with a spread of 7 to 10 percent. Monetary developments during the 1994–96 period were dominated by shortages of foreign currency and commercial payments arrears.

38. IMF Country Report 96/46.

The central bank introduced a pipeline scheme (or queuing) for the allocation of foreign exchange and a system for the allocation of foreign exchange
to seven categories of expenditures.[39] At the root of the external pressures during
the second half of the decade was the rising fiscal deficit (14 percent of GDP
during 1996–99), fueled by the expanding welfare system, rising wage bill,
transfers to parastatals, and a big capital spending program. The authorities
responded to balance of payments pressures with further tightening of trade
and exchange restrictions in 1998 and 2001. Since that time, IMF staff reports
have been pushing for the dismantling of price, trade, and exchange controls.
While real GDP fell more than 15 percent from 1998 to 2001, and the current
account deficit averaged 17 percent of GDP during 1999 through 2001, there
was a massive accumulation of external debt and arrears and falling reserves.
There is anecdotal evidence that the rupee seems far overvalued. The authorities' current program focuses on the resolution of the large monetary overhang
resulting from the excessive public financing.

Cape Verde operated a basket peg until 1998. Although central planning
and an economically dominant public sector determined strategy from 1975 to
1991, relatively prudent policies (and large foreign transfers) allowed solid economic growth through the 1980s. Toward the decade's end, however, the government did not respond to declining aid and remittances by cutting large
expenditures, but instead used bank credit to finance deficits. Unemployment
and inflation rose, and official reserves fell. An adjustment program starting in
1992 restored reasonable growth, with significant contributions from services
and foreign investment in export-oriented manufacturing. Until 1997, however, fiscal policies were unsustainably lax, leading to accumulation of domestic debt and depletion of foreign exchange reserves.[40] Rapid progress was
made under the precautionary arrangement with the IMF in 1998. Real GDP
growth increased to 8 percent in 1998–99 and inflation was reduced from
6 percent in 1997 to 4.3 percent in 1999. Current account and capital transactions were liberalized in mid-1998, policies aimed at ensuring the escudo's convertibility. In order to signal a commitment to low inflation and macroeconomic stability, the basket peg was replaced with a fixed link of the Cape
Verdean escudo to the Portuguese escudo. Since the replacement of the latter
by the euro in 1999, Cape Verde's currency has been pegged to the euro, the
EU's common currency. Overly expansionary fiscal policies in 1999, however, partially financed by credit from the central bank and a credit line facil-

39. The pipeline scheme requires rupee deposits, which queue for foreign exchange allocation, while the allocation system by categories does not require previous deposits in rupees.
IMF Country Report 00/162.
    40. IMF Country Report 99/58.

ity from Portugal (designed to ensure convertibility between the two coun-tries' currencies), led to a widening current account deficit (14 percent of GDP). The authorities responded to the pressure on reserves by temporarily introducing foreign exchange rationing.[41] Fiscal deterioration worsened in 2000, however, in the run up to elections, endangering the peg to the euro. With limited statutory independence, the central bank was unable to prevent monetization of the deficit, financed also by accumulation of domestic and external arrears. The balance of payments deteriorated, reflecting lower for-eign direct investment and the suspension of aid. In particular, since they had not repaid the credit line with Portugal by the previous year's end, access to this facility was supposed to be blocked, raising further questions about the sustainability of the peg.[42]

41. By the end of the year, however, inflows of foreign direct investment, related to privat-ization and aid inflows, turned the overall balance of payments into a surplus.

42. The credit line was subsequently reopened in 2001, when Cape Verde and Portugal agreed to transform the outstanding payments into a long-term bridge loan. IMF Country Report 01/174.

References

Abdel-Salam, Osman Hashim. 1970. "The Evolution of African Monetary Institutions." *Journal of Modern African Studies* 8 (October): 339–62.

Adam, Christopher S., and David L. Bevan. 2000. "The Cash-Budget as a Restraint: The Experience of Zambia." In *Investment and Risk in Africa*, edited by Paul Collier and Catherine Pattillo, pp. 185–215. St. Martin's Press and MacMillan Press.

Agénor, Pierre-Richard, and Nadeem Ul Haque. 1996. "Macroeconomic Management with Informal Financial Markets." *International Journal of Finance and Economics* 1 (2): 87–101.

Alesina, Alberto, and Robert Barro. 2002. "Currency Unions." *Quarterly Journal of Economics* 117 (2): 409–36.

Alibert, Jacques. 1999. "Un nouveau satellite pour l'euro: le Cap Vert et la zone 'Escudo.'" *Afrique contemporaine* 189 (Janvier-Mars): 30–32.

Alweendo, Tom K. 1999. "Mr. Alweendo Discusses Namibia's Current Exchange Rate Arrangement and Its Implications for the Country's Monetary Policy." *Bank for International Settlements Review* 127: 1–10.

Aron, Janine, Ibrahim A. Elbadawi, and Brian Kahn. 2000. "Real and Monetary Determinants of the Real Exchange Rate in South Africa." In *Development Issues in South Africa*, edited by Ibrahim A. Elbadawi and Trudi Hartzenberg, pp. 195–236. St. Martin's Press and MacMillan Press.

Austen, Ralph A. 1987. *African Economic History: Internal Development and External Dependency*. London: James Currey Ltd.

Badiane, Ousmane, Louis Goreux, and Paul Masson. 2002. "Cotton Sector Strategies in West and Central Africa." Working Paper 02/173. Washington: International Monetary Fund.

Bank of France. 2002. *Rapport annuel de la zone franc 2001*. Paris.

Barro, Robert, and David Gordon. 1983. "A Positive Theory of Monetary Policy in a Natural Rate Model." *Journal of Political Economy* 91 (4): 589–610.

Baumol, William J., Richard R. Nelson, and Edward N. Wolff, eds. 1994. *Convergence of Productivity: Cross-National Studies and Historical Evidence.* Oxford University Press.

Bayoumi, Tamim, and Paul Masson. 1995. "Fiscal Flows in the United States and Canada: Lessons for Monetary Union in Europe." *European Economic Review* 39: 253–74.

Beaugrand, Philippe. 1997. "Zaïre's Hyperinflation, 1990–96." Working Paper 97/50. Washington: International Monetary Fund.

Bevan, David, Paul Collier, and Jan Willem Gunning. 1990. *Controlled Open Economies: A Neoclassical Approach to Structuralism.* Oxford: Clarendon Press.

Bigsten, Arne, and Beatrice Kalinda Mkenda. 2002. "Kenya and the East African Community: A Report for Sida." Mimeo. Göteborg University.

Birmingham, David, and Phyllis M. Martin. 1983. *History of Central Africa,* vol. 2. New York and London: Longmans.

Bleaney, Michael, and Lisenda Lisenda. 2001. "Monetary Policy after Financial Liberalisation: A Central Bank Reaction Function for Botswana." Working Paper 01/17. University of Nottingham, Centre for Research in Economic Development and International Trade.

Botswana Institute for Development Policy Analysis (BIDPA) and Centre for the Study of African Economies (CSAE). 2001. *The Prerequisites for Progress toward a Single Currency in COMESA: Medium to Long-Term Perspective Study.* University of Oxford.

Boughton, James M. 1991. "The CFA Franc Zone: Currency Union and Monetary Standard." Working Paper 91/133. Washington: International Monetary Fund (December).

_____. 1993. "The Economies of the CFA Franc Zone." In *Policy Issues in the Operation of Currency Unions,* edited by P. R. Masson and M. P. Taylor, pp. 96–107. Cambridge University Press.

Broda, Christian. 2001. "Coping with Terms-of-Trade Shocks: Pegs versus Floats." *American Economic Review* 91 (2): 376–80.

Buffie, Edward, and others. 2004. "Exchange Rate Policy and the Management of Official and Private Capital Flows in America." *Staff Papers* 51: 126–60. Washington: International Monetary Fund.

Calvo, Guillermo, and Carmen Reinhart. 2000. "Fixing for Your Life." *Brookings Trade Forum 2000*: 1–39.

_____. 2001. "Fear of Floating." Mimeo. University of Maryland, College Park.

_____. 2002. "Fear of Floating." *Quarterly Journal of Economics* 117 (2): 379–408.

Cashin, Paul, Luis Céspedes, and Ratna Sahay. 2002. "Keynes, Cocoa, and Copper: In Search of Commodity Currencies." Working Paper 02/223. Washington: International Monetary Fund.

Cashin, Paul, John McDermott, and Catherine Pattillo. 2004. "Terms of Trade Shocks in Africa: Are They Short-Lived or Long-Lived?" *Journal of Development Economics* 73 (2): 727–44.

Casteleijn, A. J. H. 2001. "South Africa's Monetary Policy Framework." Conference Papers on the Monetary Policy Frameworks in Africa. Pretoria, South Africa Reserve Bank, September 17–19.

Clément, Jean A.P., and others. 1996. "Aftermath of CFA Franc Devaluation." Occasional Paper 138. Washington: International Monetary Fund.

Cobham, David, and Peter Robson. 1994. "Monetary Integration in Africa: A Deliberately European Perspective." *World Development* 22 (3): 285–99.

Cohen, Benjamin. 1998. *The Geography of Money.* Cornell University Press.

_____. 2000. "Monetary Unions: The Political Dimension (Dollarisation: la dimension politique)." *L'Economie politique* 5 (1): 88–112.

Collier, Paul. 1991. "Africa's External Economic Relations, 1960–90." *African Affairs* 90: 339–56.

Collier, Paul, and Jan Willem Gunning. 1999. "Exchange Rate Management in Liberalising African Economies, Vol. 1." In *African Economies in Transition*, edited by Jo Ann Paulson, 169–92. New York: St. Martin's Press.

Cooper, Richard. 1984. "A Monetary System for the Future." *Foreign Affairs* 63 (Fall): 166–84.

Crick, Wilfred Frank, ed. 1965. *Commonwealth Banking Systems.* Oxford: Clarendon.

d'A.Collings, Francis, and others. 1978. "The Rand and the Monetary Systems of Botswana, Lesotho, and Swaziland." *Journal of Modern African Studies* 16 (1): 97–121.

Debrun, Xavier. 2003. "Regional Currencies." Mimeo. (July.)

Debrun, Xavier, Paul Masson, and Catherine Pattillo. 2002. "Monetary Unions in West Africa: Who Might Gain, Who Might Lose and Why?" Working Paper 02/226. Washington: International Monetary Fund.

_____. 2004 (forthcoming). "Monetary Unions in West Africa: Who Might Gain, Who Might Lose and Why?" *Canadian Journal of Economics.*

Devarajan, Shantayanan, and Jaime de Melo. 1987. "Evaluating Participation in African Monetary Unions: A Statistical Analysis of the CFA Zones." *World Development* 15 (4): 483–96.

Doré, Ousmane, and Paul Masson. 2002. "Experience with Budgetary Convergence in the WAEMU." Working Paper 02/108. Washington: International Monetary Fund.

Easterly, William, and Ross Levine. 2003. "Tropics, Germs, and Crops: The Role of Endowments in Economic Development." *Journal of Monetary Economics* 50 (January): 3–39.

Eichengreen, Barry. 1994. *International Monetary Arrangements for the 21st Century.* Brookings Institution.

Eichengreen, Barry, and others. 1999. "Transition Strategies and Nominal Anchors on the Road to Greater Exchange-Rate Flexibility." *Essays in International Finance* 213. Princeton University Press.

Elbadawi, Ibrahim A. 1997. "The Parallel Market Premium for Foreign Exchange and Macroeconomic Policy in Sudan." In *Parallel Exchange Rates in Developing Countries*, edited by Miguel Kiguel, J. Saul Lizondo, and Stephen O'Connell, pp. 221–46. New York: St. Martin's Press.

Ellyne, Mark. 2000. "The Failure of Real Targets for Monetary Policy: The Case of Zimbabwe." Mimeo. Washington: International Monetary Fund.

Emerson, Michael, and others. 1991. *One Market, One Money.* Oxford University Press.

Fischer, Stanley. 2001. "Distinguished Lecture on Economics in Government—Exchange Rate Regimes: Is the Bipolar View Correct?" *Journal of Economic Perspectives* 15 (2): 3–24.

Foroutan, Faezeh, and Lant Pritchett. 1993. "Intra-sub-Saharan African Trade: Is It Too Little?" *Journal of African Economies* 2 (1): 74–105

Frankel, Jeffrey. 1999. "No Single Currency Regime Is Right for All Countries or at All Times." *Essays in International Finance* 215. Princeton University Press.

Frankel, Jeffrey, and Andrew Rose. 1998. "The Endogeneity of Optimum Currency Area Criteria." *Economic Journal* 108 (July): 1009–25.

Glick, Reuven, and Andrew Rose. 2001. "Does a Currency Union Affect Trade? The Time Series Evidence." Mimeo. Federal Reserve Bank of San Francisco (November).

Gnassou, A. Laure. 1999. "*Après l'euro: quel statut juridique pour la zone franc africaine?*" *Afrique contemporaine* 189 (Janvier-Mars): 6–22.

Goldstein, Andrea, and Njuguna S. Ndung'u. 2001. "Regional Integration Experience in the Eastern African Region." *OECD Development Centre Technical Papers* 171.

Guillaume, Dominique M., and David Stasavage. 2000. "Improving Policy Credibility: Is There a Case for African Monetary Unions?" *World Development* 28 (8): 1391–407.

Guillaumont, Patrick, and Sylviane Guillaumont. 1984. *Zone franc et développement africain.* Paris: Economica.

Gupta, Sanjeev, Hamid Davoodi, and Erwin Tiong. 2000. "Corruption and the Provision of Health Care and Education." Working Paper 00/116. Washington: International Monetary Fund.

Gupta, Sanjeev, Keiko Honjo, and Marijn Verhoeven. 1997. "The Efficiency of Government Expenditure: Experiences from Africa." Working Paper 97/153. Washington: International Monetary Fund.

Hall, Robert E., and Charles Jones. 1999. "Why Do Some Countries Produce So Much More Output per Worker Than Others?" *Quarterly Journal of Economics* 114 (1): 83–116.

Hanink, Dean, and J. Henry Owusu. 1998. "Has ECOWAS Promoted Trade among Its Members?" *Journal of African Economies* 7 (3): 363–83.

Hausman, Roberto, Ugo Panizza, and Ernesto Stein. 2001. "Original Sin, Passthrough, and Fear of Floating." Mimeo. Washington: Inter-American Development Bank.

Hawkins, John, and Paul Masson. 2003. "Economic Aspects of Regional Currency Areas and the Use of Foreign Currencies." *Regional Currency Areas and the Use of Foreign Currencies*, BIS Papers 17, pp. 4–42. Basel: Bank for International Settlements (May).

Hazlewood, A. 1952. "Sterling Balances and the Colonial Currency System." *Economic Journal* 62 (248): 942–45.

Helleiner, Eric. 2001. "The Southern Side of Embedded Liberalism: The Politics of Postwar Monetary Policy in the Third World." Working Paper 01/5. Trent International Political Economy Centre, Trent University, Peterborough, Canada.

——————. 2003. *The Making of National Money: Territorial Currencies in Historical Perspective.* Cornell University Press.

Helleiner, Gerald. 2002. "Marginalization and/or Participation: Africa in Today's Global Economy." *Canadian Journal of African Studies* 36 (3): 531–50.

Hermans, H.C.L. 1997. "Bank of Botswana: The First 21 Years." In *Aspects of the Botswana Economy: Selected Papers,* edited by J. S. Salkin and others, pp. 177–222. Oxford: James Currey.

Hernández-Catá, Ernesto, and others. 1998. *The West African Economic and Monetary Union: Recent Developments and Policy Issues.* Occasional Paper 170. Washington: International Monetary Fund.

Hoffmaister, Alexander W., Jorge E. Roldos, and Peter Wickham. 1998. "Macroeconomic Fluctuations in Sub-Saharan Africa." *Staff Papers* 45 (1): 132–60. Washington: International Monetary Fund

Honohan, Patrick, and Philip Lane. 2000. "Will the Euro Trigger More Monetary Unions in Africa?" WIDER Working Paper 176. United Nations University World Institute for Development Economics Research, Helsinki.

Honohan, Patrick, and Stephen A. O' Connell. 1997. "Contrasting Monetary Regimes in Africa." Working Paper 97/64. Washington: International Monetary Fund.

Indian Ocean Newsletter. 1986. "Mozambique: Key-Sectors of the Economy." 1986 Edition. Paris.

Institut Royal des Relations Internationales. 1963. "Décolonisation et indépendance du Rwanda et du Burundi." *Chronique de politique etrangère 16* (4–6): 439–718.

International Monetary Fund. 2002a. "IMF Concludes Article IV Consultation with Namibia." Public Information Notice 02/13 (February 22). Washington.

_____. 2002b. "IMF Concludes Discussion on Recent Developments and Regional Policy Issues with the Central African Economic and Monetary Community." Public Information Notice 02/96 (September 3). Washington.

Jenkins, Carolyn, and Lynne Thomas. 1996. "Is Southern Africa Ready for Regional Monetary Integration?" Working Paper 51. Centre for the Study of African Economies. (November). Oxford.

_____. 1998. "Divergent Growth Experience in the Southern African Development Community." Mimeo. Centre for the Study of African Economies and Centre for Research into Economics and Finance in Southern Africa. Oxford and London.

Jensen, Henrik. 2003. "Explaining the Inflation Bias without Using the Word 'Surprise.'" Mimeo. University of Copenhagen (February).

Johnson, Marion. 1970. "The Cowrie Currencies of West Africa. Part II." *Journal of African History* 11 (3): 331–53.

Kapur, Ishan, and others. 1991. "Ghana: Adjustment and Growth, 1983–91." Occasional Paper 86. Washington: International Monetary Fund.

Kaufmann, David, Aart Kraay, and Pablo Zoido-Lobaton. 1999. "Aggregating Governance Indicators." Working Paper 2195. Washington: World Bank.

Kenen, Peter. 1969. "The Optimum Currency Area: An Eclectic View." In *Monetary Problems of the International Economy*, edited by Robert Mundell and Alexander Swoboda, pp. 41-60. University of Chicago Press.

Kraus, Christiane. 2003. "Concept Paper—Toward an East African Customs Union." Mimeo. Washington: World Bank.

Levy-Yeyati, Eduardo, and Federico Sturzenegger. 2002. "Classifying Exchange Rate Regimes: Deeds vs. Words." Working paper. University of Torcuato di Tella.

Martin, Philippe. 1995. "Free-Riding, Convergence and Two-Speed Monetary Unification in Europe." *European Economic Review* 39 (7): 1345–64.

Masalila, Kealeboga, and Oduetse Motshidisi. 2003. "Botswana's Exchange Rate Policy." *Regional Currency Areas and the Use of Foreign Currencies*, BIS Papers 17, pp. 123–28. Basel: Bank for International Settlements (May).

Masson, Paul R. 2001. "Exchange Rate Regime Transitions." *Journal of Development Economics* 64: 571–86.

Masson, Paul R., and Heather Milkiewicz. 2003. *Africa's Economic Morass—Will a Common Currency Help?* Brookings Policy Brief 121. July.

Masson, Paul, and Catherine Pattillo. 2001. "Monetary Union in West Africa (ECOWAS)—Is It Desirable and How Could It Be Achieved?" Occasional Paper 204. Washington: International Monetary Fund.

_____. 2002. "Monetary Union in West Africa: An Agency of Restraint for Fiscal Policies?" *Journal of African Economies* 11 (September): 387–412.

McCarthy, Colin. 2003. "The Southern African Customs Union: Executive Summary." Workshop Case Study, FAO Workshop on Regional Integration, Common Agriculture Policies and Food Security. Pretoria, South Africa, May 6-9.

Mkenda, Beatrice Kalinda. 2001. "Is East Africa an Optimum Currency Area?" *Working Papers in Economics* 41. Göteborg University.

Mládek, J.V. 1964a. "Evolution of African Currencies, Part I: The Franc Area." *Finance and Development,* a Quarterly Publication of the International Monetary Fund and the World Bank 1 (2): 81–88.

_____. 1964b. "Evolution of African Currencies, Part II: The Sterling." *Finance and Development* 1 (3): 184–91.

Monga, Célestin, and Jean-Claude Tchatchouang. 1996. *Sortir du piège monétaire.* Paris: Economica.

Montiel, Peter, Pierre-Richard Agénor, and Nadeem Ul Haque. 1993. *Informal Financial Markets in Developing Countries: A Macroeconomic Analysis.* Cambridge, Mass.: Blackwell.

Moser, Gary, and others. 1997. "Nigeria: Experience with Structural Adjustment." Occasional Paper 148. Washington: International Monetary Fund.

Mundell, Robert. 1961. "A Theory of Optimum Currency Areas." *American Economic Review* 51 (September): 657–65.

_____. 1972. "African Trade, Politics, and Money." In *African and Monetary Integration,* edited by R. Tremblay, pp. 11–67. Montreal: Les Editions HRW.

_____. 1999. "The Euro: How Important?" *Cato Journal* 18 (3): 441–44.

_____. 2002. "Does Africa Need a Common Currency?" In *Defining Priorities for Regional Integration,* pp. 45–57. Addis Ababa: UN Economic Commission for Africa.

Mussa, Michael, and others. 2000. "Exchange Rate Regimes in an Increasingly Integrated World Economy." Occasional Paper 193. Washington: International Monetary Fund.

Ndiaye, Mansour. 2000. *The Demand for Money in the UEMOA Countries: An Application of Recent Developments in Econometrics.* Dakar: BCEAO (September).

Ndung'u, Njuguna S., and Rose W. Ngugi. 1999. "Adjustment and Liberalization in Kenya: The Financial and Foreign Exchange Markets." *Journal of International Development* 11 (3): 465–91.

Ng'eno, Nehemiah. 2002. *The Status of Regional Trade Liberalization in East Africa.* Kenya: African Centre for Economic Growth.

Ngwenya, Sindiso. 2000. "Reviewing the Differences and Common Goals of SADC and COMESA." Paper presented at Conference on Reviewing Regional Integration in Southern Africa: Comparative International Experiences, June.

Nitsch, V. 2002. "Honey, I Shrunk the Currency Union Effect on Trade." *World Economy* 25 (4): 475–79.

Obstfeld, Maurice, and Kenneth Rogoff. 1995. "The Mirage of Fixed Exchange Rates." *Journal of Economic Perspectives* 9 (4): 73–96.

OECD. 2002. *African Economic Outlook* (with United Nations Economic Commission for Africa). Paris. December.

Parmentier, J. M., and R. Tenconi. 1996. *Zone franc en Afrique: Fin d'une ère ou renaissance?* Paris: L'Harmattan.

Pellechio, Anthony, and others. 2001. "Ghana: Economic Development in a Democratic Environment." Occasional Paper 199. Washington: International Monetary Fund.

Quah, Danny T. 1995. "Empirics for Economic Growth and Convergence." Discussion Paper 1140. London: Centre for Economic Policy Research.

_____. 1996. "Twin Peaks: Growth and Convergence in Models of Distribution Dynamics." *Economic Journal* 106 (437): 1045–55.

Rajaram, A. A., and others. 1999. "Putting the Horse before the Cart: On the Appropriate Transition to an East African Customs Union." Mimeo. World Bank report prepared for the East African Community Secretariat. Washington.

Reinhart, Carmen, and Kenneth Rogoff. 2002. "The Modern History of Exchange Rate Arrangements: A Reinterpretation." Working Paper 8963. Cambridge, Mass.: National Bureau of Economic Research.

Rogoff, Kenneth S., and others. 2003. "Evolution and Performance of Exchange Rate Regimes." Working Paper 03/243. Washington: International Monetary Fund.

Rose, Andrew. 2000. "One Money, One Market: Estimating the Effect of Common Currencies on Trade." *Economic Policy* 30: 9–45.

Sala-i-Martin, Xavier, and Jeffrey Sachs. 1993. "Fiscal Federalism and Optimum Currency Areas: Evidence for Europe from the United States." In *Establishing a Central Bank: Issues in Europe and Lessons from the United States*, edited by Matthew B. Canzoneri, Vittorio Grilli, and Paul R. Masson, pp. 195–227. Cambridge University Press.

South African Reserve Bank. 2002. *Quarterly Bulletin* (December).

Stasavage, David. 1997. "The CFA Franc Zone and Fiscal Discipline." *Journal of African Economies* 6 (1): 132–67.

_____. 2003. *The Political Economy of a Common Currency: The CFA Franc Zone since 1945*. Aldershot, U.K.: Ashgate.

Subramanian, Arvind, and Natalia Tamirisa. 2001. "Africa's Trade Revisited." Working Paper 01/33. Washington: International Monetary Fund (March).

Tenreyro, Silvana, and Robert Barro. 2003. "Economic Effects of Currency Unions." Working Paper 9435. Cambridge, Mass.: National Bureau of Economic Research (January).

Tjirongo, M. 1995. "Short-Term Stabilization versus Long-Term Price Stability: Evaluating Namibia's Membership of the Common Monetary Area." Centre for the Study of African Economies. Working Paper 95-18. University of Oxford.

Uche, C.U. 1997. "Does Nigeria Need an Independent Central Bank?" *African Review of Money Finance and Banking* 21: 141–58.

U.K. Treasury. 2003. *U.K. Membership of the Single Currency: An Assessment of the Five Economic Tests*. London: Stationery Office.

Valério, Nuno. 2002. "The Escudo Zone—a Failed Attempt at Colonial Monetary Union (1962–71)." Paper presented at session thirty-nine of the 13th International Economic History Congress. Buenos Aires, July 22–26.

Van Zyl, Lambertus. 2003. "South Africa's Experience of Regional Currency Areas and the Use of Foreign Currencies." *Regional Currency Areas and the Use of Foreign Currencies*. BIS Papers 17, pp. 135–40. Basel: Bank for International Settlements (May).

Venables, Anthony J. 2000. "Winners and Losers from Regional Integration Agreements." Discussion Paper 2528. London: Centre for Economic Policy Research.

Vinay, Bernard. 1988. *Zone franc et coopération monétaire*. 2nd ed. Paris: Ministère de la Coopération et du Développement.

Vizy, Marc. 1989. *La Zone franc*. Paris: Centre des Hautes Etudes sur l'Afrique et l'Asie Modernes.

Wiegand, Johannes. 2002. "Fiscal Surveillance Criteria for Oil-Exporting Developing Countries—the Example of the CEMAC." Mimeo. Washington: International Monetary Fund.

World Bank. 2000. "Part II: West Africa, Key Trends, and Regional Perspectives." West Africa Regional Assistance Strategy Discussion Paper. Washington.

_____. 2003. "Regional Trade Integration in East Africa—Trade and Revenue Impacts of the Planned Customs Union." Washington.

World Bank Africa Database. 2002. CD-ROM. Washington.

Yansané, Aguibou Y. 1984. *Decolonization in West African States with French Colonial Legacy. Comparison and Contrast: Development in Guinea, the Ivory Coast and Senegal (1945–1980).* Cambridge, Mass.: Schenkman Publishing.

International Monetary Fund Staff Country Reports:

Botswana: 2002 Article IV Consultation—Staff Report. Report 02/244. November 5, 2002.

Burundi—Recent Economic Developments. Report 97/114. December 15, 1997.

Burundi: 2002 Article IV Consultation and Use of Fund Resources—Request for Post-Conflict Emergency Assistance—Staff Report; Staff Statement; Public Information Notice and Press Release on the Executive Board Discussion; and Statement by the Executive Director for Burundi. Report 02/242. November 6, 2002.

Cape Verde—Recent Economic Developments. Report 99/58. July 19, 1999.

Cape Verde: 2001 Article IV Consultation—Staff Report and Public Information Notice on the Executive Board Discussion. Report 01/174. October 3, 2001.

Democratic Republic of the Congo: 2001 Selected Issues and Statistical Appendix. Report 01/123. August 2, 2001.

Eritrea—Selected Issues. Report 97/88. October 31, 1997.

Eritrea: 2003 Article IV Consultation—Staff Report; Public Information Notice on the Executive Board Discussion; and Statement by the Executive Director for Eritrea. Report 03/165. July 1, 2003.

Ethiopia—Selected Issues. Report 96/52. June 21, 1996.

Ethiopia: Recent Economic Developments. Report 99/98. September 20, 1999.

Gambia, the: Selected Issues. Report 99/71. August 18, 1999.

Gambia, the: 2001 Article IV Consultation—Staff Report; Staff Statement; Public Information Notice on the Executive Board Discussion; and Statement by the Authorities of the Gambia. Report 01/148. August 20, 2001.

Ghana: 2001 Article IV Consultation and Third Review under the Poverty Reduction and Growth Facility and Request for Waiver of Performance Criteria. Report 01/141. August 9, 2001.

Guinea: Staff Report for the 1999 Article IV Consultation and Request for the Third Annual Arrangement under the Enhanced Structural Adjustment Facility. Report 00/33. March 8, 2000.

Guinea-Bissau: 2002 Article IV Consultation—Staff Report; Staff Supplement; and Public Information Notice on the Executive Board Discussion. Report 02/153. July 26, 2002.

Kenya: 2001 Article IV Consultation—Staff Report; Staff Supplement; and Public Information Notice on the Executive Board Discussion. Report 02/85. April 19, 2002.

Liberia: Selected Issues and Statistical Appendix. Report 00/50. April 10, 2000.

Mozambique: 2000 Article IV Consultation and Second Review under the Poverty Reduction and Growth Facility—Staff Report; Staff Statement; Public Information

Notice and Press Release on the Executive Board Discussion; and Statement by the Authorities of Mozambique. Report 01/17. January 17, 2001.

Nigeria: 2001 Article IV Consultation—Staff Report; Staff Statement; and Public Information Notice on the Executive Board Discussion. Report 01/131. August 6, 2001.

Nigeria: 2002 Article IV Consultation—Staff Report; Staff Statement; and Public Information Notice on the Executive Board Discussion. Report 03/3. January 3, 2003.

Seychelles: Recent Economic Developments. Report 96/46. June 21, 1996.

Seychelles: Recent Economic Developments. Report 00/162. December 18, 2000.

Sudan—Recent Economic Developments. Report 99/53. July 19, 1999.

Sudan: Final Review under the Medium-Term Staff-Monitored Program and the 2002 Program-Staff Report; and Staff Supplement. Report 02/245. November 5, 2002.

Sudan: 2003 Article IV Consultation and First Review of the 2003 Staff-Monitored Program—Staff Report. Report 03/390. December 19, 2003.

Swaziland: 2002 Article IV Consultation—Staff Report. Report 03/21. January 31, 2003.

Tanzania: 2002 Article IV Consultation, Fifth Review under the Poverty Reduction and Growth Facility and Request for an Extension of the Arrangement and Waiver of Performance Criterion—Staff Report; Public Information Notice and News Brief on the Executive Board Discussion; and Statement by the Executive Director for Tanzania. Report 03/1. January 6, 2003.

Tanzania: Selected Issues and Statistical Appendix. Report 03/2. January 7, 2003.

Uganda: Financial System Stability Assessment, including Reports on the Observance of Standards and Codes on the following topics: Monetary and Financial Policy Transparency, Banking Supervision, Securities Regulation, Insurance Regulation, Corporate Governance, and Payment Systems. Report 03/97. April 10, 2003.

Zimbabwe: Recent Economic Developments, Selected Issues, and Statistical Appendix. Report 01/13. January 11, 2001.

Index

Abuja Treaty (*1991*), 147–48
AEC. *See* African Economic Community
Africa: aid to, 150; central banks, 17, 20, 33, 34, 38, 148, 156–57, 163; colonies and colonization, 6, 12, 13–14; conflict and war in, 40–41; corruption, 93, 150; currencies and exchange rates, 9–10, 11, 14, 18, 26, 27–32, 38, 44, 81t, 147, 150, 152–61, 162, 164, 166–69; development banks, 39; dollarization in, 4b, 120; economic issues, 1–3, 11, 37, 53, 93, 150–51, 152, 156, 159, 163, 166, 168–69; financial markets in, 94, 166; gold and money, 13–26; history of monetary arrangements, 6, 8, 12–32; inflation, 34, 35, 38; integration of, 147–48; monetary union in, viii, 3, 12, 34–35, 37, 38, 40, 44, 46, 76, 150, 151–59, 161, 162–63; regional cooperation, 5–6, 9–10, 151–52; trade, 7, 37, 40, 54, 64, 150, 155–56, 159, 161, 164, 165, 168. *See also* individual countries and regions
Africa—sub-Saharan: central banks in, 94; corruption, 100; country experiences with flexible exchange rates, 80–92; economic issues, 152; general exchange rate issues, 77–80, 93; institutional quality indexes, 101. *See also* West Africa; individual countries
African Economic Community (AEC), 147
African National Congress (ANC), 113
African Peer Review Mechanism (APRM), 110, 160
African Union (AU), 3, 41, 147, 148, 153. *See also* New Partnership for African Development
Aid, effect of, 83–84, 92, 150, 189–92
Algeria, 19
Alweendo, Tom K., 67
Amin, Idi, 21, 131. *See also* Uganda
AMU. *See* Arab Maghreb Union
ANC. *See* African National Congress
Anglo American (mining company), 186
Angola: COMESA and, 139; conflict in, 40, 114–15; currency and exchange rate issues, 19, 82, 187; economic issues, 143, 145; financing needs, 121; monetary union and, 145; petroleum

issues, 115, 187; problems in, 153;
REER and real commodity prices, 86;
trade, 121. *See also* Africa
APRM. *See* African Peer Review Mechanism
Arab Maghreb Union (AMU), 148, 149
Argentina, 155, 165, 168
AU. *See* African Union

Bank of England, 17, 20
Banks and banking. *See* Central banks; individual countries
Banque Centrale des Etats de l'Afrique de l'Ouest (BCEAO). *See* West African Economic and Monetary Union
Banque des Etats de l'Afrique Centrale (BEAC). *See* Central African Economic and Monetary Community
Barro, Robert, 42
BCEAO (Banque Centrale des Etats de l'Afrique de l'Ouest). *See* West African Economic and Monetary Union
BEAC. *See* Central African Economic and Monetary Community
Belgian Congo, 16, 19
Belgium, 6, 16
Birr (Eritrea), 192
Botswana: abandonment of CMA monetary union, 7, 25, 65–66; central bank, 73, 74, 127, 148; currency issues, 24, 69, 73; dollarization in, 4b; economic issues, 67, 69, 74–75, 114; exchange rates, 25, 28–29, 73–74, 75, 92; financing needs, 121; as former British colony, 19; income, 67; Reserve Bank of South Africa, 16; trade, 71–72, 73, 115, 117, 121. *See also* Africa
Boughton, James M., 22
Bouteflika, Abdelaziz, 159
Bretton Woods, 8, 19, 24, 165
British Cameroons, 16, 19, 20
Buffie, Edward, 83–84
Bulgaria, 5b
Bundesbank (Germany), 39
Burkina Faso, 101
Burundi, 19, 86, 91, 139, 143, 192. *See also* Africa

CAEMC. *See* Central African Economic and Monetary Community
Calvo, Guillermo, 84, 166
Cameroon, 49, 63; as former British colony (British Cameroons), 16, 19, 20; as former French colony (Cameroun), 15, 20
Cape Verde, 17, 92, 195
Cedi (Ghana), 20, 185
Central Africa, 15, 19, 20, 23. *See also* individual countries
Central African Currency Board, 20
Central African Economic and Monetary Community (CAEMC): BEAC and, 21, 23, 168; COBAC and, 47; convergence criteria, 50, 51; economic issues, 8, 56, 57f, 58–59, 60, 62–63; exchange rates, 97; devaluation in, 109; history of, 49; members, xi, 17, 62, 150; monetary policies and currencies, 17, 24, 27, 38, 47, 48, 49; surveillance procedures, 60; trade, 51, 52, 53, 62, 64, 154. *See also* CFA franc zone
Central African Republic, 15, 47
Central Bank of Rhodesia and Nyasaland, 20
Central banks: for Africa, 17, 20, 33, 34, 38, 148, 156–57, 163; economic shocks and, 35, 44; of ECOWAS, 112; European, 34, 151; financing needs, 101, 120; fiscal deficits and, 92; government and, 42, 43–44, 171–72; independence of, 94; inflation and, 42–43, 82; interbank markets, 80; monetary unions and, 38, 42, 64–65, 98, 110, 171; national central banks, 43; pressure on, 120; regional central banks, 37–39, 43; supranational central banks, 120; in the WAMZ, 96
CFA franc zone: *agrément unique*, 47; banks and bank branches, 47, 157; business law in, 49; central banks in, 23, 38, 46, 47, 48, 49, 51, 53, 63, 156–57; consolidation of, 21–24; crises, 8, 109; currency issues, 15, 22–23, 51, 169; customs unions, 8; definition, xi–xii; devaluation of the CFA franc, 23, 24, 38, 40, 46, 49, 60, 156; durability of, 76, 154; economic

issues, 22, 39, 49, 51–63, 109; euro and, 11, 27, 32, 46, 48, 53, 164–65, 167; European attitude toward, 164–65; exchange rate issues, 23, 28, 46, 48, 53, 109, 167–69; expansion of, 9, 10, 11, 153–54; financial integration in, 39–40, 46–51; France and, 21, 22, 23, 41, 46, 111–12, 164, 167; French franc and, 19–20; future of, 165; as a monetary union, 4b, 19, 47, 75, 152; history of, 6, 12–13, 15, 17, 45, 46, 49; monetary and fiscal policies in, 46–51; political issues, 32, 41, 63, 76; prospects for evolution, 111–12; regions and members, 21, 23, 45, 47, 48–51; reserves, 46–47; sanctions, 63, 76; stability of CFA franc, 27; surveillance, 50, 51, 60–63, 75; tariffs and trade, 48, 49, 51–53, 63, 64, 75; zone overlap, 6. *See also* Central African Economic and Monetary Community; Francs; West African Economic and Monetary Union

Chad, 15, 62

Chile, 168

CIS. *See* Commonwealth of Independent States

CMA. *See* Common Monetary Area

COBAC (Commission Bancaire d'Afrique Centrale). *See* Central African Economic and Monetary Community African

Coffee, 135–36, 143, 184

Cohen, Benjamin, vii, 41, 72

Collier, Paul, 93

Colonies and colonization. *See* Africa

Colonies Françaises d'Afrique (CFA) franc. *See* CFA franc zone; Francs

COMESA. *See* Common Market for Eastern and Southern Africa

Commission Bancaire. *See* West African Economic and Monetary Union

Commission Bancaire d'Afrique Centrale (COBAC). *See* Central African Economic and Monetary Community African

Common Market for Eastern and Southern Africa (COMESA): African Union and, 148; currency and exchange rate issues, 139, 140; economic issues, 140, 143–45, 146; history and creation of, 139; members, 5–6, 129, 138, 139, 140–45, 149; monetary union, 9, 77, 139, 140, 142–43, 145–46, 152, 153; strategies and objectives, 139–40, 143–45; trade and tariffs, 5–6, 132, 135, 139, 140–43. *See also* individual members

Common Monetary Area (CMA): central bank in, 72–73; convergence and integration, 66–69; costs and benefits of membership, 122–26; currency and exchange rate issues, 25, 28, 65, 70–71, 72, 120; economic issues, 8, 66–69, 72, 75–76, 120, 122; effectiveness and durability, 26, 39, 72, 76, 122; as an exchange rate union, 4b, 25–26, 127; expansion of, 10, 25, 127, 153–54; history and creation of, 13, 24–26; members, xii, 65, 67, 122–26, 140; monetary policies in, 5b, 25–26, 69–73, 75, 120, 122; political issues, 41, 76; rand and, 45, 120; regional integration and, 4–5; SADC and, 127; South Africa and, 41, 71–72, 122, 123, 127, 154; surveillance by, 66, 76; trade, 71–72, 73, 122, 127. *See also* Botswana; Rand; Rand Monetary Area

Commonwealth of Independent States (CIS), 151–52. *See also* Soviet Union

Communauté Economique et Monétaire de l'Afrique Centrale. *See* Central African Economic and Monetary Community

Comoros, 19, 139

Conflict. *See* Wars and conflict

Congo-Brazzaville, 15

Constitutive Act (*2001*)

Convergence, Stability, Growth, and Solidarity Pact (*1999*; WAEMU), 51

Copper, 185–86

Côte d'Ivoire: Commission Bancaire, 47; corruption and institutional quality, 100t, 101; economic issues, 49, 104; financing needs, 63, 101, 103; in franc

zone, 15; political issues, 60–61; unrest and conflict in, 40, 60–61, 154; WAEMU and, 10
Cowrie shells (as currency), 13
Currencies: combination of regional currencies, 150; common currencies, 35, 65; currency blocks, 163–64; deterritorialization of, vii; devaluations, 79; dollarization, 4b, 5b, 120; great currencies, 151–52; independent currencies, 65; new currencies, 7; transactions costs and, 36–37, 72, 97, 155, 183. *See also* Africa; Economic issues; individual countries and groups
Currency boards: in Africa, 16, 28–29, 168; in Argentina, 165; in British colonies, 16; definition and characteristics, 5b, 20; dissolution of British currency boards, 20–21
Currency unions, 33, 40, 43, 52, 54, 71–72. *See also* CFA franc zones; Common Monetary Area; Optimum currency area
Customs Union Agreement (*1969*), 66n33
Customs unions, 48n5, 49, 148. *See also* individual groups

Dahomey, 15
Dakar (Senegal), 23
Debrun, Xavier, 41, 110, 175
Debt. *See* Economic issues
Democratic Republic of the Congo (DRC): COMESA and, 139; conflict in, 40, 114–15, 153; currency and exchange rate issues, 82, 186, 187; economic issues, 143, 186–87; government financing needs, 121
Developing countries, vii, 27, 90, 167. *See also* individual countries
Diamonds, 73–74, 75
Djibouti, 5b, 92, 139, 142, 143, 193–94. *See also* Africa
Dollarization. *See* Currencies
Doré, Ousmane, 60
DRC. *See* Democratic Republic of the Congo

EAC. *See* East African Community
East Africa, 4, 20–21, 138, 169

East African Community (EAC): cooperation and disintegration, 17, 40; currency and exchange rate issues, 20–21, 130, 131, 133–34, 150; customs union in, 130, 131–33, 138; EAC Secretariat, 131, 133; economic issues, 130, 131, 133–34, 136, 146; history of, 129; members, xii, 17, 20, 129; migrant labor in, 7; Monetary Affairs Committee, 134; monetary union in, 9, 20, 35, 40, 130, 136–38, 145; old EAC, 130–34, 137–38, 146; political issues, 133, 138; RECs and, 150; revitalization of, 4, 77, 153; trade and tariffs, 131, 132–33, 134–35, 138; treaties and strategies, 129-30, 133. *See also* individual members
East African Currency Board, 16, 17
East African currency union, 19
East African Development Bank, 131
Eastern Caribbean Currency Union, 39
EC. *See* European Commission
ECB. *See* European Central Bank
ECCAS. *See* Economic Community of Central African States
Economic Community of Central African States (ECCAS), 148, 150. *See also* individual members
Economic Community of West African States (ECOWAS): African Union and, 148; central bank, 112; CFA franc zones and, 6; corruption in, 100; currencies and exchange rates, 104, 112, 153; ECOMOG, 193; economic issues, 63, 65, 95–96, 102, 105–07, 112, 120–21; financing needs, 101; formation and goals, 3, 95; France and, 111–12, 164; members, 149; merger with WAEMU, 96, 104, 111–12; monetary union, 95, 104–06, 110, 152; monetary zones, 8–9, 96; net gains for, 105; political issues, 95–96, 112; regional conflict and, 40; surveillance and sanctions, 112; trade, 6, 54, 98, 105, 112. *See also* individual members
Economic issues: balance of payments pressures, 92; bond sterilization, 83;

business cycles, 107; capital mobility, 165, 166; control and rationing, 79; current account convertibility, 80; debt and deficits, 50, 79; development strategies, 2–3, 78; economic shocks, 7, 34, 35, 36–37, 38, 42, 44, 79, 82; gold standard, 14; government spending, 173; income and fiscal convergence, 53, 56–63; inflation, 35, 38, 42, 43, 44, 78, 82, 83, 84, 92, 167; interest rates, 83n12; liberalized payments and trade regimes, 3; monetary policies and expansion, 36, 38, 42, 79; real commodity prices, 85–89; reserve cover ratio, 46; saving, 79; underdeveloped financial sectors, 182–85. *See also* Currencies; Exchange rates; Labor issues; Trade; individual countries, regions, and groups

ECOWAS. *See* Economic Community of West African States
Egypt, 29, 139, 142, 145, 145–46
EMS. *See* European Monetary System
EMU. *See* European Economic and Monetary Union
Equations. *See* Methods and equations
Equatorial Guinea, 17, 62
Eritrea, 91, 139, 143, 192
ERM. *See* Exchange rate mechanism
Escudo (Cape Verde; Portugal), 16, 19, 195
Estonia, 5b
Ethiopia: COMESA and, 139, 145; currency and exchange rate issues, 81–82; East African Currency Board, 16; economic issues, 145; foreign exchange markets, 184; REER and real commodity prices, 86; trade, 142, 143
EU. *See* European Union
Euro: African peg to, 155; characteristics of, vii, 10, 152; currencies linked to the euro, 17, 32, 46, 164–65, 195; effects of, 151; introduction of, 3, 32. *See also* Euro zone
Europe: African gold and, 13; attitudes toward Africa, 164; central bank, 34, 151; coinage, 13–14; colonization by, 6; monetary union in, 35, 39, 40, 107,

120, 127, 151, 155; optimum currency areas in, 34; exchange rate crises, 27; trade with Africa, 165; World War II and, 14. *See also* European Union; Euro; Euro zone; individual countries
European Central Bank (ECB), 34, 48, 111
European Commission (EC), 4b
European Council, 111
European Monetary System (EMS), 4b, 27, 49
European Union (EU): CRA franc zone and, 111; ECOWAS and, 111, 164; exchange rates, 165–66; costs and benefits of monetary union, 37; pegs to its currency, 11, 164–65; trade, 135. *See also* Euro; Europe; Euro Zone; individual countries
Euro zone: capital movements, 48; creation of, 3; effects of, 33; expansion of, 11; as a full monetary union, 4b, 120; Stability and Growth Pact, 34, 49, 151; symmetry of, 120. *See also* Euro; European Union
Exchange rate mechanism (ERM), 5b, 120
Exchange rates: adjustable peg regimes, 78; African countries, 22, 26–32, 93–94; anchors, 167–68; auction markets, 80–81; British controls, 19; capital markets and, 10; CFA franc zone, 23, 28, 46, 48; classifications of, 78, 80; colonial powers and, 19; controls and rationing, 27; corruption and, 8, 27; currency blocs, 163–64; economic issues, 78, 80–82, 84–94, 164, 185–96; fixed rates, 78, 84, 85t–94, 165–66, 167–68; flexible rates, 42, 78, 79–94, 165–66, 182–96; floating rates, 83–84, 162, 166, 189–96; hollowing out hypothesis, 165–67; international environment, 163–64; monetary unions and, 21; pegged rates, 11, 26, 32, 97, 164, 166; preliberalization regimes, 78–80; problem areas, 80–84; REER and, 74, 82, 85–89, 93n25; reforms and, 79–80, 82, 93; stability or volatility, 10, 17, 26, 72; in sterling areas, 19; targets, 10–11; West Africa, 97. *See also*

Currencies; individual countries, regions, and organizations

Exchange rate unions: constituted by the CMA, 9, 25; definitions, 4b, 120; southern Africa and, 25, 26, 45; symmetry of, 5b

Fadiga, Abdoulaye, 23
Federal government. *See* Government
Federal Reserve (U.S.), 20
Foreign investment, 117–19
Foroutan, Faezah, 54
France: colonial and post-colonial monetary arrangements, 6, 15–16, 17, 21–22, 23; cultural links with, 21–22; ECOWAS and, 111–12; French franc, 15–16; introduction of euro, 3; pegs to its currency, 11; trade, 51–52. *See also* CFA franc zone; Euro; Europe; Euro zone
Francs: Belgian franc, 16; Colonies Françaises d'Afrique (CFA) franc, 15, 23, 45, 53, 97; Congolese franc, 16; franc zones, 18–19; French franc, 15–16, 17, 23; Rwanda and Burundi franc, 19. *See also* CFA franc zone
Frankel, Jeffrey, 107, 166
French Equatorial Africa, 15
French Somaliland. *See* Djibouti
French West Africa, 15

G-7 countries, 50
G-8 summit (*2003*), 160
Gabon, 15, 62
Gambia, the: central bank, 183; corruption and institutional quality, 100, 101; currency and exchange rate issues, 80, 81, 183; economic issues, 183; REER and real commodity prices, 86; WAEMU and, 106; West African Currency Board, 16, 20
Geography of Money, The (Cohen), vii
Germany, 3, 5b, 34, 39, 165. *See also* Euro; Europe; Euro Zone
Ghana: African central bank and, 148; economic issues, 82; government financing needs, 101; REER and real commodity prices, 86; reform program,

185; trade, 105, 185; West African Currency Board, 20. *See also* Africa
Gold, 13, 14, 16, 26
Gold Coast, 16
Gordon, David, 42
Governments: central banks and, 42, 43–44, 171–72; deficits and debt, 109; monetary unions and, 42, 43–44; reforms of, 79; taxes and spending, 36, 79, 171–81
Great Britain: colonial monetary arrangements, 6, 17, 18; currency boards, 16, 20–21; exchange rates, 19, 27; introduction of coinage, 13; protectorates in Africa, 24; sterling areas and territories, 18, 19. *See also* Bank of England; Euro; Europe; Euro zone
Great Depression, 14
Guillaume, Dominique M., 63
Guinea: banks, 80; currency and exchange rate issues, 15, 21; foreign exchange markets, 183–84; monetary union and, 105, 106; REER and real commodity prices, 86. *See also* Africa
Guinea-Bissau, 17, 87
Gunning, Jan Willem, 93

Hanink, Dean, 54
Hegemonic powers, 41
Highly Indebted Poor Country (HIPC) initiative, 50
Honohan, Patrick, 157
Houphoët-Boigny, Félix, 22
ICRG. *See* International Country Risk Guide

IFEM. *See* Interbank Foreign Exchange Market
IMF. *See* International Monetary Fund
Inflation. *See* Economic issues
Institut d'Emission de l'Afrique 0Equatoriale Francaise et du Cameroun, 15–16, 21
Institut d'Emission de l'Afrique Occidentale Française et du Togo, 15–16, 21
Institutional quality index, 100–01
Interbank Foreign Exchange Market (IFEM), 188–89

International Country Risk Guide (ICRG), 100
International Monetary Fund (IMF): Cape Verde and, 195; CFA franc devaluation, 24; Djibouti and, 194; exchange rates and, 28, 78, 80, 182; HIPC initiative, 50; Kenya and, 191; loan programs, 79; monetary harmonization program, 139–40; Seychelles and, 195; Tanzania and, 190
Israel, 168
Italy, 3, 27

Japan, 165
Jenkins, Carolyn, 56, 119, 128

Kenya: COMESA and, 139, 140; currency and exchange rate issues, 191–92; currency board issues, 16; EAC and, 17, 20, 129, 140, 146, 153; economic issues, 21, 134, 137, 191–92; financing needs, 137; interest rates, 83n12; monetary union and, 9, 137, 145; REER and real commodity prices, 87; social indicators, 134; trade and tariffs, 9, 131, 132, 135, 136, 138, 142

Labor issues, 7, 36, 37, 56, 67. See also Economic issues
Lane, Philip, 157
Latin America, 93
League of Nations, 16, 65
Lesotho: central bank for, 72–73; CMA and, 122; currency issues, 120; economic issues, 67, 72; financing needs, 121; as former British colony, 16; rand and, 6–7, 24–25, 65, 72; trade, 71, 73, 121; Union of South Africa and, 16. See also Africa
Levy-Yeyati, Eduardo, 29
Liberia, 40, 91, 193. See also Africa
Lilangeni (Swaziland), 72
Loynes, J. B., 17
Maastricht Treaty (1992), 111. See also Euro; Europe; Euro Zone
Madagascar, 23, 32, 87, 139, 142
Malagasy Republic, 19

Malawi: COMESA and, 139; currency and exchange rate issues, 20; economic issues, 114, 119; problems in, 153; REER and real commodity prices, 87; trade, 117, 121, 142
Mali, 15, 21, 101
Maputo summit (2003), 160
Martin, Philippe, 42
Masson, Paul, 60, 110, 175
Mauritania, 15, 23–24
Mauritius: CMA and, 123, 125–26; COMESA and, 139; economic issues, 114, 119; government financing needs, 121; REER and real commodity prices, 87; South Africa and, 117; trade, 142. See also Africa
Mbeki, Thabo, 159
Mboweni, Tito, 72, 114
Methods and equations: assessment of asymmetries, 63–64; budget balance, 61–62; calibration of monetary integration model, 171–81; convergence, 56–60; creation of a single currency, 157–59; evaluation of benefits of monetary unions, 101, 103–06, 136–37; exchange rate flexibility index, 84; financing needs, 101; gravity model, 54–55, 71, 73, 76, 115, 155–56
Metical (Mozambique), 19
Millennium Partnership for the African Recovery Program, 159
MMA. See Multilateral Monetary Agreement
Monetary geography, vii, 11, 162–69
Monetary policies. See Economic issues; Political issues
Monetary unions and integration: advantages of, 107, 109, 121, 151; asymmetry in, 120, 121; central banks and, 38, 42, 64–65, 98, 171; conflict and, 40–41; costs and benefits, 7, 36–37, 39–40, 43, 44, 63–65, 93, 119–26, 136–38, 155; currencies in, 7, 39, 63, 155; definition, 3; design of, 40, 119–20; economic issues, 36–37, 46, 53, 56, 63–64, 98, 100, 107, 109, 120, 172–73; exchange rates and, 35, 42, 63, 134, 172; fiscal discipline in, 7,

8–9; formation of, viii, 3; income convergence, 53–54; models and simulations, 41–44, 121–26; monetary expansion and, 35; political issues, 32, 35, 39, 41, 44; success of, 10; surveillance in, 109; symmetry in, 5b, 120, 121; trade and, 51, 53, 56, 75, 96, 107, 109, 121–22, 134, 155, 172; types of, 3–6. *See also* Africa; CFA franc zone; Central African Economic and Monetary Community; Common Monetary Area; Currency unions; Economic Community of West African States; Euro; Euro zone; West African Economic and Monetary Union; West African Monetary Zone

Morocco, 19

Mozambique: aid to, 189, 190; CMA and, 154; currency and exchange rate issues, 19, 83, 89, 189, 190; economic issues, 114, 119, 190; financing needs, 121; REER and real commodity prices, 87; trade, 117, 121. *See also* Africa

Multilateral Monetary Agreement (MMA; *1992*), 25

Mundell, Robert, 7, 34, 36, 63, 152

Nafka (Eritrea), 192

Naira (Nigeria), 20

Namibia: central bank for, 72–73; CMA and, 25, 65, 122, 140; COMESA and, 139; currency and exchange rate issues, 6–7, 16, 25, 120; economic issues, 67, 72, 114; rand and, 6–7, 25, 72; trade, 71, 73, 117, 121. *See also* Africa; South West Africa

NEPAD. *See* New Partnership for African Development

Net Open Forward Position (NOFP), 70

New Partnership for African Development (NEPAD; *1999*): agenda, 160; APRM and, 110; formation of, xii, 3; goals of, 159–60; potential effects of, 150–51; regional integration and, 10; structure of, 159. *See also* African Union

Niger, 15, 100, 105. *See also* Africa

Nigeria: black market premium, 84; central bank, 17, 96–97; corruption, 100; currency and exchange rate issues, 20,

32, 82, 97, 188–89; currency board issues, 16, 20; diversion wedges, 101; economic issues, 96, 97, 98, 110, 112, 152–53, 188; ECOWAS monetary union, 111, 152–53; financing needs, 101, 110; monetary union or zone issues, 8–9, 96, 105, 110, 112; petroleum issues, 96, 97–98, 105, 109, 153, 188; political issues, 96; REER and real commodity prices, 88; trade, 97–98, 106. *See also* West African Currency Board; West African Monetary Zone

Nyasaland, 16

Nyerere, Julius, 131

OAU. *See* Organization of African Unity

Obansanjo, Olusegun, 159, 188

Obote, Milton, 131

OCAs. *See* Optimum currency areas

OECD. *See* Organization for Economic Cooperation and Development

OHADA (Organisation pour l'Harmonisation du Droit des Affaires en Afrique), 49

Oil: African exporters, 164; Angola, 115, 187; CAEMC and, 53n11, 62, 64, 154; Ghana, 185; monetary union and, 109; Nigeria, 96, 97–98, 109; price of, 70

Optimum currency areas (OCAs): central banks, 41; economic issues, 41–44, 120–21; in Europe, 40; labor mobility and, 36; literature on, 34; model of, 41–44; monetary unions, 36–37; political issues, 41–44; world currency, 33n1, 36. *See also* Currency boards; Currency unions

Organisation pour l'Harmonisation du Droit des Affaires en Afrique (OHADA), 49

Organization for Economic Cooperation and Development (OECD), 2, 56

Organization of African Unity (OAU), 3, 147

Owusu, J. Henry, 54

Pattillo, Catherine, 110, 175

Peseta (Portuguese and Spanish colonies), 16

Petroleum. *See* Oil
Plan Omega, 159
Political issues: devaluation, 79; monetary
unions, 32, 35, 39, 41; optimum cur-
rency areas, 41–44; undemocratic poli-
tics, 2
Portugal, 6, 16, 17, 19, 92, 195–96
PPP. *See* Purchasing power parity
Preferential Trade Area (PTA), 139, 140
Pritchett, Lant, 54
PTA. *See* Preferential Trade Area
Pula (Botswana), 25, 73–74
Purchasing power parity (PPP), 1n1

Quah, Danny T., 57–58

Rand: as anchor for the CMA, 45, 120;
appreciation and depreciation of, 66,
70, 72; dollarization, 72, 120; ex-
change rate issues, 11, 25–26; mone-
tary area provisions, 25; pegging to,
6–7, 32, 74; replacement of the South
African pound, 16; use of in southern
Africa, 24, 25–26, 65
Rand Monetary Area, 16, 24–25, 152
Real effective exchange rate (REER). *See*
Exchange rates; individual countries
RECs. *See* Regional Economic
Communities
REER (real effective exchange rate). *See*
Exchange rates; individual countries
Regional Economic Communities (RECs),
xiii, 147–50, 153, 157, 156, 157t
Reinhart, Carmen, 32, 84, 90, 166
Reserve cover ratio, 46
Rhodesia, 16, 20. *See also* Africa
Roberts, J. J., 193
Rogoff, Kenneth S., 32, 90
Rose, Andrew, 40, 107
Ruble and ruble zone, 35, 40, 151–52
Rupee (Seychelles), 194, 195
Rwanda, 19, 40, 88, 139, 143
Rwanda-Urundi, 16

SACU. *See* South African Customs Union
SADC. *See* Southern African Development
Community
SADCC. *See* Southern African Develop-
ment Coordination Conference

Sanctions, 39, 63, 76, 112
SARB. *See* South African Reserve Bank
SDR. *See* Special Drawing Right
Senegal, 15, 60, 101, 103, 104. *See also*
Africa
Senghor, Leopold, 22
Seychelles: COMESA and, 139; currency
and exchange rate issues, 92, 126,
194–95; economic issues, 114, 119,
194, 195; monetary union and, 145;
trade, 121. *See also* Africa
Shilling (East Africa, Tanzania), 40, 190
Sierra Leone, 16, 20, 40, 79, 101. *See also*
Africa
Silver, 13–14, 16
Sirte (Libya) Declaration (1999), 148
Somalia, 16, 19
South Africa: apartheid, 113, 115; balance
of payments pressures, 70; central
bank, 72–73, 127; CMA and, 122;
currency and exchange rate issues, 11,
25–26, 28, 32, 69–71, 122, 164; economic issues, 65, 66, 67, 69–70, 72,
114, 117–19, 166, 167; financing
needs, 122; labor mobility, 7; macroeconomic stability, 9; monetary area,
viii, 16, 19, 24–25, 152; REER and
real commodity prices, 88; SADC and,
114, 127; trade, 8, 67, 71–72, 115,
121, 135; unemployment in, 72. *See
also* Rand; Rand Monetary Area
South African Customs Union (SACU):
customs union agreement, 24; economic issues, 59, 68, 119; members,
xiii, 66; regional integration and, 4; stability of, 153; trade, 71, 115, 121, 135.
See also individual members
South African Reserve Bank (SARB): balance of payments pressures, 70; currencies, 16; inflation and fiscal policies,
126; interest rate policies, 69–70; monetary policy responsibility, 5, 8, 9, 26,
65, 127
Southern Africa: British protectorates, 16;
colonization of, 6; creation of the
CMA, 24–26, 65; currency of, 16, 169;
economic convergence, 128; exchange
rate union in, 45; independence of,
6–7; monetary union in, 9, 45; Rand

Monetary Area provisions and, 25; regional integration, 4. *See also* Rand; Rand Monetary Zone; individual countries

Southern African Development Community (SADC): African Union and, 148; Committee of Central Bank Governors, 113, 114, 119; currency and exchange rate issues, 126–27; economic issues, 114, 117–19, 121, 127; financing needs, 121; Free Trade Protocol, 115; history of, 113; members and goals, xiii, 4–5, 114, 115t, 116–17, 138, 140, 149, 150; Memorandum of Understanding on Macroeconomic Convergence, 119; monetary union, 9, 77, 113–14, 119–28, 152, 153; surveillance in, 66, 119, 127–28; trade, 113, 114, 115–17, 121, 122t–123t, 134–35. *See also* individual members

Southern African Development Coordination Conference (SADCC), 113

Southern Rhodesia Currency Board, 16

South West Africa, 16, 65. *See also* Namibia

Soviet Union, 35, 40, 151–52. *See also* Commonwealth of Independent States

Spain, 6, 16, 17

Special Drawing Right (SDR), 23, 74, 192, 194

Stability and Growth Pact (Euro zone), 34, 49, 151

Stasavage, David, 22, 63

Sterling. *See* Great Britain

Sturzenegger, Federico, 29, 32

Subramanian, Arvind, 54

Sudan: COMESA and, 139; conflict in, 40; currency and exchange rate issues, 82, 187–88; economic issues, 84; monetary union and, 145; REER and real commodity prices, 88. *See also* Africa

Swaziland: central bank for, 72–73; CMA and, 25, 65, 66, 122, 140; COMESA and, 139; currency and exchange rate issues, 16, 120; economic issues, 66, 67, 72; rand and, 6–7, 24–25; trade, 71, 72, 73, 143; unemployment in, 72

Tamirisa, Natalia, 54

Tanganyika, 16

Tanzania: aid to, 189, 190; COMESA and, 138; currency and exchange rate issues, 83, 189, 190; EAC and, 17, 20, 129, 153; economic issues, 114, 119, 134; financing needs, 121; inflation, 83; monetary union and, 9, 137; REER and real commodity prices, 88; SADC and, 138; social indicators, 134; socialism in, 21; trade and tariffs, 121, 131, 132, 135–36, 138. *See also* Africa

Tariffs. *See* Trade

Taylor, Charles, 193

Thomas, Lynne, 56, 119, 128

Tjirongo, M., 67

Togo, 15, 61, 101

Tourism, 114, 155

Trade: CFA franc zone, 48, 49; commodity exports, 92; common currencies and, 51; continental solidarity and, 10; currency unions and, 36–37, 76; development and, 168; in diamonds, 73–74; "Dutch" disease, 73; endogenous shocks to, 109; in Europe, 155; export structures, 82, 83; fiscal deficits and, 61; foreign exchange and, 82; free trade area, 148; gravity model, 52, 54–55; imports, 78, 83; import–substitution industries, 78; inflation and, 44; monetary systems and, 14, 43, 44, 76, 172; protectionism, 78; reforms and, 79–80; tariffs, 49, 130, 148; terms of trade, 121, 135–36. *See also* Africa; Southern African Development Community; West Africa; individual countries

Treaty on European Union. *See* Maastricht Treaty

Tunisia, 19

UEMOA (Union Economique et Monaire Ouest-Africaine). *See* West African Economic and Monetary Union

Uganda: *1971* coup, 131; aid to, 189–90; COMESA and, 139, 140; conflict in, 21; currency and exchange rate issues, 17, 83, 189, 190; EAC and, 9, 17, 20, 129, 140, 153; East African Currency

Board, 16; economic issues, 134, 190; inflation, 83; monetary union and, 137, 145; REER and real commodity prices, 88; social indicators, 134; trade and tariffs, 131, 132, 135–36, 138, 142, 143
Union Economique et Monaire Ouest-Africaine (UEMOA). *See* West African Economic and Monetary Union
Upper Volta, 15

Venables, Anthony J., 133

Wade, Abdoulaye, 159
WAEMU. *See* West African Economic and Monetary Union
WAMI. *See* West African Monetary Institute
WAMZ. *See* West African Monetary Zone
Wars and conflict: in Africa, 40–41; economic effects of, 84, 91; exchange rates in war countries, 192–93; in Mauritania, 23–24; monetary unions and, 40–41; regional integration initiatives, 3, 32; tribal and ethnic conflict, 2. *See also* World War II; individual countries
West Africa: bank note issue, 15; central bank in, 39; CFA franc zone, 19; corruption and institutional quality, 100; currency boards in, 20; economic issues, 96, 99; migrant labor in, 7; monetary zones and integration, 3, 8–9, 152; petroleum issues, 109; political issues, 96; proposed single currency for, 95–112; silver mining, 13–14; trade, 96, 99. *See also* Economic Community of West African States
West African Currency Board, 3, 16, 20
West African Economic and Monetary Union (WAEMU): BCEAO and, 21, 23, 48, 110, 168; Commission Bancaire, 47; convergence criteria, 50, 51; costs and benefits of, 101, 103–07, 108; currency area, 98; devaluation in, 109; economic issues, 8, 9, 56, 57f, 58–62, 65, 97, 102, 103–04, 106–08; ECOWAS and, 150; exchange rates, 101, 103; extension of, 105–06; fi-

nancing needs, 101, 102; France and, 112; history of, 49; institutional quality indexes, 100, 101; members, xiii, 17, 102, 105; merger with ECOWAS, 96, 104–05, 111–12, 152; migration in, 65; monetary policies and currencies, 17, 24, 27, 38, 47, 49; stresses in, 154; surveillance procedures, 60; trade, 6, 51, 52–53, 64, 97, 98, 103, 104, 106; WAMZ countries and, 105–06. *See also* CFA franc zone; individual members
West African Monetary Institute (WAMI)
West African Monetary Zone (WAMZ): convergence criteria, 109–10; economic issues, 95, 97, 102; exchange rates, 98; financing needs, 102, 106; formation of, 3, 77, 95, 152; institutional quality indexes, 100, 101; joining WAEMU, 105–06; members, xiii, 3, 95n1, 102; merger with ECOWAS, 105–08, 111, 112; monetary policies and currencies, 95, 96, 110; monetary union, 97; trade, 97–98. *See also* individual members
World Bank, 20, 24, 50, 79, 133, 140
World Trade Organization (WTO), 151
World War II, 14, 15

Yaoundé (Cameroun), 23

Zaïre, 79
Zambia: COMESA and, 139; currency and exchange rate issues, 20, 32, 79, 82, 84, 185–86; economic issues, 185–86; financing needs, 121; problems in, 153; REER and real commodity prices, 89f; trade, 117, 121, 142. *See also* Africa
Zambia Consolidated Copper Mines (ZCCM), 185–86
Zanzibar, 16
Zimbabwe: CMA and, 125, 154; COMESA and, 139; conflict in, 91–92, 153; currency and exchange rate issues, 83n12, 91–92, 191; economic issues, 114, 119, 143, 145, 191; financing needs, 121; monetary union and, 145; REER and real commodity prices, 89f; trade, 117, 121, 142